Communicate What You Mean

GRAMMAR FOR HIGH-LEVEL ESL STUDENTS

CARROLL WASHINGTON POLLOCK

PRENTICE HALL REGENTS, Englewood Cliffs, NJ 07632

Library of Congress Cataloging in Publication Data

POLLOCK, CARROLL WASHINGTON. (date)
    Communicate what you mean.

    Includes index.
    1. English language—Study and teaching—Foreign
students.   2. English language—Grammar—1950–
I. Title.
PE1128.A2P64   428.2′4   81–15408
ISBN   0-13-153486-6   AACR2

Printed in the United States of America

10

Editorial/production supervision
        and interior design by Barbara Alexander
Cover design by 20/20 Services, Inc. Mark Berghash.
Manufacturing buyer: Harry P. Baisley

ISBN 0-13-153486-6

PRENTICE-HALL INTERNATIONAL, INC., *London*
PRENTICE-HALL OF AUSTRALIA PTY. LIMITED, *Sydney*
PRENTICE-HALL OF CANADA, LTD., *Toronto*
PRENTICE-HALL OF INDIA PRIVATE LIMITED, *New Delhi*
PRENTICE-HALL OF JAPAN, INC., *Tokyo*
PRENTICE-HALL OF SOUTHEAST ASIA PTE. LTD., *Singapore*
WHITEHALL BOOKS LIMITED, *Wellington, New Zealand*

for G.T.F., J.S., and T.P.H.S.

Contents

Preface

Underlying Concepts of the Text

The grammatical rules of a language do not tell us *what to say*. Rather, the grammatical rules of a language tell us *how to respond correctly* within the structural system of a language. Therefore, using a language is, to a large degree, a psychological activity in that a speaker's responses depend not only upon a knowledge of structure but also upon a knowledge of the events of a "situation" and the speaker's feelings toward those events. Students (at every level) must be expected to give semantically and situationally correct responses as well as grammatically correct ones.

Although the "formal" study of grammatical analysis and meaning are often autonomous, encoding one's thoughts into a correct as well as situationally appropriate response is not. When speaking or writing, semantics and syntax work together to transmit meaning, and a message will be anomalous if there is a mistake in one or the other. For example, the student who says, "I have been arriving in the United States," understands the grammatical formation of the present perfect continuous tense, but the meaning of the verb "arrive" in this sentence limits us to an activity that occurs "one" time.

Features of the Exercises

With few exceptions, *the exercises are contextual;* that is, they are built around a "center of interest" so that the student is "talking about something" rather than simply repeating or completing a series of unrelated statements.

Although the explanations are presented deductively, *the exercises* that follow *provide oral as well as written practice.* High-level students need just as much aural–oral practice with more complex structures as do low-level students with more basic structures.

The exercises require that the student make a grammatically correct response as well as one that is semantically appropriate. For this reason, many of the exercises allow for a number of correct responses that reflect the particular way in which a student has perceived the situation or has understood what has previously been stated. The student must "think" instead of merely filling in the blanks. Students who are only required to fill in the blanks are not provided with an opportunity to reuse previously learned structures or vocabulary.

There is a "built-in" repetition of structures from lesson to lesson so that old, previously learned material is reviewed while new material is being practiced. This built in redundancy also impresses upon the student the realization that several points of grammar operate simultaneously whenever we speak or write.

Special Features of the Text

At the beginning of each unit, introductory remarks (to the student) provide the student with a general idea of what is to be covered in the unit. This feature grew as a result of students' questions over the years. Before beginning a unit, these remarks may be read in class or assigned to the student to be read at home, but they should not be omitted.

Each unit concludes with a practice exam. This exam provides a final review of the material covered in the lessons, and it permits the teacher to identify any remaining weaknesses.

Acknowledgments

I am deeply grateful to Professor Mary Newton Bruder of the University of Pittsburgh for choosing to "class test" this text and to the ESL teachers at the University of Pittsburgh who used it in their classes for three semesters. I am particularly grateful to Miss Elaine Williams who coordinated the class testing and provided me with invaluable comments. I wish also to thank my colleagues Betsy Berriman who class tested the text at the University of Denver and Linda Peerson who proofread and assisted in the typing of the manuscript. Their training and years of experience in the field of ESL made their comments most valuable. A word of appreciation must be given to my former professors and colleagues at New York University, whose dedication to and professional pride in the field of ESL has always remained with me. Finally, I thank my husband Mel and son Matt for their patience and love.

Carroll Washington Pollock
Denver, Colorado

UNIT 1

Tense Review

There are times in speaking and writing when only one tense is used predominately; however, when speaking or writing, a person generally uses several different tenses and moves from one tense to the other correctly and quickly. As you review the tenses in this chapter, remember the following:

1. Grammar rules do not tell you *what* to say. Grammar rules tell you *how* to say something correctly. Real-life events and your feelings about these events will determine what you will communicate.

2. Certain verbs cannot be used in certain tenses because of the *meaning* of the verbs. You must often think about the meaning of a particular verb as well as the meaning of the whole sentence before you use the verb in a particular tense. At all times meaning and form must fit. Look at the following sentence from a student composition.

> incorrect: My parents have sent me to Stanford University after my graduation from high school.

The *form* of the present perfect tense is correct—have + past participle—but the *meaning* of the word *sent* in this sentence refers to an activity that usually happens only one time and is then finished. How many times can you graduate from high school? After graduation, how many times can your parents send you to the same university for the *first* time?

> correct: My parents sent me to Stanford University after my graduation from high school.

As you review the tenses in this chapter, remember that the listener or reader does not know what you are going to say or write or how you feel about something

1

until you say it or write it. Your choice of tense must *correctly* express the activities of a situation as well as your feelings about the situation. Your choice of tense must express what *you* wish to communicate.

LESSON ONE

SIMPLE PRESENT

1. Makes factual statements.

    The coffee bean **grows** well in warm, damp climates.

    Colombia **produces** good coffee.

    Roberto **is** from Colombia.

    His father **owns** a coffee plantation.

2. Expresses customs and habitual activity.

    Many office workers **take** a fifteen-minute coffee break every day.

    I **drink** three cups of coffee every morning.

3. Expresses future time when used with a future time word or phrase.

    Roberto **leaves** for Colombia next week.

    Sue:　What's the matter?
    Bob:　I didn't have time for coffee this morning.
    Sue:　Don't worry. The coffee cart **arrives** in ten minutes.

4. Expresses nonactions.

opinions:	My landlady **makes** excellent coffee.
sense perceptions:	This coffee **tastes** bitter.
emotions:	I **hate** bitter coffee.
possession:	This cup **belongs** to the secretary.

PRESENT CONTINUOUS

1. Expresses a single activity or a series of activities happening at the moment of speaking.

    I usually have a salad for lunch, but I'm **having** a sandwich now.

    It's noon, and I **am sitting** in the park. It's a beautiful day, so many office workers **are eating** their lunches outside. A few people **are standing** in line in front of a park vendor. They **are waiting** for hot dogs. A little boy **is enjoying** a huge ice cream cone.

2. Expresses a single activity or a series of activities happening over a given period of time, not necessarily at the moment of speaking.

This quarter, my roommate **is working** in the dorm cafeteria. He serves breakfast from 6:30 to 8:30 every morning. He **is taking** only two night courses this quarter, so his father agreed to let him work. His mother, however, **is trying** to convince him to quit the job.

3. Expresses future time. A future time word or phrase is necessary to distinguish between a present and future time reference. Sometimes an earlier statement makes the future time clear, and a future time word is not necessary.

Jim's plane **is arriving** in Denver **at 6:00 tonight.**

He and his wife **are meeting** with their lawyer **tomorrow.**

They're **leaving** Denver **next week.** They're **flying** to Texas.

PRESENT PERFECT

1. Expresses an action or an emotion that started in the past and has continued into the present.

Dr. Jones **has lived** in New York for many years.   (He is still there.)

He **has taught** at New York University for twenty years.   (He is still teaching.)

His students **have** always **enjoyed** his classes.   (They still do.)

2. When used with the words "just" and "already," the present perfect expresses an action that started in the past but finished recently or very close to the moment of speaking.

Husband: Don't forget to mail my package for me.

Wife: I have **already** mailed it. I went to the post office this morning.

or

It's on its way. I have **just** returned from the post office.

3. Indicates an action that happened at an indefinite time in the past. The time of the action is not given. When the time is given, the simple past is used.

Ana **has finished** her composition.	She **finished** it **two days ago.**
The teacher **has corrected** it.	He **corrected** it **last night.**
I **have received** my acceptance letter to the university.	I **received** it **the day before yesterday.**

Exercise 1: Complete the following paragraphs with the simple present, present continuous, or present perfect tense of the verbs. In some sentences more than one tense may be correct.

Ali and Roberto _____ (be) graduate students in the department of

physics at Harvard University. They _____ (be) students at

Harvard for one year. This institution of higher learning _____ (be) the oldest university in the United States, and it _____ (have) the distinction of being a very prestigious school.

This quarter, Roberto _____ (work) in the library on Friday and Saturday nights. He _____ (take) only two courses this quarter, so he _____ (have, negative) many assignments. His girlfriend _____ (try) to convince him to quit his job so that they can go out on the weekends.

It's noon now, so they _____ (eat) lunch in the student union. Many students _____ (stand) in line and _____ (wait) for someone to take their orders. Ali and Roberto _____ (be) in line for nearly twenty minutes, and they _____ (get) a little impatient. Although they _____ (have) lunch in the union a few times a week, Roberto _____ (prefer) to eat in the dorm cafeteria because the service _____ (be) faster.

Their spring break _____ (begin) next week, and Ali _____ (fly) to his country by airplane to visit his family. He _____ (receive, already) a big check from his father, so he _____ (plan) to fly first class. His flight _____ (depart) at seven o'clock in the morning. Both Ali and Roberto _____ (register) for a course in aerodynamics next quarter because the phenomenon of flying _____ (fascinate) them since they were children.

The Present Continuous Tense: *Special Notes*

Remember that there are several verbs that do not usually occur in the present continuous tense.

Group I:	Verbs expressing sense perceptions are not used in this tense.			
feel (touch)	**hear**	**see**	**smell**	**taste**

The five words in this group usually refer to actions of the senses that are *involuntary:* we do not consciously think about the actions.

Involuntary Actions

1. I **feel** cold air. Close the window.
2. I **hear** voices. Someone is downstairs.
3. These shirts are too expensive. Wait a minute! I **see** a sale on shirts over there.
4. I **smell** something burning.
5. Your soup **tastes** great.

Sometimes speakers of English use these verbs to express a *voluntary* (conscious) use of their senses, and they use some of these verbs in the present continuous.

Voluntary Actions

1. Sue **is feeling** the material *to see* if it is real silk.
2. What are you doing? I'm **smelling** this meat *to see* if it is spoiled.
3. What is Bob doing in the kitchen? He's **tasting** the soup *to see* if it needs salt.

Note the use of the infinitive "to see" to express purpose.

FEEL   in a medical sense can be used in the present continuous.

How is your father **feeling** now?   He's **feeling** much better.

What's the matter with you?   I'm not **feeling** well today. I have a cold.

SEE   is used in the present continuous when it has the following meanings.

a. meet by appointment: Ali **is seeing** the director today.
(Ali has an appointment with . . .)

b. visit (places of interest):   Where's Maria? She's out **seeing** the sights of Paris. She'll be back soon.

Group II: Verbs of thinking, attitudes, or opinions are not used in this tense.

appear(seem)	**feel(think)**	**mean**	**remember**
believe	**forget**	**need**	**seem**
consider	**guess**	**prefer**	**sound**
doubt	**know**	**realize**	**think**
			understand

FEEL   when it means "think" can never be used in the present continuous.

correct: I feel that I got an A on the reading test.
incorrect: I am feeling that I got an A on the reading test.

CONSIDER and **THINK** can be used in the present continuous if the speaker is not giving an opinion.

Not Giving an Opinion	**Giving an Opinion**

1. What are you doing?
   I'm **thinking** about the exam.
	1. What do you think about it?
	   I **think** it was too long and difficult.

2. Jim **is considering** buying my old car.	2. He **considers** it a good bargain.

Group III: Verbs expressing emotion are not used in this tense.

care	**forgive**	**like**	**refuse**	**wish**
desire	**hate**	**love**	**want**	

Notice the *simple present tense* form of these verbs as a mother speaks to her sixteen-year-old son.

1. Your father and I **care** about you. You are our only child.
2. We don't **want** to make you miserable. We **desire** the best in life for you.
3. Don't worry. Your father **forgives** you for wrecking the family car.
4. Remember, however, he **hates** careless drivers.
5. You realize, of course, that I don't **like** reckless drivers either.
6. We know teenagers **love** speed; nevertheless, we **refuse** to let you use the car again until you slow down.
7. We don't **want** to see you in the hospital.
8. I **wish** you would think about this conversation carefully.

Note the following use of "wish" in the present continuous.

Mother: Why do you have your eyes closed and your fingers crossed?
Little Girl: I'm **wishing** for a baby brother to play with.

Group IV: Verbs expressing possession are not used in the present continuous.

belong	**have**	**own**	**possess**

HAVE may be used in the present continuous when it does not express possession.

Compare the following sentences:

6

Possession

1. We're **having** a grammar test today.	The teacher **has** the tests upstairs.
2. Bob **is having** a party tomorrow.	He **has** a beautiful apartment.
3. The Smiths **are having** a good time in Paris.	They **have** a lot of money.
4. My sister **is having** a baby in June.	She already **has** five children.

Complete the following dialogue with the simple present or present continuous form of the verb. Remember the use of the present continuous indicates a voluntary (conscious) use of the senses.

Voluntary versus Involuntary—TASTE

Yuko: This international party was a great idea.

Ana: It certainly was. Look at all the food.

Yuko: That dish from Libya _____ great. What are you doing?

Ana: I _____ the Mexican dish I cooked.

Yuko: What's the matter with it? Does it _____ all right?

Ana: No, it doesn't. It _____ terrible. I didn't put enough salt in it.

Yuko: Don't worry about it. Nobody will notice it.

Ana: Look at our teacher. He's walking from table to table. He

_____ every dish.

Yuko: Yes. Except the one he brought.

Ana: Isn't it good?

Yuko: I didn't like it. American food _____ bland to me because Americans don't use enough spices.

Ana: Look. He _____ my dish now. Don't tell him I cooked it. I don't want to fail reading this quarter.

PRESENT PERFECT CONTINUOUS

The present perfect continuous tense is used to *emphasize* the *continuous* nature of an activity that started in the past and is still going on at the moment of speaking.

What are you doing?

I'm waiting to talk to the airlines ticket agent.

I have been waiting for almost twenty minutes.

IMPORTANT: It is possible to use either the present perfect or the present perfect continuous to express the same thought.

I **have flown** to New York a great deal this month.

I **have been flying** to New York a great deal this month.

But the present perfect continuous is *not used* to express an action that is not continuous in nature.

I **have** finally **returned** my book to the library.

REMEMBER:

1. The present perfect and present perfect continuous are often interchangeable. Native speakers of English seem to choose one or the other depending on their desire to make the listener or reader "feel" the uninterrupted nature of an activity or to make the listener or reader "feel" the speaker's attitude or emotion toward the activity.

   I **have been waiting for you for one hour** is more effective than I **have waited for you for one hour** if I want the other person to know that I really did not like waiting that long.

   Look at the following sentences. Without knowing the intonation of the speaker or the expression on his or her face, which sentence *seems to indicate* that the speaker is tired?

   a. I have reviewed this chapter for three hours.

   b. I have been reviewing this chapter for three hours.

2. Because of the meaning of many verbs, they can never be used in the present perfect continuous.

   incorrect: The plane has been arriving.

   correct: The plane **is arriving.**   (A plane "arrives" only one time.)

   or

   The plane **has arrived.**

3. The present perfect continuous seems to indicate *recency* more regularly than the present perfect.

   a. Tom has made a lot of money.   (since 1969)

   b. Tom **has been making** a lot of money.   (since he began his new job seven months ago)

4. The present perfect continuous often expresses an action that is *uninterrupted*.

Do not use it when you mention the *number of times* that something has been done or the *number of things* that have been done.

    a. **I have read** this statistics problem **five times.**

    b. I've **been reading** it for the past hour.

    c. Bob **has** already **completed six** problems.

    d. I've **been trying** to understand the same problem all night.

5. Both the present perfect and the present perfect continuous can be used to express a single action, but the *meanings* are different.

    a. Mary **has washed** the dishes.   (The job is finished.)

    b. Mary **has been washing** the dishes.   (for the past twenty minutes)

Exercise 2: Complete the following sentences with either the present perfect or present perfect continuous. For some sentences, either tense may be appropriate.

Group 1

1. Jack _____ (fail) his driving test three times because he doesn't know how to park. However, he _____ (practice) three hours every day for the past week, and I think he _____ (make) a lot of improvement.

2. My brother _____ (pass, negative) his driving test either.

3. He _____ (worry) about this for two months.

4. I _____ (study) the driver's manual for hours every day, but I _____ (take) my test yet.

5. My father _____ (help) me to review the questions.

Group 2

1. My roommate _____ (just, buy) a new stereo.

2. He _____ (play) records since six o'clock this morning, and he is driving me crazy.

3. The other students on our floor _____ (complain) to our resident assistant, but he _____ (say) anything to my roommate yet.

4. Everyone is especially annoyed because we are taking final exams this week.

My roommate _____ (take) two exams already, and he

_____ (fail) both of them because he

_____ (study, negative).

5. I _____ (think) about moving out of the dorm, but I

_____ (make) a definite decision yet.

Group 3

1. Bob _____ (receive, negative) a check from his parents in two months.

2. He _____ (look) for the lettercarrier every day.

3. His friends _____ (lend) him money so that he can buy food and toilet articles.

4. Bob _____ (just, begin) a part-time job in the library, but he _____ (get) his first paycheck yet.

5 . He _____ (work) in the library for only one week.

SIMPLE PAST

1. Describes actions of short duration in the past.

   I **met** Dr. Dance yesterday, and we **talked** for a few minutes.

2. Describes actions that took place over a period of time in the past.

   Dr. Dance **taught** at Michigan State for ten years.

3. Describes past habitual actions.

   When Dr. Dance was at Michigan State, he **rode** his bike to classes.

PAST CONTINUOUS

1. *With a point in time* the past continuous expresses an action that began before the time given and probably continued after it. The exact beginning and end of the action is unknown.

   At 12:30 we **were eating** lunch in the park.

2. *With a period of time* the past continuous expresses an action that continued for a

rather long period. Again, we do not know exactly when the action began or ended.

Yesterday morning **I was jogging** through the park.

3. *During a period of time* the past continuous expresses the beginning and ending of an action.

From eight to ten yesterday morning, **we were playing** soccer.

4. The past continuous expresses two actions that were happening *at the same time* in the past.

The **children were playing** while their **mothers were watching** them.

5. The past continuous expresses an action that began *before another action* in the simple past and probably continued after it.

As **I was jogging**, a man stopped me and asked for the time.

In some sentences either the simple past or past continuous is possible. But the speaker will use the simple past to indicate that the action started and finished.

The speaker will use the past continuous to indicate that the action started and continued for a period of time. With the past continuous, the speaker wants to *emphasize* the duration of an action. He wants us to feel the continuing nature of an action that was in progress.

REMEMBER MEANING.   The use of the simple past or the past continuous may be correct depending on the meaning of your sentence.

Example: When I got up this morning, my roommate **prepared** breakfast.   (He waited for me to get up.)

When I got up this morning, my roommate **was preparing** breakfast.   (He started before I got up.)

Exercise 3: Where possible, change the simple past tense to the past continuous. Be careful of the meaning of the verbs.

Example: The police **did** not **believe** me.

_____ no change _____

They **questioned** me about my activities all night.

They **were questioning** me about my activities all night.

1. When I arrived at the police station, the officer in charge took my fingerprints.

_____ _____

2. I sat in a small, dimly lit room for six hours.

    _____

3. Some of the police officers were very polite.

    _____

4. Other officers screamed at me the entire time I was there.

    _____

5. They asked me strange questions.

    _____

6. When I began to answer their questions, they told me to be quiet.

    _____

7. One officer interrogated me three different times.

    _____

8. A short man entered the room five times, but he never spoke.

    _____

9. Around 11:00 at night, the sergeant put six people in the cell next to mine.

    _____

10. They made noise all night.

    _____

11. From 11:00 until 2:00 in the morning, they sang songs.

    _____

12. I was finally able to go to sleep at 3:00 A.M.

    _____

13. When I awoke the next morning, one of the guards served breakfast.

    _____

14. At 2:00 in the afternoon, my brother arrived with our lawyer.

    _____

15. The captain permitted me to leave at 2:30, and I cried with relief as I got into my

    brother's car. _____

    _____

Exercise 4:   Tense discrimination. Practice the pronunciation and discuss the meanings of the following words.

en vi′ ron ment	con serve′	en thu si as′ ti cal ly
ma′ jor	pre dom′ i nate	ap prox′ i mate ly
is′ sue		

Group 1

First, close your books and *identify* the tense you hear in each question as your teacher reads it. Then, with your books closed, *answer* each question orally in a complete sentence.

Marriage

1. Do people generally marry at a young age in your country?
2. Has this always been the custom?
3. Are people still marrying young?
4. Did your parents marry when they were young?
5. Who in your family has been thinking about getting married?

Sports

1. What is the most popular sport in your country?
2. Did the national team have a successful year last year?
3. Has this always been the favorite sport in your country?
4. Are people still attending the games enthusiastically?
5. Does your country usually send a team to the Olympic games?

Personal Information

1. Which subject did you enjoy in high school?
2. Were you studying or working before you came here?
3. What are you planning to study in the United States?
4. Have you always been interested in this field?
5. Have you been enjoying your English classes so far?

Universities

1. Are universities crowded in your country?
2. Have they always been crowded?
3. Are many students still trying to enter a university?
4. Did you attend a university before you came here?
5. How long have you been studying in the United States?

Group 2

First, with your books closed, *identify* the tense you hear in each question as your teacher reads it. Then, with your books closed, *write* the answer to each question in a complete sentence.

Pollution

1. Do many countries have a pollution problem?
2. Has pollution become a problem in the large cities in your country?
3. Are industries contributing to the problem?
4. Is pollution of the environment a major issue in your country?

The Fuel Shortage

1. Does your country have a fuel shortage?
2. Approximately how many years ago did fuel become an international issue?
3. Have you been hearing much about the fuel shortage since you have been here?
4. While you were living at home, did you have to conserve fuel?

Religion

1. What is the predominant religion in your country?
2. Has it always had the largest number of followers?
3. Are most people still attending religious services regularly?
4. Have you been attending services since you have been here?

FUTURE

Speakers of English express future actions in several different tenses.

Simple present	I **leave** for Texas tomorrow.
Present continuous	I **am leaving** for Texas tomorrow.
Will + main verb	I **will leave** for Texas tomorrow.
Be + going to	I **am going to leave** for Texas tomorrow.

These ways of expressing future actions not only have different grammatical forms, but some can only be used with certain verbs and not with others.

14

The Simple Present

1. The simple present is usually used with verbs of arriving and departing to express a scheduled or planned action: *come, go, leave, arrive, depart, return.*

   My flight **leaves** Denver at 3:00 tomorrow afternoon.

   It **arrives** in Houston at around 5:00.

2. The simple present is also used with verbs of starting and finishing: *begin, commence, start, finish, end, close, conclude.*

   Final exams **begin** next week.

   The semester **ends** in two weeks.

3. The simple present may also be used with other verbs to express a *scheduled* event in the future. Use a future time word or phrase to make the time clear.

   I **have** a doctor's appointment *next Thursday.*

   If an earlier statement makes the future time clear, a future time word may not be necessary.

   I won't be in class *next Wednesday.* Our soccer team **plays** in Michigan.

The Present Continuous

1. The present continuous is also used with verbs of arriving and departing, starting and finishing.

   I'm sorry, the store **is closing** in ten minutes.

   My flight **is arriving** in Texas at 3:00 tomorrow afternoon.

2. Verbs of the senses, emotion, thinking, and possession cannot be used in the present continuous to express future actions. Exceptions to this rule are "see" when it means have an appointment with and "have" when it does not mean possession.

   My doctor **is seeing** me tomorrow at 9:00.

   I'm **having** an eye examination.

3. To avoid confusion and make the time clear, a future time word accompanies the present continuous. However, sometimes the future time is already clear because of an earlier statement.

   My parents **are arriving** *this weekend,* and I'm very excited because I haven't seen them in six months. I'm **picking** them up at the airport in my new car.

   In the last sentence, a future time word is not necessary because the time was given in the first sentence.

15

Be careful! You *cannot* use every verb in the English language in the simple present and present continuous to express future time. As you gain more practice in the language, you will become more and more aware of the verbs that native speakers usually use in these two tenses when they wish to express future time.

Will + Main Verb

1. This form is used to express expected future actions, actions that usually or normally happen.

    I'll **see** you tomorrow in class. Don't worry. I'll **sit** beside you during the test.

2. This form is used for future habitual actions that we assume will happen.

    Mr. Ray **will give** us a quiz on Friday.   (He always does.)
    I'll probably **fail** the quiz.   (I always do.)
    He **will give** me a lecture on studying.   (He always does.)

3. This form is used with verbs of the *senses, emotion, thinking,* and *possession* to express the future.

    I'll **see** you tomorrow.
    I will **forget** about your rude remarks.
    I will **forgive** you.
    We **will have** a nice apartment if we work together.

4. "Will" used as a modal is discussed in Unit Eight.

Be Going to + Main Verb

1. "Going to" is often used to express a feeling of certainty.

    Look at the sky. It's **going to be** a beautiful day.
    All students brought food from their countries. We're **going to have** a good picnic.

    The words "sure," "certain," and "know" are often used with "will" to express certainty.

    Look at the sky. I'm **sure** it **will be** a beautiful day.
    All students brought food from their countries. I **know** we **will have** a good picnic.

2. "Going to" and "will" can be used with the verb *be*.

    I'll **be** at the picnic when it starts, and I'm **going to be** there until it ends.

Be Going to versus Will

Sometimes we can use either "going to" or "will" in a future sentence but *not always*.

There is an important difference in *meaning* between these two forms, and there are times when only one of them is possible.

The "going to" form tells us that the subject has **deliberately planned** an action and has already given the action much **previous thought** and **planning.**

GOING TO   It is clear that the speaker has given the action previous thought and planning.

a. Ahmed bought a lot of food this morning and borrowed my stereo and records.

He's **going to have** a party tonight.

b. Mother: What are you doing with that hammer?

Little Boy: I'm **going to fix** our television.

c. Sue: Why are you going to the supermarket so late at night?

Jim: I'm **going to shop** while it's quiet and uncrowded.

d. We bought a new car last week, and we got some maps.

We're **going to drive** to Alaska next month.

The sentences clearly express previous thought and planning. Speakers of English would not use "will."

WILL   It is clear that the speaker has not given the action previous thought or planning.

a. Teacher: I left the grammar tests in my office.
   Student: I'll **get** them for you.

b. Jim: The phone's ringing.
   Sue: Don't get up. I'll **answer** it.

c. Bill: I won't have time to go to the cleaners tomorrow.
   Ron: Don't worry. I'll **pick up** your suit for you.

d. Ray: I'm having a lot of trouble in my statistics class.
   Mel: Stop worrying. I'll **help** you.

Be Going to or Will

Sometimes it is not clear (we don't know) whether or not the speaker has given the action previous thought or planning.

The speaker may merely be reporting a future event or asking a question about a future event.

My parents **will arrive** (are **going to arrive**) at 8:00 tonight.

Our conversation teacher is absent today. Who's **going to teach** the class?   (Who **will teach** the class?)

Is the president **going to be** in Denver tomorrow?

Will the president **be** in Texas tomorrow?

NOTE: When *you* are communicating an idea, you will not (necessarily) give all the background information on an action you want to express. The previous plans and thoughts will stay in your mind. You will simply use the "going to" form when you speak.

Note: When the verb in the main clause is in a future tense, the verb in the dependent time clause is in the present tense, not the future tense.

	Main Clause	Dependent Time Clause
correct:	I will come home, after I *leave* the library.	
incorrect:	I will come home, after *I will leave* the library.	

Exercise 5:   Complete the following paragraph with an appropriate tense to express future time. Use the simple present, present continuous, will + main verb, or going to + main verb. Do not use the same tense for every sentence. Be prepared to discuss answers different from your own.

   This semester _____ (end) three months from now. My roommate and I _____ (go) to the Bahamas for our summer vacation. I _____ (be) happy to get away from grammar tests for a while. At the moment, we're studying for a grammar test that we _____ (have) tomorrow. After the test, everyone _____ (meet) at Pedro's apartment for a party. The party _____ (start) at 5:00. Tomorrow is his birthday, and he _____ (be) twenty-one years old. All our classmates _____ (help) him to celebrate this happy occasion. He told us not to bring birthday presents, but everyone _____ (buy) him something. I _____ (give) him a poster of a beautiful French girl in a bathing suit. Pedro's from Venezuela, but we're sure that he _____ (like) the poster because he's an international girl-watcher. At the party, I _____ (worry about, negative) my grammar test. It _____ (begin) at 3:00 tomorrow and

_____ (end) at 4:00. I _____ (think about, negative) it after 4:00.

ADVERBIAL TIME EXPRESSIONS

Many students make unnecessary mistakes in using the tenses correctly in both speaking and writing simply because they do not pay attention to the time words and expressions that usually accompany the various tenses.

Remember the following points:

1. In sentences expressing only one action, a time word or expression modifies the verb and helps to make the time of the action clear. An incorrect time expression makes the sentence confusing.

    incorrect: I have not completed my assignment yesterday.

    incorrect: I did not complete my assignment already.

2. In writing, it is important to use the tenses consistently. If you begin writing in one tense, *do not* change to another tense unnecessarily or suddenly. When you change to a different tense, you must have a specific and clear reason for changing, *and* you must signal to the reader that you are going to change so that the reader will not become confused.

    The use of time words and expressions will help you to tell the reader that you are going to change the time of events.

3. Time words are very important because they signal the use of a particular tense. However, it is not necessary to use a time word in *every sentence*. The meaning of what you are talking about will make the time clear, and you will only use a time word when you *change* the time of the events.

Time Expressions

In English some words clearly indicate a specific time period.

Present Time

now	I work/am working in a bank **now**.
right now	I'm helping a customer **right now**.
at the moment	**At the moment**, I am very busy.
	The bank president is meeting with the tellers **at the moment**.

Past Time

the day before yesterday	Maria decided to quit her job **the day before yester-day**.

| yesterday | She found a new job **yesterday**. |
| last week | She was working/worked in the bank with me **last week**. |

Future Time

tomorrow	I leave for New York **tomorrow**.
the day after tomorrow	Will you be in class **the day after tomorrow?**
two days from now	We are having the test **two days from now**.

Some words do not clearly indicate a specific time period, but they are regularly used with certain tenses.

The Simple Past

| ago | I finished my report two days **ago**. |

The Past Continuous

| *while | **While** I was working, you were out dancing at a disco. |

The Present Perfect

already	Ali has **already** completed his reading assignment.
yet	Has he finished the grammar assignment **yet?** No, he hasn't done it **yet**.
for	He has been sick **for** two weeks.
since	Ali has been sick **since** last week.
so far/up to now	We have written only two compositions **so far/up to now**.
ever	Have you **ever** failed a course? No, I haven't **ever** failed one. (No, I have **never** failed one.)

The Present Perfect Continuous

| for | I have been working on this composition **for** two weeks. |
| since | We have been reviewing the tenses **since** the quarter began. |

---

* Note the *comma* after the dependent time clause when it appears at the beginning of the sentence. Compare the following sentence.

   You were out dancing at a disco *while I was working*.

Frequency words tell *how often* an activity takes place. Most of these adverbs of frequency can be used with several tenses.

Simple Present Tense

1. I **always complete** my homework assignments on time.
2. Bob's homework **is sometimes** late.
3. Sue **never finishes** her assignments on time.
4. Hers **are usually** more than two days late.
5. I **often give** my compositions to the instructor early.
6. The instructor **occasionally returns** our compositions the next day.

In the sentences just given, the meaning is habitual, repeated action.

Simple Past Tense

1. I **always completed** my homework assignments on time last semester.
2. Bob's homework **was sometimes** late.
3. Sue **never finished** hers on time.
4. Her assignments **were usually** more than two days late.
5. I **often gave** my compositions to the instructor early.
6. The instructor **occasionally returned** our compositions the next day.

In this group of sentences, the meaning is also habitual, repeated action, but for a *definite time in the past:* last semester.

Present Perfect Tense

1. I **have always completed** my homework assignments on time.
2. Bob's homework **has sometimes been** late.
3. Sue **has never finished** hers on time.
4. Hers **has usually been** more than two days late.
5. I **have often given** my compositions to the instructor early.
6. The instructor **has occasionally returned** them the next day.

The meaning here is not repeated action for a specific time period in the past, but action *from a point of time in the past to the moment of speaking.*

Additional adverbs of frequency that may accompany these tenses are *scarcely, rarely, seldom, hardly ever.*

The expression "once in a while" may also be used with several tenses to indicate how often.

1. I **see** my old high school friends **once in a while.**
2. When I was home last year, I **saw** my chemistry teacher **once in a while.**
3. Next summer, I **will help** my father in his store **once in a while,** not every day.

The word "still" is also used with several different tenses in affirmative, negative, and interrogative statements.

1. With the simple present to indicate an activity that has not changed over a period of time.

   > Do you **still have** your 1969 Ford?
   > Yes, and it **still runs** fairly well.

2. With the present continuous to indicate an activity that is happening at the moment of speaking.

   > I'll be ready in a few minutes. I'm **still combing** my hair.

3. With the simple past to indicate an activity that did not change over a period of time.

   > The teacher patiently explained my mistakes to me for two hours, but I **still didn't understand.**

4. With the past continuous to indicate an activity that is in progress at a given point in time.

   > At four o'clock, the teacher **was still trying** to help me.

5. With the present perfect to indicate activity that started in the past but not completed at the moment of speaking.

   > I **still haven't completed** last week's assignment.

6. With the future tense to indicate a situation that will not change.

   > I **will still love** you after we're old and grey.

Exercise 6:   Changing the tense to fit the time expression.

Group 1

Write the correct tense of the verb "talk" to fit the time expressions.

1. I _____ to my parents **every week.**

2. I _____ to my parents **every week last quarter.**

3. I _____ to my parents **yet.**

4. I _____ to my parents **for two straight hours.**

5. I _____ to my parents from eight to ten **yester-day evening.**

6. I _____ to my parents **two days from now.**

7. I _____ to my parents **at the moment.**

8. I _____ to my parents **occasionally.**

9. I _____ to my parents five times **since the quarter began.**

10. I _____ to my parents **three days ago.**

Group 2

Write the correct tense of the verb "protest" to fit the time expressions.

1. Some students _____ in front of the dean's office **now.**

2. They _____ again **this coming Thursday.**

3. They _____ in front of his office **since eight o'clock this morning.**

4. They _____ **while we were** in class.

5. They _____ **two weeks from today.**

6. They _____ **for the past two hours.**

7. They seldom _____ in front of the dean's office **last year.**

8. They _____ to the president **yet.**

9. They _____ **in a few minutes.**

10. They _____ **ever since this morning.**

11. They _____ **last Friday.**

12. They _____ still _____ in front of the dean's office.

13. They _____ **in two weeks.**

Exercise 7: *Before* you complete the following paragraphs with the correct form of the verbs, read the entire exercise and note the time words and expressions. *After* you have completed the exercise, discuss the use of various tenses and explain why more than one tense is correct for some sentences.

    Last week, on Wednesday, we _____ (have) our first grammar test. It _____ (be) a test on the tenses. The instructor _____ (be, negative) very happy with the results because not enough students _____ (receive) high grades. As a result, **on Thursday,** she _____ (review) the test with the class. **While** we _____ (talk) about the test and the correct use of the tenses, I _____ (think) about how difficult it _____ (be) to learn to use the tenses spontaneously. I _____ (be) a little disappointed with my grade because this test _____ (be) the first grammar exam that we _____ (have) **so far,** and I really _____ (want) to get a good grade.

    Since we _____ (be) in class, we _____ (discuss) how the tenses show meaning, but I have to say that I _____ (**still, have**) a little trouble with this. I _____ (have) trouble with meaning **since I first** _____ (begin) to study English.

    At the moment, I _____ (see) that every student _____ (concentrate on) this exercise. Our instructor _____ (stand) in front of the class **now,** but a **few minutes ago** she _____ (walk) around the room looking at our papers. After our review, **last Thursday,** I _____ (feel) better about the tenses, so **today** I _____ (feel) confident, and I _____ (believe) that I _____ (do) well on this exercise. As I _____ (mention) **earlier,** changing from one tense to another _____ (be, never) easy for me; however, I _____ (know) I _____ (continue) to improve **until the end of the quarter.**

Exercise 8: Before you complete the following exercise, read it once and note the time changes.

I _____ (visit) quite a few cities since 1960. In June of 1960, I _____ (finish) high school in Michigan. After my graduation, my parents _____ (send) me to Stanford University in California. After one year at Stanford, I

_____ (ask) my father if I could go to the Sorbonne in France. He _____ (agree) to let me go, so in June of 1961, I _____ (fly) to Paris, France.

It's now 1963, and I _____ (be) in France for two years. At first, it was difficult for me to understand the French language, but I

_____ (study) very hard, and little by little, I

_____ (learn) to speak French very well. I

_____ (like) the French language. In fact, I

_____ (like) it since I was in junior high school.

Of course, my life _____ (be) very busy since I came to Europe. I _____ (work) hard, and I

_____ (meet) many interesting people. Last month, I

_____ (go) to Italy, and next month, I

_____ (go) to Spain. While I _____

(stay) in Italy, I _____ (see) my friend Karl, whose parents live in Germany. He _____ (invite) me to meet them, so we

_____ (hitchhike) to Berlin. He

_____ (introduce) me to his mother and father, who

_____ (make) me feel very comfortable in their home. I

_____ (never, forget) their kindness.

I _____ (complete) my studies next year. Right now, I _____ (think about) my return to Michigan, but I realize that I _____ (miss) my friends in Europe.

Exercise 9:   Write a composition using the following tenses: simple present, simple past, present continuous, past continuous, present perfect, and present perfect continuous. Use the following questions to guide your composition, but *do not* merely answer the questions. *Add additional information* when appropriate. Your composition should be at least two and a half pages long.

Paragraph 1

1. Where were you living when you received your acceptance letter to the intensive English program?
2. When did you arrive here?
3. How long have you been here?
4. In which level are you studying this quarter?

Paragraph 2

1. Generally speaking, do you enjoy traveling by plane?
2. How was your plane ride to the United States?
3. What were you thinking about when the plane took off?

Paragraph 3

1. What do you like about this city?
2. What do you not like about it?
3. What have you seen since you have been here?
4. Where have you gone since you have been here?
5. What have you been doing since classes started?

Paragraph 4

1. What are you planning to do during the next vacation period?
2. What do you plan to do after you finish studying English?

LESSON TWO

PAST PERFECT

I had gone   We had gone
You had gone   You had gone
She, he, it had gone   They had gone

Speakers of English use the past perfect to talk about an action in the past that happened before another action in the past.

PAST	PRESENT	FUTURE

past perfect   simple past
action 1   action 2

The first past action is in the past perfect. The second past action is in the simple past. The past perfect indicates that the first action was *finished completely* before the second action started.

> When I **got** home, my roommate **had** already **cleaned** the apartment.

The past perfect usually occurs with the simple past, but the past perfect can be the only tense in a sentence if a *specific past time* is given.

> *By three o'clock*, Professor Larson's lecture **had ended.**
> I **had** never **heard** him speak *before last week.*
> *Until that time*, I **had** not **known** he was such a good speaker.

Time Words and Expressions

After, Before

These words *by themselves* tell which action came first. Therefore, in *informal speech* only the simple past may be used if the actions are *in order* and it is *clear* which action happened first.

a. After I **finished** reading the book, I **lent** it to Bob.
        (1)   (2)

b. The library **closed** before I **arrived.**
               (1)   (2)

If the actions are *not in order*, the first action is in the past perfect.

a. I **lent** the book to Bob after I **had finished** reading it.
   (2)   (1)

b. Before I **arrived**, the library **had closed.**
           (2)   (1)

In the *written language*, it is best to use the past perfect with the words "before" and "after" to be sure that the reader clearly understands which action happened first, even though the actions are in order.

After the president **had given** his speech, he **answered** questions.
(1)   (2)

By the Time, When

These words by themselves do not tell which action came first; therefore, the first action must be in the past perfect.

   a. The exam **had started** *by the time* I got to class.
   b. *When* I **had told** the instructor my reason for coming late, I sat down.
   c. *When* the class ended, I **had** only **finished** the first page of the exam.

If two actions happened at the same time in the past, only the simple past is necessary. Notice the difference in meaning between the following sentences.

   d. When Professor Dance **gave** his lecture, he **sat** down.
      (He was speaking and sitting at the same time.)
   e. When Professor Dance **had given** his lecture, he **sat** down.
      (He stood and gave his lecture; then he sat down.)

Just, Already, Scarcely

These words are often used with the past perfect to indicate *recency*.

   a. I had **just** gotten into bed when someone knocked on the door.
   b. When I opened it, the person had **already** left.
   c. I had **scarcely** pulled the covers over me when the phone rang.

Note the *comma* after a time clause when it appears at the beginning of the sentence.

   Before I arrived, the library had closed.
   When Professor Dance had given his lecture, he sat down.
   After the President had given his speech, he answered questions.

PAST PERFECT CONTINUOUS

The past perfect continuous is formed with had + been + present participle.

I had been sleeping	We had been sleeping
You had been sleeping	You had been sleeping
She, he, it had been sleeping	They had been sleeping

The past perfect continuous is used to emphasize the continuous nature of the earlier past action and the recency of an earlier action. Compare the following sentences.

Continuous Nature

    a. Bob **had waited** for an hour when he decided to leave.

    b. Bob **had been waiting** for an hour when he decided to leave.

Both sentences are correct. In sentence b, however, the speaker or writer *emphasizes* the "waiting."

Note that an expression of time beginning with "for" often accompanies the past perfect continuous to help emphasize the continuous nature of the action.

Recency

    c. The class **had discussed** the final exam when the instructor came in.   (They had started the discussion before she entered and were talking about something else when the instructor came in.)

    d. The class **had been discussing** the final exam when the instructor came in.   (They had started the discussion before the instructor entered and had *just* finished when she walked in.)

The past perfect continuous is not used when you mention *the number of times* something was done.

    correct: I didn't go to the movies with Sue because I **had** already **seen** it three times.

    incorrect: I didn't go to the movies with Sue because I had already been seeing it three times.

Exercise 1:   Oral practice. Complete the following statements with a sentence in the past perfect or past perfect continuous. The sentences in each group are part of the same situation, so be careful of *meaning*.

    Example: By the time I was ten years old, I (learn) to play chess very well.

               By the time I was ten years old, I **had learned** to play chess very well.

Group 1: An Excellent Athlete

1. My brother has always been a superb swimmer. By the time he was ten years old, he (win) many medals.

2. When he finished high school, he (be) captain of the swimming team for four years.

3. He is now training for the Olympic games, so by 7:30 this morning, he (jog) for two hours.

4. When I got up at 8:30, he (shower), (eat) breakfast, and (leave) for work.

Group 2: A Sick Neighbor

1. Our neighbor was very sick last night, and by the time he called us his temperature (reach) 102 degrees.

2. We called the hospital before we left home, so when we reached the emergency room, the doctor (wait) for thirty minutes.

3. The doctor gave him a shot, so by the time we returned home, he (begin) to feel a little better.

4. By the time the next morning came, he (start) to feel much better.

In the next two groups, provide your own answers.

Group 3: Late to School

1. When I got to school this morning, . . .

2. By the time I entered my classroom, . . .

3. When I reached my desk, . . .

4. Before the class was over, . . .

Group 4: A Foreign Student Reception

1. When I arrived at the reception for foreign students last night, . . .

2. I didn't know anyone there, but by the time it was over, . . .

3. The president of the university left after . . .

4. I had such a good time meeting so many people that by the time I reached the refreshment table, . . .

Exercise 2: Complete the following sentences with a statement in the past perfect. The sentences in each group are part of the same situation, so be careful of *meaning*.

Example: Before I came to the United States, . . .

Before I came to the United States, **I had** already **received** my acceptance letter to the intensive English program.

Group 1: A New Quarter, A New Roommate

1. I had sent in my housing application three months before I left my country, so when I arrived on campus, the housing office . . .

2. By the time I found my dormitory room, my new roommate . . .

3. I started unpacking my suitcases after we . . .

4. I was very tired from the long plane ride, so I overslept the first morning. By the time I got to the cafeteria, . . .

5. My roommate ate breakfast because he (she) . . .

6. My roommate's father was in the army for twenty years, and they traveled all over the world. By the time my roommate was eleven, he (she) . . .

7. My roommate always got A's in French because he (she) . . .

Write the sentences in Group 2 in paragraph form.

Group 2: Ali's Troubles

1. Last week we had a test. Ali overslept, so when he got to class, . . .

2. By the time he began the test, the other students . . .

3. He had a lot of trouble with Part I of the test, so when the instructor asked for the papers, Ali . . .

4. As soon as Ali had given the instructor his paper, she returned it because he . . .

5. When he got home, his apartment door was open and the place was a mess. Someone . . .

6. He ran to the closet and looked for his new coat, but it was gone. He felt terrible because his parents . . .

7. He began to clean the apartment immediately, so by the time I arrived, he . . .

8. I was surprised when he told me what . . .

Exercise 3: Use the simple past, past perfect, or past perfect continuous of the verbs to complete each sentence.

1. Carla _____ (go) to the department store and

   _____ (return) the dress she

   _____ (buy).

2. She _____ (return) home after the clerk

   _____ (refund) her money.

3. After she _____ (eat) dinner, she _____
   (begin) to watch a movie on television.

4. She _____ (change) from Channel 7 to Channel 4

   because she _____ (see, already) the movie
   on Channel 7.

5. After she _____ (watch) the movie for a while, she

   _____ (become) bored.

6. She _____ (just, turn off) the set when the

   telephone _____ (ring).

7. By the time she _____ (answer) it, the person on the

   other end _____ (hang up).

8 . It was getting late, so she _____ (decide) to take a
   shower and go to bed.

9. She _____ (scarcely, get) undressed when someone

   _____ (knock) on the door.

10. After she _____ (put on) her robe, she

   _____ (open) the door and _____ (discover)

   that someone _____ (leave) her a package.

11. After she _____ (close) the door, she

   _____ (sit) down and tried to figure out who

   _____ (give) her the package.

12. When she _____ (open) the package, she

   _____ (be) surprised to see a birthday card and a beautiful
   scarf.

Exercise 4:   Read the following pairs of sentences. First, decide which action happened first. Then, combine the sentences putting the first action in the past perfect tense. Use "after," "when," "before," and "by the time" to connect the sentences.

For some sentences more than one word can be used, but choose only one. Be careful of meaning.

Situation: A Killer Snow Storm

1. The snow storm arrived. I put snow tires on my car, so I wasn't worried.

   _____

   _____

2. Eight feet of snow fell. The storm was over._____

   _____

3. It stopped snowing. Nine people died from exposure to the cold weather. _____

   _____

   _____

4. They froze to death. The police found them. _____

_____

5. The snow became very deep. Many travelers found hotel rooms for the night, so they were not in danger. _____

_____

_____

6. The police closed some highways. Many travelers found hotel rooms for the night, so they were not in danger. _____

_____

_____

7. The storm came. The weathercasters on television warned everyone to expect it, but some people were not prepared. _____

_____

_____

8. The storm came. I bought a truckload of wood, so I was ready for it. _____

_____

_____

9. The first snowflake fell. I made a warm fire and was enjoying the view. _____

_____

_____

Exercise 5:   Mixed tense review. Complete the following paragraphs with the correct forms of the verbs in parentheses. There are many past tenses in this selection.

Last Saturday, my friend and I _____ (decide) to drive to Central City. This _____ (be) a small mountain town about twenty-five miles west of Denver. In the late 1800s, Central City

_____ (be) a successful mining town where people

_____ (find) silver and gold in large quantities. Today, during the summer, the town _____ (be) full of tourists from all over the world, but in the autumn this small community usually

_____ (have) a peaceful atmosphere. However, this was not true last Saturday.

When we _____ (arrive), there _____

(be) hundreds of people standing behind thick ropes, and
huge trucks loaded with cameras and electronic equipment filled the streets.
Small groups of people dressed in the style of the old West

_____ (walk) casually along the sidewalks. As my

friend and I _____ (move) toward the crowd of people, we

_____ (stop) a local police officer and _____

(ask) him what _____ (happen). He

_____ (tell) us that a Hollywood movie studio

_____ (make) a movie and that the crowd

_____ (be) there since 6:30 in the morning. It was now

11:00 A.M. The police officer _____
(get up) at 5:00 A.M. to direct the traffic and keep order. He also told us that
George Segal and Goldie Hawn were the stars of the movie. Both these per-

formers _____ (be) excellent actors, so we

_____ (probably, see) the movie when it is

finished.

Neither my friend nor I _____ (ever, watch) a

Hollywood studio make a movie before, so we were glad we

_____ (choose) to drive west to Central City instead of
going south to Colorado Springs.

We _____ (push) through the crowd to get closer to the
camera operators, director, and actors on the other side of the rope. We were

finally in a position to see all the activity. As we _____
(stand) there waiting for the action to begin, a woman

_____ (point to) a man who was talking to the director

of the movie. The man _____ (be) George Segal. I really like

him. In fact, I _____ (see) most of his movies, but I

_____ (never, see) him in person before that day. Sud-

denly, a man _____ (yell), "QUIET!" Everyone

_____ (become) silent, and the director shouted,
"ACTION!"

LESSON THREE

FUTURE CONTINUOUS

The future continuous is formed with will + be + present participle or with going to + be + present participle.

I will be working tonight	We will be working tonight
You will be working tonight	You will be working tonight
She, he, it will be working tonight	They will be working tonight

1. The future continuous expresses an action that will be in progress at a *given time* in the future. Look at the time expressions in the following sentences.

    a. Don't call my roommate tonight **between seven and eleven.** He **will be studying** for a test in reading.

    Don't come by our room either because I'm **going to be studying,** too.

    b. This is Reza's last quarter in the intensive English program. **This time next quarter,** he'll **be taking** engineering courses.

    I have one more quarter of study, but next quarter I'm **going to be auditing** one university class in accounting.

    c. Reza has his last English exam on Friday morning. **On Friday night,** he'll probably **be celebrating** with his friends.

    I won't be with them. I'm **going to be studying** for my writing final.

2. The future continuous also expresses an action that will continue to happen at *different times* in the future.

Instructor:	Welcome to this class. In this course, you will have a test after every chapter, a midterm exam, and a final exam.
Student:	Is that all?
Instructor:	No. I **will be giving** surprise quizzes **from time to time.**
Student:	And I'll **be having** headaches **all quarter.**

3. The future continuous expresses an action that will happen at an *unknown time* in the future.

Gita:	Did you get a letter from your boyfriend in England?
Yuko:	No. Not today.
Gita:	You haven't heard from him for a month. Aren't you a little worried?
Yuko:	No. I'll **be hearing** from him **soon.**

35

FUTURE PERFECT

The future perfect is formed with will + have + past participle.

I will have finished   We will have finished
You will have finished   You will have finished
She, he, it will have finished They will have finished

1. The future perfect expresses an action that will be finished *at some time in the future*. English speakers do not usually use this tense unless the completion of the activity is clear.

   a. **The next time we meet, I will have finished** my Masters degree.
   b. Bob already has his Masters, and he **will have received** his Ph.D. **before he's twenty-three.**

2. Time expressions beginning with "by" or "before" usually accompany this tense.

   Time expressions beginning with "in" are also used: *in a week, in two hours,* and so on.

   c. **By the end of this week,** we will have finished this review of tenses.
   d. **By the end of this quarter,** we will have studied gerunds and infinitives.
   e. **Before this quarter** is finished, the students in this class will have taken twenty quizzes.
   f. Our instructor will have gotten his new car **in two weeks.**

Placement of Adverbs

Adverbs such as *already*, *probably*, and *certainly* are placed after the first auxiliary.

   g. By the end of this week, we will **certainly** have finished this review.
   h. Don't worry. Before the party begins, I will **already** have cleaned our apartment.

FUTURE PERFECT CONTINUOUS

The future perfect continuous is formed with will + have been + present participle.

I will have been studying   We will have been studying
You will have been studying   You will have been studying
She, he, it will have been studying They will have been studying

The future perfect continuous is used to emphasize the continuous nature of an activity. It is used in the same way and with the same time expressions as the future perfect.

    a. When I go home this summer, **I will have been studying** in this country for five years.

    b. By tonight, **I will have been working** for eleven hours without a break.

Meaning

When using this tense, you must be careful of meaning. Not all verbs can be used in a continuous tense because of the meaning of the verb.

Only verbs that show continuous action can be used: *study, work, travel, write, listen, watch,* and so on.

correct:	**I will have been studying** English for three quarters by the time I take the TOEFL exam.
incorrect:	I will have been finishing the review for the test by next week. (Can a person keep on finishing something? No!)

Exercise 1: Future continuous and future perfect. The leaders of two countries (a president and a prime minister) are going to meet *next week.* Look at the following schedule of the president's activities for Monday, and answer the questions that follow in complete sentences.

    Example: On Monday morning at 8:00, what will the president **be doing?**   (At this time, he'll be talking/conferring with his advisors.)

        Before 9:00 what **will** already **have happened?**   (Before 9:00, he will already have met with his advisors.)

Monday

8:00–8:50	Conference with presidential advisors
9:00–9:50	Breakfast meeting with the prime minister, the president and their interpreters
10:00–10:50	Television speech by the president on peace relations between two countries
11:00–11:50	President and prime minister and their wives will visit automobile factory.
12:00–1:00	Private lunch with presidential advisors
1:00–3:00	Discussion of import-export needs of the two countries: president, prime minister, and ministers of trade

3:00–3:30	Signing ceremonies for new trade treaty
3:35–4:00	Meeting with television and newspaper reporters: president and prime minister
4:00–5:00	Rest period in hotel
5:00	Get ready for formal dinner at 6:00

1. What **will** the president **be doing** at 9:00?

_____

_____

2. Whom **will** he **be meeting with** at 9:00? _____

3. By 10:00 what **will** the president and prime minister already **have done?**   (give two actions)

_____

4. At what time **will** the president **be making** his speech on television?

_____

5. What **will be happening** at 11:00?

_____

6. What **will** the president already **have done** by 1:00?   (give four or five actions)

_____

_____

7. Why **will** these officials **be meeting** from 1:00 to 3:00?

_____

8. By 4:00 what important document **will** they **have signed?**

_____

9. When **will** the president and prime minister **be meeting** with reporters?

_____

10. **Will** the president **be touring** the city from 4:00 to 5:00?

_____

11. By what time (approximately) **will** the president **have gotten** ready to go to dinner?

_____

12. Before the day is over, how many meetings **will** the president **have had?**

_____

Exercise 2: Oral practice. Answer the following questions in *complete* sentences.

Group 1

1. What will you probably be doing at eight o'clock tonight?
2. Which assignments will you be working on tonight?
3. Will you have finished today's homework assignments before eleven o'clock tonight?
4. At 2:00 today, which class will you be having?
5. By 1:00 today, which classes will you already have had?
6. By 12:30 today, will you have finished lunch?
7. At this time next year, what will you be doing?
8. Will you have completed your university degree by 19 . . ?
9. Will you be studying this summer?
10. Where do you think you will be living next year?
11. By next year, how long will you have been living in the United States?

Group 2

1. Will anyone be getting married this summer?
2. Will your spouse be studying in the United States next year?
3. At the end of this year, who will have been married for more than two years?
4. By the time you finish your studies in the United States, will your parents have had a chance to visit you here?

Group 3

1. The weather has been very changeable lately. What do you think it will be doing this afternoon?
2. It is supposed to snow tonight. Do you think it will have stopped by tomorrow morning?
3. If it has not stopped snowing by tomorrow morning, what will most people be doing?
4. The roads may be bad tomorrow, but don't be late for your nine o'clock class. What will the teacher be doing?

Exercise 3

A.   Read silently as your instructor reads aloud. Be prepared to identify the different tenses in the paragraphs and discuss *why* each tense is appropriate.

I am standing in front of the student union watching a riot. I have been here since 8:00 this morning. There are approximately two thousand students and three hundred police officers on campus this morning. The students are doing many different things. Some of them are burning cars. Others are destroying books, and a group of male students is throwing rocks through the windows of the union. The police officers are arresting a few students and are beating others with night sticks. I am somewhat surprised at the officers' actions because there has recently been a great deal of publicity concerning police brutality.

The congregation of students at 9:00 yesterday morning was very peaceful and orderly. The students merely wanted to demonstrate against certain university policies. They had been requesting certain changes all year; however, the chancellor has been ignoring every opportunity to sit down and discuss the problems with the student leaders. From 9:00 to 10:00, everyone was quietly listening to speeches made by various campus leaders, and only a few people marched in front of the chancellor's office with placards announcing their grievances. At 10:20, however, a small group of students who belong to an organization called Students for a Democratic Society began shouting insults at various university officials, and the crowd began to do the same, but it never became an angry mob.

It is now 2:00 in the afternoon, and the situation in front of the union is more peaceful. The students still look angry, but the police appear to be calmer. I am standing with a group of friends. They have been here since 7:30 this morning. All of us are wondering what will happen next. Most of the people in the crowd have been talking about the brutality of the police and the chancellor's refusal to meet the student demands. Nevertheless, the crowd is beginning to break up, and many students are returning to their dorms.

The area in front of the union is full of paper, stones, and pieces of broken glass. By tonight, however, the campus workers will have cleaned up the debris. I am certain that the campus leaders will meet and organize another demonstration.

B.   Composition. Imagine that you are watching a crowd of people in Washington, D.C. in front of the White House. The people are protesting the president's decision to draft women into military service. Use the following questions to write an account of what is happening. *Do not* merely answer the questions, but provide additional information when appropriate.

Paragraph 1

1. Where are you standing? What time is it? How long have you been standing there?

2. Approximately how many people are in the crowd?

3. What are the people in the crowd doing? (give at least four different activities)
4. What are the police doing?
5. How do the police look?

Paragraph 2

6. Does your country have a draft system? Has it always had one?
7. Do you think the president's decision is a good one or a bad one? Why?

Paragraph 3

8. Has the crowd grown since you first arrived?
9. What are the people talking about now?
10. What time is it now? Is the demonstration beginning to break up?
11. What are many people still doing?
12. How many people will the police have arrested by the time the demonstration is over?
13. Had you ever witnessed a demonstration before today? (If yes) Where? When? Why were people demonstrating?

Exercise 4: Mixed review. Complete the following note from a teacher to her students.

   While I _____ (sit) at my desk at home, trying to think of an interesting way to test your understanding of the tenses, I suddenly

_____ (have) the idea of writing you a note.

   As all of you know, classes _____ (begin) eleven days ago, so we

_____ (be) together for approximately two weeks. At the start of

the quarter, our class _____ (have) only thirteen students; however,

it _____ (grow) to sixteen students on the third day. We are now in

the second full week of classes, so I _____ (know) we

_____ (get, negative) any additional students.

   By now, all of you know that I _____ (love) to teach gram-

mar. During my teaching career, I _____ (teach) many sub-

jects, but for some reason I _____

(always, enjoy, teach) grammar. All your courses _____ (be) important, but I _____ (believe) that grammar is especially important because speaking, reading, and writing well depend on a good understanding of the structure of a language.

During the time that we _____ (be) in class, some of you

_____ (complain) about doing homework. I

_____ (realize) that you _____ (take) other

classes, and I _____ (understand) that the life of a student

_____ (be) not easy. However, remember that I _____ (be) still a

student, too. Last week while I _____ (study) in the library, I

_____ (ask) myself why I was working so hard. Then I

_____ (remember) that one of my goals

_____ (be, always) to finish my Ph.D. You

_____ (have) goals, too, so you must work hard until you reach them.

As I _____ (promise) the other day, I

_____ (give, never) you an assignment that will take hours to

complete; however, during the first half of the quarter I _____ (give) you an assignment almost every night because I want you to improve your English as quickly as possible.

Some of you _____ (complete, negative) your

assignments, and as a result you _____ (have) trouble in class. Generally speaking, however, this is a good class, and all of you

_____ (be) very intelligent individuals. Work hard and accomplish your own individual goals. By the time this quarter is over, you

_____ (learn) much, and you

_____ (be) one step closer to your dream.

UNIT ONE: PRACTICE EXAM

Part I: *Underline* the incorrect verbs in the following sentences. *Write* the correct verb form on the line.

1. Pollution is a serious problem since 1970.   _____

2. In the past, nobody was caring about the problem.   _____

3. Many countries still try to solve this problem today. _____

4. Before everyone realized the dangers, pollution became a major threat to the environment. _____

5. Every day, some company has been polluting the environment. _____

6. In the early 1960s, the problem is unnoticed. _____

7. Last week, while I am listening to the news, I have heard that pollution is now _____

a major problem in several countries. _____

8. I am in the United States for two months, but I have not been buying a _____

car yet. _____

9. Last month, I am thinking about buying a used car. _____

10. My father has sent me a lot of money last month, so now I can buy a new car. _____

11. By this time next month, I am driving a new sports car. _____

12. I went to a car dealer last night, but he already closed. _____

Part II: Complete the following paragraphs.

One thing I _____ (notice) since I

_____ (be) in the United States _____ (be) the

number of cars. As is true in many large cities in the world, the streets of Denver

_____ (be) filled with automobiles. Although the automobile

_____ (become) a necessity for many people, it

_____ (be) a dangerous necessity. For example, cars

_____ (pollute) the air in cities for many years. In addition to pollu-

tion, the automobile _____ (increase) the problem of congestion in

crowded urban areas. A professor of medicine and public health from Yale

University _____ (believe) that the automobile

_____ (be) responsible for a large number of the heart attacks that

Americans have because they _____ (walk, negative) much any more.

While I _____ (read) a report on pollution in the United States the other night, I _____ (learn) that the average American family _____ (own) two cars and many _____ (have) three. It is obvious that cars _____ (contribute) a great deal to the problem of pollution that this country _____ (have). One solution, of course, _____ (be) to create better systems of public transportation. If the large cities do not create better systems of public transportation, by the year 2000 many Americans _____ (buy) gas masks, and they _____ (wear) them everywhere they go.

However, the automobile may not be a big problem in the future because of the cost of fuel. In this country at the moment, the big American oil companies _____ (have) a lot of trouble. In fact, they _____ (have) a lot of trouble since they _____ (begin) to raise the price of gasoline. In the summer of 1979, the oil companies _____ (increase) the price of gasoline dramatically, and the American public _____ (become) extremely angry. Many people _____ (believe, negative) that it _____ (be) necessary for the companies to ask for more money because they _____ (receive) very high profits for many years. Many citizens _____ (sell) their large cars, and they _____ (buy) smaller ones. This _____ (create) another problem in this country for at least one of the large automobile manufacturers, the Chrysler Corporation located in Detroit, Michigan. A few years ago, this company _____ (see, negative) the future need for small cars, so it _____ (manufacture) only big cars. Today, however, many Americans _____ (want) small automobiles. In 1979, the Chrysler Corporation _____ (ask) the U.S. government for money, so it could prepare its factories to build small cars.

Before I _____ (come) to the United States, I

_____ (think about) buying a big car, but since I

_____ (live) here, I

_____ (decide) to purchase a small economy car.

Tomorrow, I _____ (go) with an American friend to look
at the cars at his father's automobile dealership. His father

_____ (promise) to give me a good deal.

Part III: Write your own sentences using the time words and expressions indicated.

    Example: all day yesterday _____ I was studying all day yesterday. _____

1. still _____

2. by the end of this month _____

3. between seven and ten o'clock tonight _____

4. ago _____

5. for two semesters _____

6. while _____

7. by the time _____

8. yet _____

9. in a few minutes _____

10. every week _____

UNIT 2

Coordination

To the Student   Read before you begin this unit.

In the English language several methods are used to express two or more ideas in the same sentence. In this chapter, we will discuss *coordination* as a method for combining two or more complete sentences, not only to produce longer sentences but also to show the proper relationship between similar or related ideas. We will concentrate on the coordination of two or more independent clauses.

The word "clause" refers to a group of words that has a subject and a verb. In English, there are two kinds of clauses: *independent* and *dependent*. An independent or main clause has a subject and a verb and gives meaning by itself. All complete sentences are independent clauses. A dependent or subordinate clause also has a subject and a verb, but it is incomplete because it does not make sense by itself. Look at the following examples:

Independent Clauses	*Dependent Clauses*
I saw Kayoko yesterday.	when I saw Kayoko yesterday
She seemed very depressed.	why she seemed very depressed
She was going home.	because she was going home

Both the independent and dependent clauses have a subject and a verb, but only the independent clause makes sense by itself. The method of coordination connects two or more independent clauses.

LESSON FOUR

COORDINATING CONJUNCTIONS

The coordinating conjunctions are *and, or, nor, but, for, so, yet*. These conjunctions have the name coordinating, which means that they connect structures that are *the same*. Study the following examples.

Single Words

(2) Nouns	*Men* **and** *women* are in that class.
(2) Adjectives	My parents were *poor* **but** *happy*.
(2) Verbs	Last night I *was sitting* **and** *thinking* about you.
(2) Objects	This typewriter is for *the secretary* **but not** (for) *the students*.
(2) Infinitives	I have *to write* **and** (to) *type* this paper tonight.

Prepositional Phrases

There is still plenty of food *in the living room* **and** *in the kitchen*.

You can lie down *on the bed* **or** *on the sofa*.

This was *in the book* **yet not** *on the exam*.

Verb Phrases

I *am sitting here* **and** *writing a letter*.

Nobody *wants to do homework* **or** (to) *listen to records*.

We *were listening to the teacher* **but not** *understanding the lesson*.

Dependent Clauses (Incomplete Sentences)

Where you go **and** *what you do* is none of my concern.

We can talk *while you are here* **or** *when you return home*.

He is a person *whom I respect* **and** *whom I will always admire*.

Notice that in the sentences given *no punctuation is necessary*. In the following sentences, however, a comma is placed before each conjunction because it connects two *independent clauses* (complete sentences).

Independent Clauses (Complete Sentences)

Jim loves Sue, **and** she loves him.

He proposed, **so** they got married.

They lived in her hometown, **yet** they were not happy.

They stayed there, **for** they didn't have enough money to move.

Sue didn't have a good job, **nor** did Jim.

47

CONNECTING COMPLETE SENTENCES

When the coordinating conjunctions are used to connect two or more sentences, the statements on both sides of the conjunction *must have* a subject and a verb.

a. **I was going to call** you last night, but **my roommate was** on the phone for three hours.

b. **I was** too tired to wait, so **I went** to bed.

When writing, put a *comma* in front of the coordinating conjunction when it connects two complete sentences. If it connects single words, phrases, or dependent clauses, no comma is necessary.

I love you, but I can't marry you.   I love you but can't marry you.

Sometimes a comma is not necessary if the sentences are short, but it is always safe to add the comma.

Meaning

AND   shows *addition*.

The phone rang, **and** someone knocked on the door.

"And" sometimes shows cause and result.

The phone rang, **and** the baby woke up.

OR, NOR   express an *alternative* or *choice*.

You can stay home and study for the exam, **or** you can go out and enjoy yourself.
You don't have to stay home, **nor** do you have to study.

Sometimes "or" expresses a condition.

I have to study for the exam, **or** I will fail the course.   (If I don't study for the exam, I will fail the course.)

Often the word "else" is used with "or" to express a condition.

I have to study for the exam, **or** else I will fail it.

NOTE: "Nor" usually connects only independent clauses.

48

After "nor" the *question word* order is used.

> I don't speak French, nor **do I write it.**
> I haven't done my writing assignment, nor **have I done the reading one.**
> Mrs. Peerson is not here today, nor **is Mr. Ray.**

BUT, YET   show *contrast.*

> Dr. Jones was very sick, **but** he taught his class.
> His voice was very weak, **yet** the students understood him.

The words "but" and "yet" are often used with "not."

> His voice was very weak **but not** inaudible.
> He spoke slowly **yet not** very clearly.

FOR   introduces a *cause* or *reason.*

> Dr. Jones couldn't lecture for the entire hour, **for** he had a sore throat.

In informal speech "because" is more common than "for."

> Dr. Jones couldn't lecture for the entire hour **because** he had a sore throat.

NOTE: "For" only connects independent clauses (complete sentences).

SO   introduces a *result.*

> I've been studying diligently all year, **so** I'm going to take a vacation during the summer quarter.

NOTE: "So" usually connects only independent clauses.

REMEMBER:

These words have different meanings, so they show different relationships between the ideas in two sentences. However, the relationship is always *logical:* it makes sense. Look at the following sentence.

> The grammar test on tenses was very long, but it took a long time to finish.

This sentence has a subject and a verb in each independent clause. There is a comma before the conjunction. Why does the sentence sound "funny"?

The word "but" shows contrast, so after it we need a statement that contrasts with the first statement. "It took a long time to finish" is not in contrast to the first sentence. We need another conjunction or a slightly different sentence.

The grammar test on tenses was very long, **so** it took a long time to finish.

The grammar test on tenses was very long, **but** it didn't take a long time to finish.

Be careful of meaning at all times.

Exercise 1:   Meaning. Write a sentence that will complete the following statements. Be careful of the meaning indicated by each conjunction.

1. The life of a foreign student is sometimes difficult,

    yet _____

    _____

    for _____

    _____

2. The students in this English Center must pass three out of five courses,

    and _____

    _____

    or _____

    _____

3. I have always enjoyed studying languages,

    so _____

    _____

    but _____

    _____

4. Pierre has not enjoyed living in the United States,

    nor _____

Exercise 2:   Meaning. Oral practice. Complete the following sentences. There is more than one way to complete each sentence, but remember to express the correct relationship indicated by the conjunction.

Group 1

1. This quarter began approximately three weeks ago, **and** . . .
2. The students in section two are all men, **but** . . .

3. I didn't attend class yesterday, **for** . . .

4. Some students have been complaining about the amount of homework, **yet** . . .

Group 2

1. In 1978, Sadat, Begin, and Carter met at Camp David, **for** . . .

2. During their initial meetings, they spent many days together, **yet** . . .

3. During the first few meetings, they reached only a few minor agreements, **so** . . .

4. These three men worked diligently to solve many of their differences, **and** . . .

Group 3

1. Money cannot buy love, **nor** . . .

2. Some people love money more than anything else, **so** . . .

3. I've been working hard all my life, **yet** . . .

4. I've never had much money, **and** . . .

Group 4

1. I don't have a government scholarship for studying, **and** . . .

2. I was a terrible student in my country, **so** . . .

3. My friend's embassy pays for his tuition, books, and food, **but** . . .

4. After I finish my studies, I will get a job, **or** . . .

CONNECTING MORE THAN TWO SENTENCES

When you combine more than two sentences, it is sometimes necessary to make certain changes in the sentences, so that they will sound smoother.

Example: My parents wanted me to have the experience of studying in a foreign country.

My parents wanted me to have the experience of learning another language.

My parents do not want me to remain in a foreign country too long.

My parents do not want me to change my cultural beliefs.

Connected: My parents wanted me to have the experience of studying in a foreign country **and** learning another language, **but** they do not want me to remain here too long, **nor** do they want me to change my cultural beliefs.

The connected sentence (1) combines similar structures, (2) connects complete sentences, and (3) uses pronouns to avoid repeating the same nouns.

When writing your own sentences DO NOT PRODUCE A STRING of sentences.

Poor Connection:	You can study in the university library, *or* you can study in the dormitory quiet room, *but* you must find a quiet place to work, *and* you must find it soon.
Better:	You can study in the university library or in the dormitory quiet room, but you must find a quiet place to work soon.

Exercise 3:   Combine the following groups of sentences into one sentence. Make changes when necessary. Be careful of punctuation.

1. I haven't had an opportunity to see much of this city.
   I haven't had an opportunity to spend much time with my friends.
   The teachers have been giving us a lot of homework.
   The teachers have been giving us a lot of tests.

2. This quarter, I really like my classmates.
   This quarter, I really like the teachers.
   The teachers are very strict.
   The teachers expect us to study hard.

3. My reading instructor is very good.
   My reading instructor is extremely patient.
   Learning new vocabulary words is very difficult for me.
   I spend more time studying for my reading class than for any other.

4. We have just finished a review of the tenses.
   I'm still having a little trouble with the tenses.
   I will continue to study the tenses on my own.

5. We're going to have a test on the conjunctions next week.
   I won't be able to go anywhere this weekend.
   I want to do well on the test.
   I want to make sure that my final grammar grade is high.

6. Juan, my roommate, is very fortunate.
   Juan doesn't have to worry about tuition.
   Juan doesn't have to worry about clothes.
   I don't have a scholarship.
   My father doesn't have much money.

7. One of my classmates was very upset last week.
   His embassy told him it would not continue to pay for his wife's studies.

This classmate will try to convince the embassy to change its mind.
His wife is intelligent.
His wife is interested in learning.

8. Ali will complete his English studies this quarter.
   Ali is not going to begin university work immediately.
   Ali is not planning to visit his country.
   Ali wants to travel around for a while.

LESSON FIVE

CORRELATIVE CONJUNCTIONS

Correlatives are conjunctions with two parts. The most common correlatives are the following:

either . . . or   neither . . . nor   not only . . . but also   both . . . and

Correlatives may connect

1. Complete sentences (independent clauses)

   a. **Either** I will come, **or** I will call you.

   b. **Neither** am I rich, **nor** am I poor.

   c. **Not only** is Bob here, **but** his roommates are **also** here.

2. Similar structures: words and phrases of the same kind

   a. I will **either** come **or** call you.   (two verbs)

   b. I am **neither** rich **nor** poor.   (two adjectives)

   c. **Not only** Bob **but also** his roommates are here.   (two nouns)

Either . . . Or

Either . . . or means "one or the other." It indicates a choice or alternative.

Connecting Two Complete Sentences

1. You must tell the truth. You must go to jail.

   Either you must tell the truth, **or** you must go to jail.

2. A person is honest. A person is dishonest.

   Either one is honest, **or** one is dishonest.

3. I will see you at home. I will see you in jail.

   Either I will see you at home, **or** I will see you in jail.

4. I can call your father. I can call your mother.

   Either I can call your father, **or** I can call your mother.

5. You tell the truth. I will report you to the police.

   Either you tell the truth, **or** I will report you to the police.

Connecting Similar Structures

1. You must tell the truth. You must go to jail.

   You must **either** *tell the truth* **or** *go to jail*.   (two verb phrases)

2. A person is honest. A person is dishonest.

   A person is **either** *honest* **or** *dishonest*.   (two adjectives)

3. I will see you at home. I will see you in jail.

   I will see you **either** *at home* **or** *in jail*.   (two prepositional phrases)

4. I can call your father. I can call your mother.

   I can call **either** *your father* **or** *your mother*.   (two noun objects)

5. You tell the truth. I will report you to the police.

NOTE: The subjects of the two sentences are different in sentence 5, so the two verb phrases cannot be connected.

---

   incorrect: You either tell the truth or report you to the police.

PUNCTUATION:

When connecting two complete sentences, use a comma after the first sentence.

   Either the baby is sick, or he is tired.

Do not use a comma when connecting similar structures.

   The baby is **either** sick **or** tired.

Word Order

When connecting two complete sentences, the auxiliary + verb combination is in its usual order for statements: Either you must tell the truth . . .

When connecting two verbs or verb phrases with auxiliaries, "either" is after the auxiliary verb. Do not repeat the auxiliary after "or."

You *must* either *tell* the truth or go to jail.

He *has* either *lost* his watch or misplaced it.

She *is* either *crying* or *laughing* very hard.

When there are two auxiliary verbs, "either" is after the first one.

You *have* either *been sleeping* or watching television.
  (1)   (2)

When using "either . . . or" to connect similar structures, remember to place "either" as close as possible to the structure it is identifying.

correct: I can call **either** *your father* **or** *your mother*.

incorrect: I can either call your father or your mother.

Subject–Verb Agreement

Singular subjects joined by either . . . or take a *singular verb* after "or."

Either my roommate or I am going to go to the party.

If both *subjects are plural*, the *verb is plural* after "or."

Either my parents or my sisters are going to visit me this summer.

If *one subject is singular* and the *other subject is plural*, the *verb agrees with the subject after "or."*   (the subject closest to the verb)

Either my parents or my **sister is** going to visit me.

Either my sister or my **parents are** going to visit me.

Exercise 1:   Connect the following sentences in the two ways discussed on page 54.

Example: I will study during the summer quarter. I will take a vacation.

  a. **Either** I will study during the summer quarter, **or** I will take a vacation.

  b. I will **either** *study* **or** *take a vacation* during the summer quarter.

55

1. Jim and Bob jog every morning. They do push-ups.

   a. _____

   b. _____

2. Jim runs around the park. He runs around the block.

   a. _____

   b. _____

3. They will make the U.S. Olympic team. They will be very disappointed.

   a. _____

   b. _____

4. Bob won a gold medal. He won a silver medal four years ago. I'm not sure.

   a. _____

   b. _____

5. Jim is running. He is doing push-ups at the moment.

   a. _____

   b. _____

6. He will represent the United States this year. He will have to wait four more years.

   a. _____

   b. _____

7. Peggy Fleming was an Olympic ice skater. She was an Olympic skier.

   a. _____

   b. _____

8. My brother is going to the next Olympic games. My sisters are going.

   a. _____

   b. _____

Neither . . . Nor

Neither . . . nor means "not one or the other."

Connecting Two Complete Sentences

1. Money is not important to me. Success is not important to me.

   Neither is money important to me, **nor** is success important to me.

2. I don't want fortune. I don't want fame.

> **Neither** do I want fortune, **nor** do I want fame.

3. The director is not here. His secretary is not here.

> **Neither** is the director here, **nor** is his secretary.

4. Your son isn't outside. He isn't inside.

> **Neither** is your son outside, **nor** is he inside.

5. This coffee is not good. It isn't hot.

> **Neither** is this coffee good, **nor** is it hot.

6. Sue has not arrived. She has not called.

> **Neither** has Sue arrived, **nor** has she called.

NOTE: When connecting two complete sentences (independent clauses), after the words "neither" and "nor" the sentence is in the form of a question. But do not use a question mark.

1. is money important to me	is success important to me
2. do I want fortune	do I want fame
6. has Sue arrived	has she called

Connecting Similar Structures

1. Money is not important to me. Success is not important to me.

> **Neither** *money* **nor** *success* is important to me.   (two noun subjects)

2. I don't want fortune. I don't want fame.

> I want **neither** *fortune* **nor** *fame.*   (two noun objects)

3. This coffee is not good. It isn't hot.

> This coffee is **neither** *good* **nor** *hot.*   (two adjectives)

4. Your son isn't outside. He isn't inside.

> Your son is **neither** *outside* **nor** *inside.*   (two adverbs)

5. Sue has not arrived. She has not called.

> Sue has **neither** *arrived* **nor** *called.*   (two verbs)

PUNCTUATION:

When connecting two complete sentences, use a comma after the first sentence.

Neither has Sue arrived, nor has she called.

Do not use a comma when connecting similar structures.

Sue has **neither** *arrived* **nor** *called.*

Word Order

Remember the question word order after "neither" and "nor" when connecting complete sentences.

Neither do I love you, nor do I want to marry you.

When connecting two verbs or verb phrases with auxiliaries, "neither" is after the auxiliary verb.

I *have* neither finished my composition nor completed the reading assignment.
Sue *is* neither coming nor planning to call.

When there are two auxiliary verbs, "neither" is after the first one.

I *have* neither been watching television nor sleeping.
   (1)   (2)

When using "neither . . . nor" to connect similar structures, remember to place "neither" as close as possible to the structure it is identifying.

correct: I am **neither** *happy* **nor** *sad* today.
incorrect: I neither am happy nor sad today.

Subject–Verb Agreement

The rules are the same as for "either . . . or," but let's review them.
Singular subjects joined by neither . . . nor take a *singular verb* after "nor."

Neither Maria nor Jabria is coming to the party.

When both *subjects are plural,* the *verb is plural.*

Neither the teachers nor the students want an extra week of classes.

If *one subject is singular* and the *other subject is plural,* the *verb agrees with the subject* after "nor."   (the subject closest to the verb)

Neither the director nor the **teachers want** an extra week of classes.

Neither the teachers nor the **director wants** an extra week of classes.

Exercise 2: Connect the following sentences in the two ways discussed on page 57.

> **Example:** Bob isn't studying this quarter. He isn't working this quarter.
>
> a. **Neither** is Bob studying this quarter, **nor** is he working.
>
> b. Bob is **neither** *studying* (this quarter) **nor** *working*.
> Bob is **neither** *studying* **nor** *working* (this quarter).

Group 1

1. Our test wasn't long. It wasn't difficult

   a. _____

   b. _____

2. I haven't been getting very high grades. I haven't been getting very low grades.

   a. _____

   b. _____

3. I didn't review very much. I didn't study very hard.

   a. _____

   b. _____

4. Ali has not passed a test yet. Jose hasn't passed a test yet.

   a. _____

   b. _____

5. The next test will not cover Chapter 1. It will not cover Chapter 2.

   a. _____

   b. _____

Group 2

1. The bank would not cash my check. The supermarket would not cash it.
2. I haven't gotten a student I.D. yet. I don't have a U.S. driver's license.
3. I don't have any food to eat. I don't have any money to buy food.
4. Nevertheless, I'm not sad about this. I'm not worried about it.
5. I will not ask my parents for money. I will not borrow any money from my friends.

Not Only . . . But Also

Connecting Complete Sentences

There are several ways to use this correlative. We will study the two most commonly used patterns.

Pattern 1: In the first pattern, "but also" is kept together.

> We need a new stove. We need a new refrigerator.

> **Not only** do we need a new stove, **but also** we need a new refrigerator.

Pattern 2: In the second pattern, the subject or the subject + verb separates "but also."

> **Not only** do we need a new stove, **but** we **also** need a new refrigerator.

> **Not only** is our stove old, **but** it is **also** ugly.

NOTE: The word order after "not only" is in the form of a question.

---

1. Bob has a car. He has a motorcycle.

   > **Not only** does Bob have a car, **but also** he has a motorcycle.
   > **Not only** does Bob have a car, **but** he **also** has a motorcycle.

2. He is a fast driver. He is a good driver.

   > **Not only** is he a fast driver, **but also** he is a good one.
   > **Not only** is he a fast driver, **but** he is **also** a good one.

3. He knows how to ride a motorcycle. He knows how to repair a motorcycle.

   > **Not only** does he know how to ride a motorcycle, **but also** he knows how to repair one.
   > **Not only** does he know how to ride a motorcycle, **but** he **also** knows how to repair one.

Connecting Similar Structures

1. Bob has a car. He has a motorcycle.

   > Bob has **not only** *a car* but also *a motorcycle*.   (two noun objects)

2. He is a fast driver. He is a good driver.

   > He is **not only** *a fast driver* but also *a good one*.   (two adjectives + nouns)

3. He repairs motorcycles. He teaches motorcycle repair.

   He **not only** *repairs* motorcycles **but also** *teaches* motorcycle repair. (two verbs)

NOTE: "Not only" and "but . . . also" must be as close as possible to the structures they identify.

Exercise 3: Connect the following sentences in the three ways given in the example.

   Example: That book is boring. It is difficult.
   1. **Not only** is that book boring, **but also** it is difficult.
   2. **Not only** is that book boring, **but** it is **also** difficult.
   3. That book is **not only** *boring* **but also** *difficult.*

1. I enjoy living in another country. I enjoy learning a second language.
2. The French language is beautiful to me. It is easy for me to learn.
3. The customs are different. They are interesting.
4. The French people are friendly. They are hospitable.
5. I love French music. I love French art.
6. I have traveled all over France. I have been in other parts of Europe.
7. I have met many French people. I have met many Italians.
8. I like French food. I like Italian food.
9. My parents are coming to Paris next month. They are bringing my younger sister.
10. My sister wants to see me. She wants to stay with me.

Both . . . And

This correlative is usually used to connect only words and phrases that are similar in structure. It is rarely used to connect complete sentences.

Connecting Similar Structures

1. Our grammar teacher is sick today. Our reading teacher is sick today.

   Both *our grammar teacher* **and** *our reading teacher* are sick today. (two noun subjects)

2. I have been having trouble with grammar. I have been having trouble with reading.

I have been having trouble with **both** *grammar* **and** *reading*.   (two noun objects)

3. Bob jogs every morning. He does push-ups every morning.

   Bob **both** *jogs* **and** *does* push-ups every morning.   (two verbs)

4. There is more food on the table. There is more food in the refrigerator.

   There is more food **both** *on the table* **and** *in the refrigerator*.   (two prepositional phrases)

Subject–Verb Agreement

Subjects joined by "both . . . and" always take a *plural verb.*

My mother is coming. My father is coming.
Both my mother and my father **are** coming.

My sister is coming. My brothers are coming.
Both my sister and my brothers **are** coming.

My brothers are arriving tonight. My sister is arriving tonight.
Both my brothers and my sister **are** arriving tonight.

Exercise 4:   Use "both . . . and" to connect the following sentences. Connect only similar structures.

1. Most students enjoy living in another country.
   Most students enjoy studying in another country.
2. My best friend is an excellent student.
   His wife is an excellent student.
3. They study at home.
   They study in the library.
4. They encourage each other.
   They criticize each other.
5. His parents are coming to visit them.
   His grandfather is coming to visit them.
6. They have always wanted to see California.
   They have always wanted to see Nevada.
7. California has Hollywood.
   California has Disneyland.
8. My friend's father has made a lot of money in the restaurant business.
   His father has made a fortune in the import–export business.

1. _____

_____

2. _____

_____

3. _____

_____

4. _____

_____

5. _____

_____

6. _____

_____

7. _____

_____

8. _____

_____

Exercise 5: Connecting similar structures (no punctuation). First, read each sentence and underline the structures you will connect. Then, rewrite each sentence with the correlative in parentheses.

> **Example:** My husband's family doesn't live near us. My family doesn't live near us.   (neither . . . nor)
>
> **Neither** my husband's family **nor** my family lives near us.

1. (either . . . or)   Bob and Nancy will have their wedding in June. They will have it in July.

_____

2. (neither . . . nor)   Bob's brother can't come. His sisters can't come.

_____

3. (both . . . and)   His brother is living in another country this year. His sisters are living in another country this year.

_____

4. (not only . . . but also)   They have invited the members of their family. They have invited their friends.

_____

5. (either . . . or)   After the ceremony, the guests can dance. They can walk around the garden.

_____

6. (neither . . . nor)   They do not plan to serve beer. They do not plan to serve whiskey.

_____

7. (both . . . and)   Bob's parents are against having liquor at the wedding. Nancy's parents are against having liquor at the wedding.

_____

8. (not only . . . but also)   For their honeymoon, they're planning to visit Spain. They're planning to visit Italy.

_____

9. (either . . . or)   In Italy, they will drive around the country. They will tour it on bicycles.

_____

10. (both . . . and)   Bob says that Nancy is beautiful. He says she is intelligent.

_____

Exercise 6: Connecting similar structures. Use the appropriate correlative to connect the following sentences so that **similar structures** are connected. Remember to place the correlatives as close as possible to the words they identify. For some sentences, more than one correlative may be appropriate.

Example: I will have coffee. I will have tea.

I will have **either** coffee **or** tea.

1. Coffee is not good for some people. Tea is not good for some people.
2. Coffee contains caffeine. Tea contains caffeine.
3. Coffee keeps some people awake. It makes them nervous.
4. My father doesn't drink coffee. My mother doesn't drink it.
5. For some people, coffee keeps them awake. For these people it helps them relax.
6. I have always preferred hot chocolate. I have always preferred cold milk.
7. When I was at home, I never drank coffee. I never drank tea.

8. My friend must have several cups of coffee in the morning. His wife must have several cups of coffee in the morning.

9. They prefer black coffee, so they don't take cream. They never have sugar.

10. They drink coffee in the morning. They drink coffee throughout the day.

11. They are nervous. They are irritable.

12. Coffee has been a popular beverage for thousands of years. Tea has been a popular beverage for thousands of years.

13. Most restaurants offer coffee. Most restaurants offer Sanka for people who can't have any caffeine.

14. Coffee has risen in cost over the past few years. Tea has risen in cost over the past few years.

LESSON SIX

CONJUNCTIVE ADVERBS

Here is a list of the most common conjunctive adverbs. Notice that some of them consist of more than one word.

however	**moreover**	**hence**	**otherwise**
nevertheless	**furthermore**	**therefore**	**then**
still	**also**	**consequently**	**afterward**
on the contrary	**besides**	**thus**	**later (on)**
	in fact	**as a result**	

Like the coordinating conjunctions, these words also join complete sentences (independent clauses) and express a logical relationship between the ideas in the sentences.

However, conjunctive adverbs *cannot* join single words, phrases, and incomplete sentences (dependent clauses).

Meaning

These words show a *contrast* between the ideas in two sentences.

however   still
nevertheless   on the contrary

Studies show that cigarette smoking is dangerous to one's health; **however,** millions of people continue to smoke.

; **nevertheless,** millions of people continue to smoke.
; **still,** millions of people continue to smoke.

The phrase "on the contrary" also indicates contrast but in a slightly different way. Therefore, it is not always possible to use this expression in place of "however," "nevertheless," and "still."

The phrase "on the contrary" usually connects two sentences that express ideas that are clearly the opposite of one another.

Very often (not always, but often) to make the opposition clearer, the complete sentence on the left side of the expression is a negative statement, and the complete sentence on the right side of the expression is an affirmative statement.

Examples: Our last exam **wasn't** difficult; on the contrary, it **was** easy.

The teacher **wasn't** angry with the test scores; on the contrary, she **was** very happy with them.

The word "however" cannot be used in the sentences above. But in some sentences either "on the contrary" or "however" is possible.

A good student usually gets good grades; **however,**   a poor student gets
                                            ; on the contrary,
poor grades.

Exercise 1:   Write "on the contrary," "however," or both when applicable in the following sentences.

1. My roommate and I do not plan to study during the winter quarter;

   _____, we are going to take a vacation.

2. I had planned to drive to Mexico; _____, my car is too old.

3. I had planned to drive to Mexico; _____, my roommate
   wants to go to Canada.

4. I don't speak French very well; _____, I speak it very poorly.

5. I don't speak French very well; _____, I speak Spanish
   beautifully.

6. For some reason, I always had trouble with French in high school;

   _____, Spanish was very easy for me.

7. My roommate doesn't like hot weather; _____, he prefers
   cold weather.

8. My roommate doesn't like hot weather; _____, he doesn't
   mind it sometimes.

9. I prefer water skiing; _____, my roommate likes to ski in
   snow.

10. Water skiing isn't difficult; _____, it's quite easy.

11. Water skiing isn't difficult; _____, I still have a lot to learn about it.

12. I have been water skiing for many years; _____, I still have to be very careful.

These words give *additional information*. They add to the idea in the first sentence.

moreover	also	in fact
furthermore	besides	

"In fact" also adds emphasis to the idea in the first sentence.

Bill passed all his examinations; **in fact,** he graduated with honors.

His biology professor encouraged him to go to graduate school; **moreover,** he nominated Bill for a graduate scholarship.

These words show a *cause–result* relationship. The second sentence gives the result of the idea in the first sentence.

hence	consequently	as a result
therefore	thus	

I can't speak French very well; **therefore,** I didn't enjoy my trip to France.

Many French people didn't understand English very well; **as a result,** I used a lot of gestures.

This word expresses a *condition*.

otherwise

                                                          ; **if we don't,**
We must find solutions to the problem of pollution; **otherwise,**   we may all be wearing gas masks one day.

                                        ; **if we don't,**
We must clean up our rivers and lakes; **otherwise,** the fish will die.

                              ; **if you are,**
Don't be absent from class; **otherwise,** you will miss the review.

The following words show a *time sequence*.

then   afterward   later (on)

The student demonstrators destroyed the student union; **then** they marched toward the library.

The campus police asked them to go home; **afterward** the police began to arrest some of the demonstrators.

At first, I was going to join the demonstration; **later on** I changed my mind.

Position and Punctuation

There are four punctuation patterns for complete sentences joined by conjunctive adverbs. Study the position of the conjunctive adverb and the punctuation marks carefully.

Pattern 1:   Conjunctive adverb *between two sentences.* (Note the semicolon and comma.)

I'm studying English in Denver; **however,** my best friend is in Houston.

Pattern 2:   Conjunctive adverb *at the beginning of the second sentence.* (Note the period, capital letter, and comma.)

I'm studying English in Denver. **However,** my best friend is in Houston.

Pattern 3:   Conjunctive adverb *within the second sentence.* (Note the period, capital letter, and commas.)

I'm studying English in Denver. My best friend, **however,** is in Houston.

NOTE: The conjunctive adverb is usually placed after the complete subject, in front of the main verb or the auxiliary verb.

Pattern 4:   Conjunctive adverb *at the end of the second sentence.* (Note the periods, capital letter, and comma.)

I'm studying English in Denver. My best friend is in Houston, **however.**

IMPORTANT: Then, afterward and later (on) appear in pattern 1 more than in any other pattern. However, these time words are not followed by commas.

I gave the instructor my test; **then** I asked about the third question.

Exercise 2:   Punctuation practice. Punctuate the following sentences. You need commas, periods, and semicolons.

1. In some parts of the United States there is a shortage of water   **thus**   residents in these areas can only water their lawns every three days

2. Local governments urge the residents of these cities to use water conservatively   **Otherwise**   there will not be enough water for everyone

3. The governments of many industrialized nations have been worried about the rising costs of fuel for several years   Most private citizens   **on the contrary**   have just begun to realize the problem

4. Gasoline has become a major problem for many Americans   **therefore**   many people have sold their large cars and have bought smaller ones

5. Scientists believe that heat from the sun is an important new source of energy   They realize that solar technology is still in its infancy   **however**

6. Ecologists are also concerned about new sources of energy   **nevertheless**   they want future sources that will not harm the environment

7. Water and fuel shortages are not the only kinds of shortages many American cities have   **In fact**   some cities have electric shortages during the summer

8. Many cities have been studying the possibility of converting trash into fuel to produce steam   **then**   they would like to use the steam to manufacture hydrogen as a fuel for buses

9. There are many different possible sources of fuel   The problem   **however**   is the time and cost of developing them

10. In the meantime, people in the industrialized nations must learn to conserve energy   **otherwise**   they may find themselves walking, not driving

Exercise 3:   Meaning. Complete the following sentences. Remember, there may be more than one way to complete each sentence logically.

1. Married students may not feel as homesick as single students; **however,** . . .

2. Single foreign students do not have any of their relatives nearby; **thus,** . . .

3. Single students usually have more free time than do married students; **moreover,** . . .

4. A single student has only himself or herself to worry about; **on the contrary,** . . .

5. During the week, a married student cannot spend too much time with his or her family; **otherwise,** . . .

6. The married student may sometimes wish that his or her spouse and children were in their native country; **still,** . . .

7. Some married students find it difficult to study in their apartments; **consequently,** . . .

8. Married students often eat food from their native countries every night; **however,** . . .

9. Before coming to the United States to study, the single male student has probably never cooked a complete meal; **in fact,** . . .

10. The married student with a wife and children spends more money on food; **furthermore,** . . .

11. The married student's wife often misses her family and friends; **therefore,** . . .

12. During the first few months, the wife might feel excited and happy about being in the United States; **then** . . .

13. A married student's wife often stays at home and takes care of young children all day; **as a result,** . . .

14. At first, married and single students enjoy attending classes for five hours every day; **later on** . . .

Exercise 4:   Meaning and punctuation. Complete the following paragraph with the following words: "however," "therefore," "as a result," "moreover," "furthermore," "nevertheless," "still," "then," "also," "consequently." Use each word only *one time.* Include the *correct punctuation* for each sentence.

At the beginning of the quarter   the students in the section 3 nine o'clock grammar class were miserable   They could not enjoy a cup of coffee during the

break _____ they asked the instructor if she would think of a way to solve this serious problem   She told them she would buy a large cof-

fee pot if everyone gave her two dollars _____ she told them she would buy coffee, sugar, and cream if everyone gave her seventy-

five cents a week   The instructor _____ didn't collect the

money for many days _____ the students became

more miserable _____ they couldn't stay awake during the second hour of her class   One student from Saudi Arabia was especially thirsty for a

good cup of coffee _____ every day for the next two weeks he reminded the teacher to get the money from the students   Finally   he decided to collect the money himself   He collected two dollars and seventy-five

cents from everyone in the class _____ he gave the money

to the teacher   Now everyone is happy   The teacher _____ is worried about the mess in her office every day after the students get their cof-

fee _____ she is happy, too, because the students are

satisfied _____ they will be awake for her class

Exercise 5: Review. Rewrite the following paragraphs so that they read more smoothly. *Be careful!* Do not overuse the connectors! Do not produce strings of sentences!

The English Language Center began three years ago. It has been a part of the university for only a short time. It has already received much respect from the entire university. It has received much respect from its own students. The members of the faculty are experienced teachers. The students are serious. The program began with only thirty-seven students in the fall quarter. It grew rapidly. In the winter quarter, there were seventy-six students. There were almost one hundred students in the spring quarter.

During the first year of operation, the center was in a beautiful building. There was not enough room. It was growing very quickly. It had to move to a larger building. The second home for the center was larger than the first one. The building was very old. The students did not like it. The teachers did not like it. The rooms were small. The rooms were uncomfortable. There were not enough blackboards. There was no lounge area for the students.

The university prepared a new, permanent home for the English Language Center. It was beautiful. Finally, students were happy. Teachers were happy.

UNIT TWO: PRACTICE EXAM

Part I: Use a *coordinating conjunction, conjunctive adverb,* or *correlative conjunction* to complete the following sentences. Punctuate each sentence when necessary.

1. Many parents in America are upset. Their children are not learning good reading and math skills in school.   (cause or reason)

2. Many parents in America are upset over their children's poor reading and math skills. They are worried abut the problem of discipline in the schools.   (addition)

3. The parents are upset over these problems. They are demanding better teachers and stricter punishment for problem children.   (result)

4. In some states, school officials want permission to spank children. Many parents are against this.   (contrast)

5. School officials believe that spankings are necessary for some children. They will continue to disrupt their classes.   (condition)

6. When they were children, many parents had a lot of homework. Children today have very little.   (contrast)

7. Children today have very little homework. They don't get a chance to review the work they have had in class.   (result)

8. At the moment, most problem students are sent to the office. Most problem students are sent home.   (either . . . or)

9. Parents want to improve the schools. School officials want to improve the schools.   (both . . . and)

10. Problem children interrupt their classes. They prevent themselves and others from learning.   (not only . . . but also)

11. Most problem children don't like school. They don't feel comfortable there. (neither . . . nor)

Part II: Complete and punctuate the following sentences.

1. I was a quiet child in elementary school   **therefore** . . .

2. I had to be quiet   **or** . . .

3. I paid attention in class   **furthermore** . . .

4. I studied very hard   **but** . . .

5. I studied very hard   **consequently** . . .

6. My father worked at my school   **in fact** . . .

7. Most of my friends hated math   **on the contrary** . . .

8. I usually made _____ A's _____ B's on math tests.

9. I completed elementary school in my hometown   **then** . . .

10. I have always enjoyed school   **so** . . .

11. Learning is _____ easy _____ exciting for me.

12. This quarter has been interesting so far   **yet** . . .

13. _____ the teachers _____ the students are enjoying this quarter.

UNIT 3

Indirect Speech

In the English language, there are primarily two ways of reporting what a person has said: *direct speech* and *indirect speech.* In direct speech, we report the speaker's exact words, as in the following sentence:

He said, "It's late, so I'm going to bed."

Notice that in writing a comma follows the introductory verb, and the person's words are placed between quotation marks. The quotation marks indicate that we are reporting exactly what the speaker said without changing any of his or her words. Notice also that the period, question mark, or exclamation point at the end of the statement is placed within the quotation marks.

In indirect speech, we do not give the speaker's exact words, but we keep the exact meaning of a remark or a speech. Whereas direct speech is found in conversations in books, in plays, and in quotations, indirect speech is normally used in live conversations and in written reports where we tell what an author has said.

When you begin academic work, you will discover that you will use indirect speech a great deal in both speaking and writing. In seminars and other small classes, your professors will expect you to contribute to classroom discussions by expressing your own ideas on the topics you are studying. However, your professors will also expect you to demonstrate an understanding of the information in textbooks, articles, and journals. Therefore, you will find that you will be using indirect speech to report what others have written or said about the subject you are discussing in your classroom.

In like manner, you will discover that indirect speech will also be used in your written reports, term papers, and essay exams. Your goal at the beginning of this chapter should be to master the rules of indirect speech so that you are able to report quickly and correctly what you have heard or read.

LESSON SEVEN

TENSE CHANGES IN INDIRECT SPEECH

When the introductory verb (say, ask, tell, etc.) is in the simple past, the verbs in the indirect statement must change. Study the changes for the following tenses.

Direct Statement	*Indirect Statement*
Bill said, "Gail **knows** that man."	Bill said Gail **knew** that man.
Joe said, "Mark **is leaving** today."	Joe said Mark **was leaving** today.
Bob said, "I **have seen** that movie."	Bob said he **had seen** that movie.
Tom said, "We **saw** it too."	Tom said they **had seen** it too.
Jim said, "I **was thinking** about it."	Jim said he **had been thinking** about it.
Sue said, "**I'm going to see** it soon."	Sue said she **was going to see** it soon.
Roy said, "Joan **will go** with us."	Roy said Joan **would go** with them.
Pat said, "I **can drive** us there."	Pat said she **could drive** them there.

NOTES:

1. The verbs in the indirect statements are past in form but not in meaning; in addition to past time, the verbs may indicate present or future time.

2. Sometimes native speakers do not change the tense of the verb after an introductory verb in the past

   a. When the statement reports an *historical fact* or *general truth.*

      He **said** (that) Florida **is** in the southeastern United States.

      She **said** (that) the best coffee **comes** from South America.

   b. When the indirect statement is given *very soon after* the original statement.

      Bob: I'm tired.

      Jim: What did you say?

      Bob: I **said** I'm tired.

3. The word "that" may or may not be used after most introductory verbs.

   He said (that) he was going to come.

4. Never change the infinitive of the verb.

> *Instructor:* I want **to see** you after class.
>
> *Student:* She said she wanted **to see** me after class.

5. Change *all* the verbs in a statement.

> She said, "When I **see** Bob, I **will** tell him the truth."
>
> She said (that) when she **saw** Bob she **would** tell him the truth.

Notice that the main verb after the modal does not change.

6. Pronouns and possessives change to the second or third persons except when the speaker is reporting his own words.

> Jim said, "I like my new car."
>
> Jim said **he** liked **his** new car.   (another speaker's reporting Jim's words)
>
> I said **I** liked **my** new car.   (Jim reporting his own words)

Sometimes a noun is used to avoid confusion and make the speaker clear.

> Jim said, "**He** was very nice when we bought the car."
>
> Jim said **the salesman** had been very nice when they bought the car.   ("Bought" did not change. See page 77, note 3.)

When the introductory verb is in the present tense, there is no tense change in the indirect statement.

Direct Statement	**Indirect Statement**
Bill says, "Gail **knows** that man."	Bill says Gail **knows** that man.
Joe says, "Mark **is leaving** today."	Joe says Mark **is leaving** today.
Bob says, "I **have seen** that movie."	Bob says he **has seen** that movie.
Tom says, "We **saw** it too."	Tom says they **saw** it too.
Jim says, "I **was thinking** about it."	Jim says he **was thinking** about it.
Sue says, "I'm **going to see** it soon."	Sue says she **is going to see** it soon.
Roy says, "Joan **will go** with us."	Roy says Joan **will go** with them.
Pat says, "I **can drive** us there."	Pat says she **can drive** them there.

Say versus Tell

In indirect speech "say" and "said" are usually used *when the person spoken to is not mentioned.*

> Bob said (that) the movie was excellent.

When the person spoken to is given, "tell" or "told" is always used, and it is always followed by an indirect object.

Bob told **Gail/her** (that) the movie was excellent.

It is possible to use "said to me/her, etc."

Exercise 1:   Tense changes. Change the following statement to indirect speech. Change the tense in the indirect statement when necessary.

1. He **said**, "The police know who committed the crime."
2. The police **say**, "We will catch the guilty persons."
3. Mrs. Jones **says**, "I'm going to tell the police everything I know."
4. The police captain **said**, "Our investigation has already begun."
5. The reporter **said**, "My paper will cover the trial in court."
6. Mr. Jones **said**, "I did not see the men."
7. One old man **said**, "I was sleeping when everything happened."
8. The lawyer **said**, "I told the witnesses to tell the truth."
9. The witnesses **said**, "We can identify the men who are guilty."
10. One female witness **says**, "I'm not afraid to tell the truth."
11. Then she **said**, "I have always obeyed the law."
12. The judge **said**, "It is difficult to find honest and brave citizens."
13. The judge **says**, "My court will punish the guilty."
14. Then the judge **said**, "The crime rate in this city has increased 50 percent."
15. The jury **said**, "We found the defendants guilty."
16. The judge **said**, "The defendants are going to jail."
17. The defendants' lawyer **said**, "We are going to appeal the court's decision."
18. The reporter **says**, "This trial was an unusual one."
19. He also **said**, "The jury deliberated for only twenty minutes."
20. The defendants **said**, "We will never change our plea of innocent."

NOTES: SIMPLE PAST AND PAST CONTINUOUS

1. The simple past usually changes to the past perfect in indirect speech. However, sometimes in spoken conversational English there is no tense change if the meaning does not change.

   a. direct: Ray said, "Sue **arrived** last week."
   b. indirect: Ray said Sue **arrived/had arrived** last week.

Compare the following statements:

Direct	Meaning	Indirect
c. Ray said, "I love her."	He still **loves** her.	Ray said he **loved** her.
d. Ray said, "I loved her."	He doesn't love her anymore.	Ray said he **had loved** her.

For sentence d, we must change the simple past to the past perfect to indicate that his feelings are *finished*.

2. In spoken English, the simple past does not usually change to the past perfect if the report is made *soon* after the person has spoken.

    e. Larry: Hi, Bob. *Did* your check **come** this morning?

        Bob: Larry just asked me if my check **came** *this morning.*

        Bob: *(Two days later)* Larry asked me if my check **had come.**

3. In written English, the simple past and past continuous usually change to the past perfect and past perfect continuous. However, in *dependent time clauses, the simple past and past continuous do not usually change.*

Dependent Time Clauses

    f. Bob said, "*When I saw the police,* I stopped."
        Bob said when he **saw** the police, he stopped.

    g. He said, "*When I was driving home,* I saw Gail."
        He said when he **was driving** home, he saw Gail.

Notice that the verbs in the independent clause can change or stay the same.

    Bob said when he was driving home, he saw/had seen Gail.

ADDITIONAL CHANGES IN INDIRECT SPEECH
Time Expressions

> **Today, this morning, yesterday, now, tomorrow, next week,** and so on

If the indirect report is made very *soon* after the direct statement or on the same day, it is not necessary to change the time word.

In the following conversation, Bob is speaking to Pete on *Monday morning.*

Pete: Hi, Bob. What are you doing?

Bob: Hi, Pete. I'm packing. My vacation begins **today,** and I am leaving for Mexico **tomorrow.**

Pete is speaking to Tom on *Monday afternoon.*

Pete: Hello, Tom. I talked to Bob this morning, and he told me that he was packing because his vacation began **today,** and he was leaving for Mexico **tomorrow.**

Notice that the time word changes when Pete speaks to Bill *on Friday.*

Bill: Hi, Pete. Have you spoken to Bob this week?

Pete: Sure. I talked to him **four days ago/on Monday.** He told me that he was packing because his vacation began **on that day/on Monday,** and he was leaving for Mexico **on the following day/on Tuesday.**

Demonstrative Pronouns: This, That, These Those

The demonstrative pronouns usually change to "the."

   a. He said, "I bought **this** diamond ring for my wife."

      He told me he had bought **the** diamond ring for his wife.

   b. She heard the noise of breaking glass, so she went into the living room. She returned with two large rocks and said, "I found **these** on the floor under the window."

     She told me she had found **the rocks** on the floor under the window.

A place expression usually replaces the word "here."

   a. She said, "You can sit here."

     She said I could sit on the floor/beside her/in the big chair, and so on.

Modals

can, will, must, may

In indirect speech, *can* changes to *could; will* changes to *would; must* meaning necessity remains the same or changes to *had to; may* changes to *might.*

"Could," "would," "might," and "should" do not normally change.

   b. "**Could** I use your phone?" he said.
     He asked if he **could** use my phone.

   c. She said, "I **would** help you, but I don't have time today."
     She said she **would** help me, but she didn't have time today.

d. Bob said, "I **might** go to the party tomorrow."
Bob said he **might** go to the party tomorrow.

e. She said, "You **should** work harder."
She told me that I **should** work harder.

REPORTING STATEMENTS

"Say" and "tell" are usually used to introduce indirect statements. However, you may add variety to your speaking and writing by using other introductory verbs that fit the sentence and the speaker.

The following verbs are often used to introduce indirect statements. If you are not sure of the meaning of any of these words, look them up in your dictionary before you begin the exercise that follows.

announce	**declare**	**remark**	**reply**	**predict**	**deny**
complain	**state**	**mention**	**answer**	**promise**	**explain**

IMPORTANT: In indirect speech, these words are not followed immediately by an indirect object *except* the word "promise."

She remarked that . . .   She promised **me** that . . . (or) she promised that
She answered that . . .

Exercise 2:   Replace "said" with one of the words supplied. Choose the word that best fits the sentence and the speaker. Some words may be used more than once.

Example: While we were standing in line, the man behind us **said,** "I have already seen this movie three times."

While we were standing in line, the man behind us **remarked** that he had already seen the movie three times.

1. The speaker on the radio said, "The concert in the part will begin at 8:00."
2. The angry customer said, "My new radio doesn't work."
3. The weathercaster said, "We will not get any rain tonight."
4. After the instructor's explanation, she asked Jim a question, but he said, "I don't know the answer."
5. I didn't know the answer either, so the instructor said, "The answer and explanations are in Chapter 4 of your text."
6. In his televised speech, the president said, "My administration will cut taxes in this country."

7. The children were crying, so their mother said, "I will take you to the movies after dinner."

8. The little boy said, "I didn't eat all the cookies."

9. After he had told us about our quiz, the instructor said, "The midterm exam is going to be in two weeks."

10. The T.V. news commentator said, "This station will present a special report on bikinis."

REPORTING YES/NO QUESTIONS

Yes/no questions are reported with "if" or "whether (or not)."

The president asked, "Did you vote for me?"	He asked **if** I had voted for him. He asked **whether** I had voted for him. He asked **whether** I had voted for him **or not.**

Instead of "ask" as an introductory verb, the expression "want to know" may be used.

The president **wanted to know** if I had voted for him.

Exercise 3:   Use "wanted to know" and "whether" or "whether or not" to report the following questions.

Example: Bob asked, "Did Mr. Fox finish the report?"

Bob **wanted to know whether** Mr. Fox had finished the report.

1. Mr. Smith asked, "Is the next sales meeting in January?"
2. The manager asked, "Has everyone finished his or her report for the meeting?"
3. The secretary asked, "Do I have to attend the meeting?"
4. The receptionist asked, "Did I get a raise?"
5. The manager asked, "Have you been working late every night?"
6. The secretary asked, "Has the receptionist been answering the phone correctly?"
7. The clerk asked, "Do we get two hours for lunch?"
8. The manager asked, "Is the typewriter repairman coming today?"
9. The repairman asked, "Are the broken typewriters in the manager's office?"

10. The manager asked, "Will the company replace these typewriters for no charge?"

11. The repairman asked, "Was anyone using this machine a few minutes ago?"

12. The repairman asked, "Can I use this desk for my work area?"

13. The clerk asked, "Is the repairman going to fix the typewriters after lunch?"

REPORTING YES/NO ANSWERS

Yes/no answers are expressed in indirect speech by subject + appropriate auxiliary verb.

Examples: 1. He asked, "Can you swim?" and I said, "No."
He asked me if **I could** swim, and I said (that) **I couldn't.**

2. He asked, "Will you have time to help me?" and I said, "Yes."
He asked me if **I would** have time to help him, and I said I **would.**

NOTE: The words "yes" and "no" do not appear in the reported (indirect) statement.

Exercise 4:   Report the following questions and answers in indirect speech.

1. He asked, "Do you like parties?" and I said, "Yes."

2. He asked, "Will you be at Mohammed and Carlos's party on Friday night?" and I said, "Yes."

3. She asked, "Are you bringing any records?" and I said, "No."

4. She asked, "Did Mohammed and Carlos send out invitations to their party?" and I said, "No."

5. He asked, "Will their landlord get angry if the guests make a lot of noise?" and I said, "Yes."

6. He asked, "Have they had many parties this semester?" and I said, "No."

7. She asked, "Were they shopping for food last night?" and I said, "Yes."

8. She asked, "Are they going to fix food from their countries?" and I said, "No."

9. He asked, "Are our instructors going to the party?" and I said, "Yes."

10. She asked, "Do you plan to take a date with you?" and I said, "Yes."

11. He asked, "Can I ride with you and your date?" and I said, "No."

12. She asked, "Is Fidel bringing his girlfriend to the party?" and I said, "Yes."

13. He asked, "Has she arrived in town yet?" and I said, "No."

14. She asked, "Have you met his girlfriend before?" and I said, "No."

REPORTING INFORMATION QUESTIONS

When reporting information questions, the word order in the indirect statement is as follows:

question word	+	subject	+	verb	+	remainder of sentence
where		I		lived		in Michigan

He asked, "Where do you live in Michigan?"

He asked me **where I lived** in Michigan.

Exercise 5:   Report the following questions in indirect speech with "He asked" or "He wanted to know."

1. What area of linguistics are you planning to study after you finish your English language courses?
2. Why has Marcella decided to study the child's use of language?
3. When does a human baby usually speak his or her first word?
4. Which word does a baby usually utter first, mama or papa?
5. How many vocabulary words has a child learned by the time he or she is one year old?
6. What kinds of words does a child first use, nouns or verbs?
7. When did you speak your first word?
8. How long will a child continue to produce only single-word sentences?
9. How old is your little boy?
10. Why hasn't he formed any sentences yet?
11. Where was Rafael living when his first child began to speak?
12. How long had he lived there?
13. Why do children seem to learn a second language faster than adults?
14. Whose child speaks both his native language and English?
15. How long has Ali's little girl been attending an American school?

REPORTING COMMANDS

When reporting commands, the word order in the indirect statement is as follows:

affirmative:	Sit down!	She told me **to sit** down.
negative:	Don't sit down!	She told me **not to sit** down.

In addition to "tell," the following words are often used to introduce commands.

82

order	command	warn	direct

The finance company said, "Pay immediately!"

The finance company **ordered** him **to pay** immediately.

The police officer said, "Move back!"

The police officer **commanded** us **to move** back.

The thief said, "Don't try anything funny!"

The thief **warned** Mr. Jones and his wife **not to try** anything funny.

The parking attendant said, "Park your car over there."

The parking attendant **directed** us **to park** our car on the left.

Exercise 6: Report the following commands using "tell," "order," "command," "warn," or "direct." Don't forget to add an appropriate *indirect object* after each introductory verb.

1. The army captain said, "Don't shoot until I give the order."
2. The lifeguard said, "Stop pushing people into the pool."
3. Gail's mother said, "Don't swim in the deep end of the pool."
4. The president said, "Be more careful about conserving energy."
5. Dr. Hurst said, "Hurry and give the patient more blood."
6. The teacher said, "Boys, sit in the front of the bus."
7. The old man said, "Don't go near the house because there is a gas leak."
8. The police officer said, "Put your hands over your head!"
9. The flight attendant said, "Fasten your seat belts quickly because we have to make an emergency landing."
10. The teacher said, "Stop fighting immediately!"

Exercise 7: The following statements, questions, and commands were taken from a composition written by Mr. Mohammed Kurashi in September 1975. Report each sentence in indirect speech with he said, asked, advised, mentioned, and so on.

Example: I miss my hometown.

Mr. Kurashi/he/this student said (that) he missed his hometown.

1. Jeddah is my beloved city.
2. I am thinking of it at this moment.
3. I can see its beautiful streets and architecture.
4. I will visit my love next summer.
5. One of my American friends went there last year.
6. I have always been in love with Jeddah.

7. Go there.

8. Enjoy yourself.

9. Visit the old houses downtown.

10. Do not be like some Americans abroad.

11. Do not stay in your own community all the time.

12. Enjoy the Saudi social life.

13. Do you like to travel?

14. Do you want to visit Jeddah?

15. Have you ever been there?

16. Are you planning to go in the near future?

17. Which countries are you planning to visit?

18. When can you visit the Middle East?

19. Be careful when you ride a camel for the first time.

20. I know you will love Jeddah as much as I do.

REPORTING REQUESTS

A command is an order given by someone who is in authority. A request is something asked for, usually in a polite manner.

"Will you," "would you," and "could you" are often used to introduce requests. When used for requests, they are expressed in indirect speech by ask + indirect object + infinitive.

She said, "Will you hold my packages for me?"
She **asked me to hold** her packages for her.

He said, "Could you tell me the time, please?"
He **asked me to tell** him the time.

Exercise 8:   Report the following requests.

1. She said, "Could you direct me to the airlines ticket desk?"

2. She said, "Would you please watch my little boy for a minute?"

3. She said, "Will you please change my ticket for me?"

4. She said, "Could you give me a seat near the window?"

5. The flight attendant said, "Will all passengers put their small bags under their seats?"

6. The captain said, "Would you please observe the 'No Smoking' sign until we are in the air?"

7. The little boy said, "Could you take me to the bathroom?"

8. His mother said, "Could you please wait a few minutes?"
9. The old man said, "Could you find me a seat in the nonsmoking section?"
10. The flight attendant said, "Would you please wait until all the passengers have boarded?"

Exercise 9: Rapid oral drill. Report the following groups of sentences with your **books closed** as different students read the sentences in each group.

Group 1

Why are you driving so fast?
Do you always drive this fast?
Don't drive so recklessly!
Would you slow down, please?
I don't want to die.

Group 2

Why are you raising your voice?
Do you always talk this way?
Don't talk so loudly.
Could you please be quiet?
I'm trying to watch television.

Group 3

When are we going to have the test?
Are we having it today?
Don't give it to me today.
Could I take it next week?
I've been sick for three days.

Group 4

When did you start smoking?
Have you always smoked so much?
Don't smoke so many cigarettes.
Your cough will get worse.
Will you please stop blowing smoke in my face?

Group 5

Are you going to throw your math notes away?
Don't throw them out.
Could I have them?
I can use them.
Why do you want to get rid of them?

Group 6

Who asked about Chapter 4?
Do you have a question about it?
Don't skip it.
Read it carefully.
It will be on the test tomorrow.

Group 7

When are you going to finish the problems?
Are you almost finished?
Don't try to add all those numbers.
Use your calculator.
There are too many numbers.

Group 8

When are you going to wear something else?
Do you have a nice pair of slacks?
Don't wear blue jeans every day.
Buy some new clothes.
You have been wearing the same jeans since the quarter began.

REPORTING EXCLAMATIONS

Exclamations become *statements* in indirect speech.

"What a terrible day!"	He said it was a terrible day.
"What a beautiful car!"	He said I had a beautiful car.

Exclamations such as "Oh no!" and "Ugh!" are usually expressed by a sentence that explains the person's feelings.

"Oh no! I have a run in my stocking."	She exclaimed with *disgust* that she had a run in her stocking.
	or
	She gave an exclamation of *disgust* and said that she had a run in her stocking.

Familiar expressions such as the following are reported in statement form.

He said, "Thank you."	He thanked me.
She said, "Good morning."	She greeted me.
They shouted, "Congratulations."	They congratulated me.
He said, "Okay."	He agreed with me.
He said, "Aw, come on."	He didn't believe me.
She said, "You're kidding."	She didn't believe me.
He said, "Really?"	He was surprised.

REPORTING MIXED SENTENCES

The following speech contains statements, questions, and commands.

Instructor:	Why is everyone so upset? Don't worry about the exam. Everybody will do well. I have not included any questions on the chapter we have just finished.
Reported (indirect) statement:	The instructor **wanted to know** why everyone was so upset, **and** he told them not to worry about the exam **because** everybody would do well. After that, he **added that** he had not included any questions on the chapter they had just finished.

In the report given, notice that each statement is either introduced by an appropriate introductory verb or connected to the next statement.

Exercise 10: Report the following mixed sentences using connecting words from Unit Two to combine sentences. Use the expressions "first," "second," "then," "after that," "next" to help you move from one idea to the next.

1. *Bob:*   Are you deaf? Turn the stereo down. I'm trying to concentrate on my notes for a test tomorrow.

   Roommate: Okay. Remember this when I have a test.

2. *Police Officer:*   Give me your driver's license.
   Foreign Student: I'm sorry. I left it at home.
   Officer: Where's your home?
   Foreign Student: It's in Germany.
   Officer: Follow me to the station.

3. *Student:* Did the Spanish give California its name?
   Teacher: Yes.
   Student: What does the name mean in Spanish?
   Teacher: It means "heat of the ovens."

4. *Radio Announcer:* The pollution in the city is becoming a major health problem for people with respiratory ailments. Don't drive to work alone. Car pool and drive with a friend.

5. *T.V. News Reporter:* The state legislature has agreed on 55 miles per hour as the lawful speed limit. The police department urges motorists to observe the limit or pay expensive fines.

6. *Sergeant to Captain:* Don't order the men to attack tonight. They are too weak from lack of food. When do you expect our supplies to arrive?

7. *Mother:*   What are you going to build?
   Little Boy: I'm not going to build anything.
   Mother: What are you doing with the screwdriver and hammer?
   Little Boy: I have to fix my television set.
   Mother: Don't you touch that television!

8. *Flight Attendant:* Can I get you anything, sir?
   Passenger: Would you bring me a blanket? The cabin temperature is extremely cold.
   Attendant: I'll be happy to provide you with a blanket. I have reported the problem to the captain. There isn't much we can do until we land.

9. *Ali:*   What have you been doing all afternoon?

   Reza: I've been trying to get my driver's license.

   Ali: Did you take the test today?

   Reza: Yes.

   Ali: What happened?

   Reza: I failed it again.

   Ali: You're kidding! This is the fourth time.

10. *Frank:*   Why were you standing at the bus stop last night?

    Jim: I was waiting for the bus.

    Frank: Is your car in the shop?

    Jim: No. I sold it.

    Frank: Why?

    Jim: I can't afford to buy gas anymore.

11. *Store Clerk:*   Who's next?

    Customer: I am. I've been standing here for ten minutes while you were talking to your friend.

    Clerk: Can I help you with something?

    Customer: Yes. You can give me the name of your supervisor.

12. *Travel Agent:*   When are you planning to visit Disneyland?

    Customer: I intend to go in two months.

    Agent: Will you be traveling with children?

    Customer: Yes.

    Agent: Have you made hotel reservations?

    Customer: No, not yet.

    Agent: Make them now. This is a busy time of year.

    Customer: Is it too late to get rooms in the hotel across the street from Disneyland?

    Agent: I don't think so.

    Customer: Thank you for your help.

INTRODUCTION TO NOUN CLAUSES

When reporting yes/no and information questions, you have been using the following word order:

She asked   where   the book was.
        (question word) (subject) (verb)

She asked if   I had taken the book.
    (if/whether) (subject) (verb)

Native speakers of English use this same word order to *answer* (as well as to report) questions.

Question:	Why is Bob absent today?
Ind. speech:	He wants to know *why Bob is absent today.*
Answer to question:	I don't know *why Bob is absent today.*
Question:	Is he sick?
Ind. speech:	He asked me *if Bob was sick.*
Answer to question:	I didn't ask anyone *if he was sick.*

NOTE: In both the reported question and the answer, the group of words following "don't know" and "didn't ask" is a noun clause. We will discuss these clauses in greater detail in Lesson Ten.

In the *answer*, the verb in the noun clause does not change tenses after an introductory verb in the present tense: "don't know . . . is." However, the verb changes tense after "didn't ask . . . was."

There are many introductory expressions that may begin this type of answer.

1. I don't know . . .
2. I have no idea . . .
3. I can't tell you . . .
4. I'm not sure . . .

5. He (she, they) didn't say . . .
6. I didn't ask (him, her, them) . . .
7. He (she, they) didn't explain . . .
8. He (she, they) couldn't tell anyone . . .

Exercise 11: Student 1: Ask the question.
      Student 2: Answer the question using the expressions above.

1. Why is Jamal returning to his country before the quarter is over?
2. Did his parents ask him to go home?
3. Is he going to return to the States?
4. How long will he stay?
5. Has he received an acceptance letter to a university here?
6. Was he packing last night?
7. What's he going to do with his car?
8. Will he work at home or continue his studies?
9. Does he have to leave immediately?
10. When does he have to leave?

11. Had he been expecting this to happen?
12. Are his brothers going home, too?
13. Why didn't they tell anyone about this?
14. What were they telling the director about this situation?

UNIT THREE: PRACTICE EXAM

Change the following dialogue to indirect speech. Write your report in the form of a paragraph. Do not forget to use the connecting words from Unit Two. Use expressions such as "first," "second," "after that," and "finally" to help you move through the paragraph. *Introduce your report with the following sentence:*

Before Mary registered for the fall quarter, she met with her advisor, Dr. John Smith.

Advisor:	Have you decided which courses you are going to take?
Mary:	I want to take Economics 102, Statistics 203, German 101, and Speech Communication 212.
Advisor:	You're planning to take too many courses. Do you think you will be able to do all the work?
Mary:	Yes. I plan to study diligently this quarter.
Advisor:	I believe you. But when will you have time to sleep?
Mary:	Do you really think it is too much work?
Advisor:	I certainly do. Don't take so many courses the first quarter. I have seen many discouraged freshmen students who could not keep up with their assignments.
Mary:	Okay. I will drop the statistics course.
Advisor:	That's a good idea.
Mary:	Thanks for your time.
Advisor:	Where is your schedule of classes?
Mary:	I left it in the dorm.
Advisor:	Take it with you to registration. It contains all the courses, their times, and their locations.
Mary:	Could you give me a map of the campus?
Advisor:	Certainly.

UNIT 4

Subordination

In the English language there are two types of clauses: *independent* and *dependent.* Remember that an independent clause has a subject and a verb and makes sense by itself. A dependent clause also has a subject and a verb, but it does not make sense by itself.

Dependent	Independent
because I was tired	I was tired.
where the bookstore is	Where is the bookstore?
whom you were talking about	You were talking about him.

In Unit Two, we studied coordination as a means of connecting two or more independent clauses (complete sentences).

I went to Hawaii on my vacation, but my roommate returned home.

I went to Hawaii on my vacation, and I had a wonderful time.

In Unit Four we will begin the study of subordination that joins an independent clause with a dependent clause.

Although I had a wonderful vacation, it was too short.
    (dependent clause)   (independent clause)

I went to the beach every day while I was in Hawaii.
    (independent clause)   (dependent clause)

The method of subordination allows the speaker or writer to (1) express a larger variety of relationships between ideas and (2) show the relationships between facts or ideas more clearly and specifically. Compare the following sentences.

a. I opened the medicine cabinet, and a bottle fell out.

b. When I opened the medicine cabinet, a bottle fell out.

In sentence a, the coordinating conjunction *and* simply adds one fact to another. In sentence b, however, by changing one of the independent clauses to a dependent adverb clause of time, we are able to bring out the relationship between the two facts more clearly.

In this unit, we will concentrate on adverb clauses, adjective clauses, and noun clauses.

LESSON EIGHT

TYPES OF ADVERB CLAUSES

Adverb clauses can be grouped according to the type of relationship they express.

Time

after	**After it had stopped snowing,** I went outside.
as	**As I was walking to the store,** it began to snow again.
as long as	I will never like snow **as long as I live.**
as soon as	**As soon as I returned home,** I made a fire.
before	My roommate had decided to go skiing **before I returned.**
since	She has been a good skiier **since she was a child.**
until	I had never seen snow **until my family moved from Florida to Boston.**
when	**When I was a young child,** I thought snow was only in Alaska.
whenever	In Boston, my father tried to get me outside **whenever it snowed.**
while	**While he was putting on his boots,** I was hiding in my room.

Place

where	I prefer to live **where the sun shines all year.**
wherever	**Wherever it's sunny and warm,** I am happy.

Reason

because	My brothers are studying in California **because they don't like snow either.**
since	**Since it is so beautiful there,** my parents are going to move.

Purpose

so that	I'm planning to live with my brothers **so that I can be near the beach.**
in order that	I want to be near the beach **in order that I might learn to water ski.**

Manner

as	In California, we can enjoy the beach **as we used to in Florida.**
as if	My brothers swim **as if they were fish.**
as though	In California, I will feel **as though I were alive again.**

Condition

as long as	I will enjoy living with my brothers **as long as they keep the apartment clean.**
if	**If they keep it clean,** I will stay with them.
in case	**In case they become too messy,** however, I'm going to save enough money to get my own apartment.
provided that	I will become a good water skiier **provided that I can find a good teacher.**
unless	**Unless the lessons are very cheap,** I won't be able to take any.
whether or not	I'm definitely planning to take surfing lessons, **whether they are cheap or not/whether or not they are cheap.**

Result

so . . . that	California is **so** beautiful **that I can't imagine staying in Boston.**
such . . . that	It is **such** a beautiful state **that I can't imagine staying in Boston.**

Contrast

although	**Although Boston is a beautiful city,** I just don't like cold weather.
though	**Though my father likes mountains and snow,** I'm sure he will learn to like beaches and sand.
even though	He'll probably enjoy water skiing, **even though he prefers to ski in snow.**
while	**While I will never miss the cold weather,** I will miss my friends in Boston.
in spite of the fact that	I'll probably visit Boston from time to time, **in spite of the fact that I will never live there again.**

Function of Adverb Clauses

An adverb clause is used as a single-word adverb or an adverbial expression.

Single-word adverbs and adverbial expressions modify a verb by answering questions such as "when?," "where?," "how?," and so on about the verb. Look at the following sentence.

Yousef bought a new car **recently/last week.**

"Recently" is a single-word adverb of time and "last week" is an adverbial expression of time. Both answer the question "when?" about the verb.

An adverb clause of time also answers the question "when?" about the verb.

Yousef bought a new car **after he had wrecked his Mustang.**

Compare the following sentences:

a. When? I'll meet you **at 3:30.**   I'll meet you **when the class is over.**
b. Why? He works **for his tuition money.**   He works **because he has to earn his tuition money.**
c. How? She sang **terribly.**   She sang **as if she had a frog in her throat.**

Punctuation of Adverb Clauses

You may put an adverb clause

1. In front of the independent clause: Use a comma after the adverb clause.

    When I was a child, I loved Dracula movies.

    Before I could go to sleep, I asked my father to check under my bed.

2. Within the independent clause: Use a comma before and after the adverb clause.

    Once, after I had seen a Dracula movie, I had a nightmare.

3. After the independent clause: Do not use a comma.

    My mother would not let me watch any more Dracula movies because they gave me nightmares.

NOTE: After the independent clause, a comma is usually used before the words "though," "although," "even though," "while," "in spite of the fact that" because they often introduce ideas that are unnecessary or connected loosely with the idea in the independent clause.

My sister still has nightmares from Dracula movies, **even though she is twenty years old.**

I don't watch them anymore, **although they don't frighten me now.**

Group I.	**TIME**	These subordinating conjunctions answer the question "when?"

when	**whenever**	**before**	**since**	**as**
while	**as soon as**	**after**	**until**	**as long as**

---

a. John F. Kennedy became the president of the United States **when he was forty-three years old.**

b. **While he was in office,** he created the Peace Corps.

c. The American people listened carefully **whenever he spoke.**

d. **As soon as he became president,** he pledged to help people everywhere.

e. He had been a naval officer **before he was elected president.**

f. **After he had died,** Lyndon B. Johnson became president.

g. Two American presidents have been assassinated **since this country began.**

h. **Until an assassin's bullet killed him,** he was one of the most beloved American presidents.

i. I cried bitterly **as I was watching the news of his death.**

j. I will remember President Kennedy **as long as I live.**

NOTES:

1. *When* indicates a

   specific point in time: When I met Kennedy **in 1965,** I liked him immediately.

   during a period of time: When he was **in office,** he introduced many new programs.

2. *Just* is often used before the words "as" and "when":

   He was killed **just as/when** he was beginning to accomplish so much.

3. *While* indicates

   period of time during which another simultaneous action takes place: While I **was writing** my report on his life, I **was thinking** about my reaction to his death.

   during a period of time: While he was **in office,** he introduced many new programs.

4. *Whenever* means "any time":

   Whenever I think about Kennedy's death, I become sad.

5. *Until* indicates from an unknown point in the past *up to the time that something happens:*

> I refused to believe that someone had assassinated President Kennedy **until I saw the reports of his death on television.**

Verb Tenses When Using Time Clauses

1. When the verb in the main (independent) clause is in a future tense, the verb in the time clause is in the present tense, not the future tense.

   After I leave the library, I will return home.

   I will finish **before you return home.**

2. When using "Since," the present perfect, present perfect continuous, or past perfect is used in the main (independent) clause, and the simple past is used in the "since" clause if the verb refers to an action that started and finished in the past.

   My roommate **has been** in the cafeteria since it **opened** this morning.

   He **has been eating** since the servers **put** out the food.

   If the verb in the "since" clause refers to an action that started in the past and continues into the present, the present perfect is appropriate.

   My roommate **has** not **missed** breakfast since he **has lived** in the dorms. (He's still living in the dorms.)

Oral Drill A: Complete the following sentences. Remember that the group of words following the subordinator *must have* a subject and a verb.

1. Most politicians smile a lot **when** . . .
2. Many people approved of Kennedy's decisions **while** . . .
3. I vote in an election **whenever** . . .
4. My brother wants to enter politics **as soon as** . . .
5. I had thought that all politicians were dishonest **before** . . .
6. A large investigation into Kennedy's death was carried out **after** . . .
7. My brother has wanted to be in politics **since** . . .
8. I really didn't have much respect for politicians **until** . . .
9. I learned about Kennedy's death **as** . . .
10. Kennedy was a member of Congress **before** . . .
11. **Whenever** he made a speech, . . .
12. **While** I was watching the news about his assassination on television, . . .

Where means a "definite place." *Wherever* means "any place."

a. Please sit **where the view is good.**

b. **Wherever we sit,** we have a good view.

c. Put the packages **wherever you want.**

d. Did you find the packages **where I had put them?**

Oral Drill B: Complete the following sentences. Remember, the group of words following the subordinating conjunction must have a subject and a verb.

1. Our grammar teacher usually writes the homework assignments **where** . . .

2. I try to do my homework **wherever** . . .

3. In the library, I like to sit **wherever** . . .

4. I always put my finished assignments **where** . . .

5. After I finish my homework, I take a break and go **where** . . .

These subordinating conjunctions answer the question "why?"

Group III.	**REASON**	because	since
Group IV.	**PURPOSE**	so that	in order that

---

a. I didn't want to go anywhere on Friday night **because I was very tired.**

b. I didn't set my alarm on Friday night **since I didn't want to get up early on Saturday morning.**

c. My roommate didn't set his alarm either **so that he wouldn't wake me up.**

d. In fact, he slept in the living room **in order that he wouldn't disturb me.**

NOTES:

1. *Because* and *since* introduce the reason for the situation expressed in the independent clause.

2. *Since* has two different meanings: *reason* and *time*.

    reason: He took an extra quarter of English **since his TOEFL score was so low.**

    time: He has been studying very diligently **since the new quarter began.**

3. *So that* is usually followed by the modal auxiliaries can, could, may, might, will, would.

   Can, may, will are used when the verb in the independent clause is in a present, present perfect or future tense.

   Could, might, would are used when the verb in the independent clause is in a past tense.

   We make airline reservations early **so that we will be sure of a seat.**

   We made airline reservations early **so that we would be sure of a seat.**

   Both *so that* and *because* provide an answer to the question "Why?" but the grammatical construction of the sentence is different.

   We make airline reservations early **because we want to be sure of a seat.**

   We made airline reservations early **because we wanted to be sure of a seat.**

4. *In order that* is more formal than *so that* and is usually only followed by may and might. There is, however, no difference in meaning.

   CBS cancelled all T.V. programs scheduled for 8:00 **in order that the president might give his speech to the nation.**

5. *So* by itself can also introduce a clause of purpose.

   We made airline reservations early **so we would be sure of a seat.**

   No comma is used before "so" when it introduces a clause of purpose. Review Lesson Four for **so** as coordinating conjunction to introduce a result.

Oral Drill C: *Time* versus *reason, since* versus *since.* Complete the following sentences with an appropriate response.

Examples: time: I have been searching for a good lawyer **since I received my speeding ticket last week.**

reason: I need the name of a good lawyer **since I have to appear in court next month.**

1. time: Joan has wanted to be a teacher **since** . . .
   reason: She will probably be an excellent teacher **since** . . .
2. time: Richard Nixon has not made many public appearances **since** . . .
   reason: The American public forced him to leave office **since** . . .
3. time: My roommate has not received one letter from his (her) family **since** . . .
   reason: I don't read my letters in front of him (her) **since** . . .

4. time: I have been working on this composition **since** . . .
   reason: I have to make a good grade on it **since** . . .

5. time: **Since** this quarter started, . . .
   reason: **Since** we don't have any homework for Monday, . . .

6. time: Bob has wanted to marry Sue **since** . . .
   reason: **Since** she doesn't love him, . . .

7. time: I have had a terrific headache **since** . . .
   reason: **Since** my headache is so bad, . . .

8. time: I have been an excellent student **since** . . .
   reason: **Since** I have always been so studious, . . .

Group V. MANNER These subordinating conjunctions answer the question "how?" (*As* means "the way.")

as   as if   as though

---

a. I backed the car into the parking space **as my driving teacher had taught me.**

b. The driving examiner looked at me **as if I had done a good job.**

c. I felt **as though I had passed the driver's test with a high score.**

NOTE: The verb **be** usually becomes **were** after **as if** and **as though.**

She looked as though she **were** sick.

They spoke as if they **were** angry.

Oral Drill D: Answer the following questions using adverb clauses introduced by "as," "as if," "as though."

Example: How did you feel after you passed your test and received your license?
             I felt **as if I had just conquered the world.**

1. On the day you left for the United States, how did your mother cry? How did your father tell you to act?

2. When you learned that you had received a scholarship to Harvard, how did you feel?

3. When you took the test on indirect speech, how did you complete the exam?

4. After you helped the firefighters save three small children, how did you feel?

5. How did you feel when you received your acceptance letter to the university?

6. How do you generally treat other people?

7. How does your grammar teacher look at you when you are late?

8. You look very tired today. How do you feel?

9. Last night, you cooked spaghetti for the first time. How did it taste?

10. How does your spouse's best friend spend money?

Group VI   CONDITION   These subordinating conjunctions answer the question "on what condition?"

if	**provided that**	**whether or not**
unless	**in case**	**as long as**

Oral Drill E: Complete the following sentences.

1. I'll fly instead of drive to Mexico with you **if** . . .

2. **Unless** I can get a reduced fare to Mexico, . . .

3. When we get to Mexico, we can save money by staying in a youth hostel **provided that** . . .

4. I really wouldn't mind staying in a youth hostel **as long as** . . .

5. I don't have much money, so I have to stay in a hostel **whether or not** . . .

6. Let's plan to take our camping equipment **in case** . . .

Unless introduces the condition under which an earlier action will or will not happen.

a. I will sell Jim my stereo **unless** Bill offers me more money.

EXPLANATION:

The earlier action "will sell" will occur under one condition.

The condition: Bill **doesn't** offer more money.

NOTE: Unless + affirmative verb = if + negative verb.

I will sell Jim my stereo **if** Bill doesn't offer me more money.

b. Bob will not stop smoking **unless** his doctor **orders** him to stop.
   Bob will not stop smoking **if** his doctor **doesn't order** him to stop.

c. The next reading test will be easy **unless** we **have to define** vocabulary words.
   The next reading test will be easy **if** we **don't have to define** . . .

Exercise 1: A. Restate the following sentences using if + negative verb.

1. The air pollution in this city will get worse **unless more people car pool.**
2. I won't buy a large car **unless the price of gas goes down.**
3. Most cars will continue to pollute the air **unless automobile manufacturers build cleaner-burning engines.**
4. **Unless more people start using public transportation,** the quality of our air will become worse.
5. I plan to ride the bus everywhere next quarter **unless the fare goes up.**
6. **Unless the service gets better,** however, many people will stop riding the bus.
7. I really don't mind waiting for the bus **unless the weather is bad.**
8. I'll be taking the bus every day this quarter **unless my roommate gets a car.**

B. Complete the following sentences.

1. The bus fare will probably remain the same **unless . . .**
2. The bus company will not hire more drivers **unless . . .**
3. No one can become a bus driver **unless . . .**
4. My roommate refuses to ride a bus **unless . . .**
5. It's usually easy to find an empty seat **unless . . .**
6. A bus will not stop at every stop **unless . . .**
7. Most men will let an older woman get on first **unless . . .**
8. The buses in this city usually run on time **unless . . .**
9. Buses are usually comfortable **unless . . .**
10. For traveling long distances, however, I prefer to fly **unless . . .**

Exercise 2: "Until" versus "unless." Complete the following sentences.

Group 1

1. Bob and Sue will not get married **until . . .**
   Bob and Sue will not get married **unless . . .**
2. After they are married, they'll probably stay in New York **until . . .**
   After they are married, they'll probably stay in New York **unless . . .**
3. They're planning to go to Mexico on their honeymoon **unless . . .**
   They're planning to stay in Mexico **until . . .**
4. A honeymoon can be a beautiful experience **unless . . .**
   Jim and Nancy were really enjoying their honeymoon **until . . .**
5. Today, most people cannot take an expensive honeymoon **unless . . .**
   Many newlyweds will continue to choose Mexico as a honeymoon spot **until . . .**

Group 2

1. **Until** you can afford a new car, . . .
   Unless you can afford a new car, . . .

2. **Unless** the price of gas goes down, . . .
   Until the price of gas goes down, . . .

3. **Until** I am able to get my car repaired, . . .
   Unless I am able to get my car repaired, . . .

4. **Until** the weather becomes very cold, . . .
   Unless the weather becomes very cold, . . .

5. **Until** my roommate bought his new car, . . .
   Unless my roommate gets a better job, however, . . .

Group VII.   RESULT   so . . . that   such (a/an) . . . that

In these constructions, the word "that" *introduces the result.*

1. *so . . . that* occurs in the following patterns:
   a. so + adjective + that

      It was **so hot that** we couldn't sleep.

   b. so + adverb + that

      The air conditioner was humming **so loudly that** it kept me awake.

   c. so + many + plural noun + that

      There were **so many students** in the small room **that** I couldn't breathe.

   d. so + few + plural noun + that

      There were **so few windows that** the air circulation was poor.

   e. so + much + uncountable noun + that

      There was **so much noise** in the hall **that** I couldn't hear the professor.

   f. so + little + uncountable noun + that

      There was **so little time** to finish the exam **that** I gave up.

2. *such (a/an) . . . that* occurs in the following patterns:
   a. such + article + adjective + singular noun + that

      He had **such a low grade that** he hid his exam paper.

      This is **such an interesting book that** I can't stop reading it.

b. such + adjective + uncountable noun + that

She makes **such good coffee that** it's impossible to drink only one cup.

c. such + adjective + plural countable noun + that

She wears **such beautiful dresses that** I hate to go anywhere with her.

Oral Drill F: Student 1: Complete the sentence with "so...that."
                      Student 2: Restate the sentence with "such (a/an)...that."

Example: The line to see the movie was _____ long _____

                Student 1: The line to see the movie was **so long that** we had to wait one hour to get our tickets.

                Student 2: There was **such a** long line to see the movie **that** we had to wait one hour to get our tickets.

1. The theater was _____ crowded _____
2. The people sitting behind us talked _____ loudly _____
3. The movie, *Star Wars*, was _____ exciting _____
4. The popcorn tasted _____ salty _____
5. I became _____ thirsty _____
6. The seats were _____ comfortable _____
7. The movie was _____ good _____
8. The end of the movie was _____ happy _____
9. There were _____ many cars in the parking lot _____
10. There was _____ much traffic on the way home _____

Group VIII.	CONTRAST	though	even though
		although	while
			in spite of the fact that

---

a. **Although it may be necessary to spend some time in a hospital,** most people do not enjoy the stay.

b. Most doctors and nurses are friendly and good-natured, **even though their jobs carry a lot of pressure.**

c. **Though my brother has never made good grades in chemistry and biology,** he wants to become a doctor.

d. **While I generally like doctors,** the doctor I had last year was gruff and rude.

e. Actually, he is an excellent surgeon, **in spite of the fact that he has a terrible personality.**

Oral Drill G: Complete the following sentences.

1.   **Even though** there are many people in the world who are afraid to fly, . . .
2.   On Memorial Day weekend in 1979, an American Airlines DC–10 jumbo jet lost its engine over Chicago's O'Hare International Airport, **although** . . .
3.   **In spite of the fact that** the Federal Aviation Administration immediately grounded all DC–10s for several weeks, . . .
4.   After the crash, many pilots and flight attendants refused to work, **in spite of the fact that** . . .
5.   **While** I am generally not afraid to fly, . . .
6.   **Although** the price of airline tickets has risen in the past few months, . . .
7.   Most business executives have to fly, **even though** . . .
8.   My uncle has always wanted to be a pilot, **in spite of the fact that** . . .

REMEMBER:

After the independent clause a comma is usually used before the words "though," "although," "even though," "while," "in spite of the fact that" because they often introduce ideas that are connected loosely with the idea in the independent clause.

Exercise 3:   Practice with "while" to show contrast. When "while" shows contrast, it means "although" and is usually placed at the beginning of the sentence. Complete the following sentences.

1.   **While** I believe our grammar instructor is a good teacher, . . .
2.   **While** I do not think that 50 percent of our grammar grade should depend on homework, . . .
3.   **While** I know it is necessary to take tests, . . .
4.   **While** I don't agree with all of the university's rules, . . .
5.   **While** I believe that this is a good English program, . . .
6.   **While** I believe that it is necessary to have more than three hours of classes every day, . . .
7.   **While** I enjoy our conversation class, . . .
8.   **While** I dislike memorizing vocabulary words, . . .
9.   **While** I believe that studying in a foreign country is usually exciting, . . .
10. **While** I believe that it is important to adjust to the customs of a foreign country, . . .
11. **While** I have been happy here, . . .

Sequence of Tenses

When using sentences that contain independent and dependent clauses, it is important to be careful of the *choice of tenses* in each clause. Two or more actions must be put into the correct relationships with each other. Remember that meaning also plays an important part in your decision to combine various tenses.

Read the sentences that follow and study the various combinations of tenses.

	Independent (Main) Clause	Dependent (Subordinate) Clause
1.	**Simple Present**	**Simple Present**
	I eat Chinese food every night	because I like it.
	I have complete concentration	whenever I study.
	I always study carefully	, even though I am tired.
		Present Continuous
	I eat Chinese food every night	because I'm working in a Chinese restaurant this quarter.
	I must have silence	when I'm trying to study.
	I feel calm	, although I'm waiting for the dentist.
		Present Perfect/Present Perfect Continuous
	I eat Chinese food every night	because I have always liked it.
	I can't concentrate on homework	after I have had a tiring day.
	I am not tired	, even though I've been working all day.
		Future/Future Continuous/Future Perfect
	I am worried	since we are going to have four final exams on the same day.
	She is angry	because he will be leaving ahead of time.
	They are disappointed	because the plane will have left before they leave work.

	Simple Past
I feel calm	because I had a good night's sleep.
	Past Continuous
I feel calm	, even though I was shaking earlier.
	Past Perfect
I believe	that she had taken an aspirin before she boarded the plane.

NOTE: The simple present tense in the main clause can be followed by any tense in the subordinate clause.

Independent (Main) Clause	**Dependent (Subordinate) Clause**
2. **Present Continuous**	**Simple Present**
I'm taking five courses this quarter	, even though I only need three to graduate.
	Simple Past
This little boy is doing his homework carefully	since his father promised him a reward.
	Future
I'm saving my money carefully	so that I'll have enough for a trip.
	Present Perfect/Present Perfect Continuous
She's trying to do extra work	since she has made/has been making poor grades all quarter.

3. **Simple Past**   **Simple Past**

I ate Chinese food every night   because I liked it.

                                     Past Continuous

I ate Chinese food every night   because I was working in a Chinese res-
                                     taurant.
In high school, I had to have silence   when I was studying.

                                     **Past Perfect/Past Perfect
                                     Continuous**

I couldn't concentrate   after I had had a tiring day.
I wasn't tired   , although I had been working all day.

4. **Past Continuous**   **Simple Past**

I was taking five courses   , although I only needed three to grad-
                                     uate.

                                     Past Continuous

At that time, I was eating Chinese   because I was working in a Chinese res-
   food every night   taurant.

                                     Past Perfect

I was going to an oriental cooking   since I had always wanted to cook good
   school   Chinese food.

                                     Past Perfect Continuous

Bob was trying to get a taxi   because he had been waiting for Jim to
                                     pick him up at the airport for two
                                     hours.

NOTE: When the verb in the main clause is in a past tense, the verb in the subordinate clause must also be in a past tense.

Independent (Main) Clause	Dependent (Subordinate) Clause
5. **Present Perfect**	**Simple Present**
	, even though I think about her often.
	Present Continuous
	because I'm waiting for her to apologize to me.
	Simple Past
	since she never answered my first letter.
I have not written to my girlfriend	**Present Perfect**
	because I have been very busy.
	Present Perfect Continuous
	since I have been working so hard.
	Future
	since her mother will not give her any of my letters.
	Future Continuous
	because she will be arriving soon.
	Future Perfect
	since she will have left by the time the letter reaches her.
6. **Past Perfect**	**Simple Past**
He had finished the exam	before the instructor asked for it.

7.	*Future*	*Simple Present*

I will see you   before you leave.

Present Continuous

My parents are going to visit me   while I'm studying in this country.

Future Continuous

I'll help you with your work next quarter   because you will be taking a heavy load.

Future Perfect

They will finish   before we will have started.

Exercise 4: Tense correction. Read the following sentences and correct all errors in tense usage. Write the correct tenses on the lines provided.

1. We can have the party in my apartment next Saturday unless my parents came a day early. _____

2. I didn't want to have the last party at my place because my roommate is sick.

   _____

3. The party last week was so good that many people have stayed very late.

   _____

4. Our landlord never minds parties as long as the guests were quiet.

   _____

5. Our next door neighbor had a very loud party two months ago, and at 1:00 in the morning the landlord was knocking on his door as though he will tear it down. _____

6. As soon as he leaves, our neighbor's party became less noisy.

   _____

7. As the guests are leaving, I noticed that they were speaking in low voices.

   _____

8. My roommate and I finally got to sleep after everyone has gone home.

   _____

9. At our party next Saturday we will tell our guests not to get too loud so that we didn't disturb the other people in the building.

_____

10. The landlord probably won't bother us provided that everyone paid attention to our request. _____

11. Since we were living in this apartment for two years, and we like it, we really don't want any trouble. _____

12. Although everyone is having the right to entertain his personal friends, we must respect the rights of the other people in the building.

_____

Exercise 5:   Meaning. Complete the following sentences. Be careful of tense usage.

1. The instructor told us to sit **wherever** . . .
2. **Before** the instructor handed out the history exams, . . .
3. **While** I was taking the exam, . . .
4. **Even though** I had studied for two weeks, . . .
5. I answered the questions in Part 2 quickly **so that** . . .
6. Part 3 of the exam was so difficult **that** . . .
7. **Since** I didn't answer all the questions, . . .
8. **So that** the instructor could read my answers, . . .
9. **Since** I have been in this class, . . .
10. **In spite of the fact that** I had really studied, . . .
11. **Although** I did the best I could, . . .
12. **Provided that** the instructor agrees with my answers, . . .
13. **If** he grades the papers strictly, . . .
14. **As soon as** I see my grade, . . .
15. **Until** I get my grade, . . .
16. **While** I usually don't worry about grades, . . .
17. **When** the exam was finished, . . .
18. I may get a passing grade on the exam **unless** . . .
19. I'm studying for a make-up test **in case** . . .
20. I will never take another history class **as long as** . . .

Exercise 6: *Think and respond.* Read the following paragraphs. Use your dictionaries to find the meanings of the underlined words. Then, complete the sentences based on the reading, in writing.

Albert Einstein (1879–1955)

In his early years, Einstein showed no <u>obvious</u> sign of genius. He did not even talk until the age of three. In high school, in Germany, he hated the system of <u>rote</u> learning and the <u>drill sergeant</u> attitude of his teachers; as a result, he annoyed them with his <u>rebellious</u> attitude. One of his teachers remarked, "You will never amount to anything."

Yet there were also some <u>hints</u> of the man to be. At five, when he was given a <u>compass</u>, he was fascinated by the mysterious force that made the needle move. Before <u>adolescence</u> Einstein went through a very religious period, and he frequently <u>argued</u> violently with his <u>freethinking</u> father because his father <u>strayed</u> from the path of Jewish <u>orthodoxy</u>. However, Einstein calmed down after he began studying science, math, and philosophy on his own. He especially loved math. At age sixteen he <u>devised</u> one of his first "thought experiments." These are experiments that an individual must do in the mind; they cannot be done in a laboratory.

Within a year after his father's business failed and the family moved to Northern Italy to start a new business, Einstein <u>dropped out</u> of school and <u>renounced</u> his German citizenship. He spent a year hiking in the Apennine Mountains of Italy, visiting relatives, and touring museums so that he could forget the bitter memories of his high school days in Germany. He then decided to enroll in the famous Swiss Federal Institute of Technology in Zurich. It is interesting to note that he failed the entrance exam because of <u>deficiencies</u> in botany and zoology as well as in languages. However, after a <u>year's study</u> at a Swiss high school, the institute admitted him. Eventually, he became a Swiss citizen.

Even at the Institute of Technology, however, Einstein's rebellious attitude continued. He <u>cut</u> lectures, read what he wanted to read, used the school's lab illegally, and made <u>his</u> teachers hate him. One of his teachers, mathematician Hermann Minkowski, who later made valuable contributions to Einstein's new physics, called him a "lazy dog." Einstein was able to pass his two major exams and graduate in 1900 because he borrowed the <u>scrupulous</u> notes of one of his classmates, Marcel Grossman, and <u>crammed</u> for the exams.

Complete the following sentences on a separate piece of paper.

1. **When** Einstein was in high school, . . .
2. **In spite of the fact that** his high school teachers said he would never be anything, . . .
3. **Until** he was three years old, . . .
4. **Even though** he failed the entrance exam to the Institute of Technology, . . .

5. His high school teachers in Germany didn't like him **because** . . .

6. **Before** he became a teenager, . . .

7. **After** he had studied for one year in the Swiss high school, . . .

8. In school, he annoyed his teachers **whenever** . . .

9. Einstein had to take courses in botany, zoology and languages **before** . . .

10. He treated his teachers **as if** . . .

11. His father's business in Germany failed, so the family moved **in order that** . . .

12. **Although** he cut most of his classes at the institute, . . .

13. His attendance at the Institute of Technology was **so** poor **that** . . .

14. He borrowed his friend's lecture notes **so that** . . .

Exercise 7:   Oral review. Complete the following sentences. Be careful of the tense you use.

1. When I was living in my country, my father always let me drive the family car **provided that** . . .

2. Before I would leave the house, he often gave me money **so that** . . .

3. My father is a generous man, but he would never let me use the car **unless** . . .

4. **Because** I came home past my curfew one night, . . .

5. **Even though** I was always a careful driver, . . .

6. One night I had an accident, **in spite of the fact that** . . .

7. Another time the police stopped me **as soon as** . . .

8. Nevertheless, my father usually agreed to let me use the car **since** . . .

9. One night, however, something happened to me, and I began driving **as though** . . .

10. **Until** I get a driver's license for the state I'm studying in now, . . .

11. I have been thinking about buying a used car **since** . . .

12. I had thought about getting a Volkswagen **until** . . .

13. **Wherever** I go in the United States, . . .

14. People in my country drive safely, but the people here drive **so** recklessly **that** . . .

15. **Before** I try to take the driver's test, . . .

16. **While** my mother knows that I am a good driver, . . .

Building Sentences with Adverb Clauses

As students on a high level of study, your sentences in both speaking and writing should contain enough information to make the idea you wish to express clear. The use of one or more adverb clauses in a sentence enables you to add necessary information.

Exercise 8: Rewrite the following sentences so that some of the ideas are expressed in adverb clauses.

> **Example:** I enjoy fall. I prefer summer. The trees and flowers are in bloom.
>
> **Although I enjoy fall,** I prefer summer **because the trees and flowers are in bloom.**

1. Yesterday, John went to the bank after class. He had to cash a check. He would have enough money for the weekend.
2. He has an account at City Bank. They would not let him cash a check. He could present them with the proper identification.
3. John was protesting their refusal to cash his check. The other customers looked at him. He was crazy.
4. John reached in his pocket for his wallet. He discovered he had left it home.
5. His apartment is near the bank. He decided to go home. He could get his wallet.
6. John was angry with the teller. He couldn't think clearly.
7. John had gotten angry with the teller. He knew that the teller was only doing his job. His supervisor had instructed him.
8. Nevertheless, the experience was an unpleasant one. He couldn't concentrate on his assignments. He returned home.
9. John knew that he would not have that experience again. He remembered to put his wallet in his pocket. He left for classes in the morning.
10. That night, John left his wallet. He could find it easily in the morning.

Exercise 9: Complete the following sentences with the type of adverb clause indicated. Be careful of *tense, meaning,* and *punctuation.*

> **Example:** _____ I must work diligently this quarter _____
> (reason)   (independent clause)   (purpose)
>
> _____
> (time)
>
> **Since my embassy gives a student only one year to study English,**
> (reason)
> I must work diligently this quarter **so that I can begin academic work**
> (purpose)
> **as soon as I can.**
> (time)

1. _____ the waitress told us to sit
          (time)

   _____.
        (place)

2. _____ the food was terrible.
        (contrast)

3. The food was _____ salty
              (reason)

   _____.
        (result)

4. _____ I had to write a check
        (time)

   _____.
        (reason)

5. We didn't leave the waitress a tip, and she looked at us

   _____.
        (manner)

6. _____ we will never go to that restaurant again.
        (reason)

Choose one of the following topics and write five sentences of your own. Each sentence must relate to the topic.

1. A current issue in the news
2. Life at your English program
3. Family life
4. American customs
5. Weekend activities when you were in your country
6. Studying and living in a foreign country

Exercise 10: Combine sentences whenever you think it necessary in order to produce a better sounding paragraph. You may use the following words. Try not to use any one word more than once. Be careful of punctuation. Do not over connect.

and	however	still
but	moreover	also
so	otherwise	on the other hand
for	nevertheless	besides
nor	furthermore	thus
or	therefore	in fact
yet	then	as a result

when	as	if
while	until	unless
whenever	where	although
as soon as	wherever	even though
before	because	while
after	so that	whenever
since	as if	in spite of the
so . . . that		fact that

Not every culture in the world eats every kind of meat. Nearly everybody enjoys chicken. One of the most famous names in chicken is Kentucky Fried Chicken. The man who started this business was not always a wealthy man. At one time, he owned a small gas station next to a main highway. Many truck drivers stopped at his gas station. They wanted to get gas and rest. Many of the drivers had been driving for many hours. They were hungry. Mr. Sanders realized they were hungry. He began serving sandwiches and coffee. He served *only* sandwiches and coffee. The sandwiches were good. The sandwiches didn't cost too much. More and more drivers began to eat at his place. Mr. Sanders began serving fried chicken. The drivers had eaten it. They told their friends. His new business grew rapidly. It did not last long. The highway department built a new main highway. Much of the traffic bypassed Mr. Sanders' station and restaurant. He had to close the restaurant. This happened. He was sixty-five years old. He knew his recipe for fried chicken was good. He went around the country trying to sell his idea of opening small restaurants that would specialize in fried chicken. By 1967, there were almost five thousand Kentucky Fried Chicken restaurants. You go anywhere in the United States. You will see one. You like fried chicken. You will enjoy eating the colonel's chicken. Colonel Sanders died in 1980. His name will live on.

Reduction of Adverb Clauses

Sometimes we can reduce a longer, more complicated word group to a shorter, simpler word group. This is called *reduction.* To reduce a word group means to simplify it without changing the meaning of your statement.

Some adverb clauses can be reduced to phrases without changing the meaning of your idea. Study the following examples.

Full Clauses	*Reduced Phrases*
a. I fell **while I was running down the stairs.**	b. I fell **while running down the stairs.**
c. **While I was walking to the library,** I saw my psychology professor.	d. **While walking to the library,** I saw my psychology professor.

e. **Before I left the class, I** asked about the exam.

f. **Before leaving the class, I** asked about the exam.

g. **Since I began this class, I** have learned a lot.

h. **Since beginning this class, I** have learned a lot.

i. **After I had taken the class, I** understood more about human nature.

j. **After taking the class, I** understood more about human nature.

NOTE: You cannot change an adverb clause to a phrase if the subjects of the dependent and independent clauses are different.

> **Example:**   While I was taking the exam, the student beside me was looking at his notes.

The following types of adverb clauses can be reduced in the following ways.

1. Omit the subject and *be* form of the verb in the adverb clause.

   k. I was very sad while **I was** packing my suitcases.

   l. I was very sad while   packing my suitcases.

2. When there is not a *be* form of the verb in the adverb clause, omit the subject and change the verb to *-ing*.

   m. Before **I left** my country, I was worried about my new life.

   n. Before **leaving** my country, I was worried about my new life.

   o. Since **I came** here, I have been very happy.

   p. Since **coming** here, I have been very happy.

Sometimes the subordinating conjunction that introduces the adverb clause is also omitted

   q. **When** my mother **saw** me board the plane, she began to cry.

   r. **Seeing** me board the plane, my mother began to cry.

Note the change from "she" to "my mother" in the independent clause.

---

   s. **Because I wanted** to be brave, I simply smiled.

   t. **Wanting** to be brave, I simply smiled.

3. An adverb clause beginning with *so that* or *if* can often be reduced to an infinitive phrase.

   u. I watched the movie on the plane **so that I would forget about my loneliness.**

    v. I watched the movie on the plane **to forget about my loneliness.**

    w. I had to listen carefully **if I wanted to hear the dialogue.**

    x. I had to listen carefully **to hear the dialogue.**

Exercise 11:   Reduce the adverb clauses to phrases.

1. **While Bob and I were camping in the mountains,** we had many wonderful experiences.
2. **Before we left for the mountains,** we checked all of our equipment.
3. We made a list **so that we would be sure to take everything.**
4. **After we had found the perfect place for our camp,** we put up our tent.
5. **When Bob looked around at the beautiful scenery,** he was breathless.
6. We saw many beautiful birds **while we were fishing in a beautiful little lake.**
7. **When Bob saw me catch fish after fish,** he began using the same bait.
8. I had told him before we left to use that bait **if he wanted to catch a lot of fish.**
9. **After we had caught six fish,** we returned to our camp.
10. We talked about the beautiful day **while we were eating our dinner.**
11. **Before we went to bed,** we put out our campfire completely.
12. That night, we slept in sleeping bags inside the tent **so that we could stay warm.**
13. **Because we wanted to remember our camping trip,** we took many pictures.

LESSON EIGHT: PRACTICE EXAM

Part I: Identification and meaning. First, underline the adverb clauses in the following paragraph. Then, tell what kind of relationship is expressed by the adverbial word, for example, time, place, contrast, and so on.

    Although the institution of marriage has suffered in many countries, in the past few years, there has been an unusually large number of divorces in the United States. In the past, when two people married each other, they did so with the idea of staying together for life, while today many individuals seem to enter marriage with the feeling that they can always get a divorce, provided that the marriage does not work out. In the past, a large majority of Americans frowned at the idea of divorce. Furthermore, many people believed that getting a divorce was a luxury that only the rich could afford. Indeed, getting a divorce was very expensive. However, since so many people have begun to take a more casual view of marriage, it is interesting to note that the costs of getting a divorce are lower. In fact, wherever you go in the United States today, it is not unusual to see newspaper ads that provide information on how and where to go to get a "cheap divorce."

    In spite of the fact that Hollywood has always been known as the divorce capital of the world, today the divorce rate among the movie stars is so high that it is difficult to know who is married to whom, if you are interested in this kind of information. Today, many movie stars change husbands and wives as though they were changing clothes. Until the institution of marriage again becomes a serious and important part of many people's lives, we will probably continue to see a high rate of divorce.

First Word of Adverb Clause	*Relationship Expressed*
1. _____although_____	_____contrast_____
2. _____	_____
3. _____	_____
4. _____	_____
5. _____	_____
6. _____	_____
7. _____	_____
8. _____	_____
9. _____	_____
10. _____	_____
11. _____	_____

Part II: Give the relationships expressed by the following subordinators.

1. while _____
2. as _____
3. since_____
4. so that_____
5. such (a/an) . . . that _____

6. unless_____
7. as long as_____
8. as soon as_____
9. whether _____
10. after_____

Part III: Building sentences. A. Combine the following groups of sentences using adverb clauses to subordinate the ideas.

1. The test on Chapter 2 was difficult. I received a high grade on it. I had studied for it.
2. Part 3 of the test was long. I almost didn't finish it.
3. Miss Peerson is very nice. She permitted some of her students to finish Part 3 in her office at noon. She was eating lunch.
4. A few students start studying. They will not pass the class.

B. Complete the following sentences with the type of adverb clauses indicated.

1. _____, both Miss Berriman and Mrs. Peerson give
             (contrast)
  too much homework.

2. During a test, they usually let their students sit

  _____ _____
          (place)   (condition)

3. _____, she was checking our writing assignments.
            (time)

4. During the last test, Mrs. Peerson looked at one of her students

  _____ _____
          (manner)   (reason)

C. Reduce the adverb clauses to phrases.

1. I ran out of gas *while I was driving home from the mountains.*

  _____

2. *Before we left,* we had forgotten to check the gas gauge.

  _____

3. *When a friendly motorist saw us standing beside the car*, she offered us a ride to
the nearest gas station.

  _____

4. *Because we were cold and tired*, we didn't talk very much in the car.

  _____

5. The kind woman waited *so that she could drive us back to our car.*

  _____

LESSON NINE

ADJECTIVE CLAUSES

An adjective clause is a subordinate (dependent) clause used as an adjective. Like single-word adjectives, adjective clauses describe and modify nouns.

The following *relative pronouns* introduce adjective clauses.

> **who** refers only to persons.

> > The man is a police officer. He lives next door.
> > The man **who lives next door** is a police officer.

whom   is the objective form of who and refers only to persons.

He is one police officer. I respect him very much.

He is one police officer **whom I respect very much.**

which   refers to animals.

Last week someone hit his son's dog. The dog was only a puppy.

Last week someone hit his son's dog, **which was only a puppy.**

refers to things.

The driver ran through a stop sign. The stop sign is on the corner.

The driver ran through a stop sign **which is on the corner.**

refers to groups of people (the audience, crowd, class).

Officer Smith often lectures to high school classes. These classes are learning safe driving principles.

Officer Smith often lectures to high school classes **which are learning safe driving principles.**

that   refers to persons.

The police officers respect him, too. Officer Smith works with them.

The police officers **that Officer Smith works with** respect him, too.

refers to animals.

He was very happy with the new puppy. I gave him the puppy last night.

He was very happy with the new puppy **that I gave him last night.**

refers to things.

I also gave his son a book. The book tells about caring for pets.

I also gave his son a book **that tells about caring for pets.**

whose   indicates possession and is used for animals.

The first puppy was six weeks old. His coat was really beautiful.

The first puppy, **whose coat was really beautiful,** was six weeks old.

used for people.

He is a little boy. His love for animals is very strong.

He is a little boy **whose love for animals is very strong.**

used for groups of people.

We should report pet owners. Their animals are mistreated.

We should report pet owners **whose animals are mistreated.**

used for things.

> This dog house is very old. Its roof has holes in it.
>
> This dog house, **whose roof has holes in it,** is very old.

The subordinators *when, where,* and *why* also introduce adjective clauses.

when   introduces adjective clauses describing nouns referring to time.

> This is the time of year. There are good sales now.
>
> This is the time of year **when there are good sales.**

where   introduces adjective clauses describing nouns referring to location.

> This is the record store. My friend works here.
>
> This is the record store **where my friend works.**

why   introduces adjective clauses that modify words such as reason and explanation, and so on.

> My friend didn't tell me the reason. He quit his job.
>
> My friend didn't tell me the reason **why he quit his job.**

NOTE: The subordinators *where/when* can also introduce adverb clauses. (See page 92.)

However, if the *where/when* clause modifies a verb it is an adverb clause. But if the *where/when* clause modifies a noun it is an adjective clause.

a. I eat at the restaurant **where I work.**
       (noun)   (adjective clause)

b. I eat **where I work.**
    (verb) (adverb clause)

c. My parents called on a day **when I was out.**
                 (noun) (adjective clause)

d. They called **when I was out.**
       (verb) (adverb clause)

REMEMBER:

When using adjective clauses, it is important to place the adjective clause *immediately after* or *as close as possible* to the noun it describes.

Necessary versus Unnecessary Adjective Clauses

An adjective clause is either *necessary* to identify the noun it follows, or it is *unnecessary*.

Necessary Adjective Clauses

A necessary (restrictive) adjective clause is needed to identify the noun and to make the meaning of the sentence clear. Look at the following examples.

    a. All students **who do not study** will fail this course.
       (Will *all* students fail the course? No. Only those *who do not study.)*

    b. Our English Language Center doesn't have any classrooms **that are not comfortable.**

    c. Students **whose native language is English** do not study here.

    d. The man **to whom I was just talking** is one of the new teachers.

    e. This English program has one instructor **who has taught for thirty years.**

    f. The bathrooms **that are on the second floor** are for women only.

Unnecessary Adjective Clauses

An unnecessary adjective clause gives additional information about the noun, but it is *not needed* to identify the noun or to make the meaning of the sentence clear.

    a. My brother **who lives in Chicago** got married yesterday.

    b. My brother, **who lives in Chicago,** got married yesterday.

In sentence a, the speaker has two or more brothers. *Which* brother got married? The adjective clause tells us it is the brother in Chicago, not the brother in Texas.

In sentence b, the speaker only has one brother. The adjective clause gives additional information about him, but it is not needed to identify which brother.

PUNCTUATION:

An unnecessary adjective clause always has commas *around* it or *before* it.

    a. My father, **who is very tall,** played tennis in college.

    b. I learned how to play tennis from my father, **who is an excellent player.**

NOTE: The relative pronoun "that" can only be used to introduce *necessary* (restrictive) adjective clauses.

Here are a few guidelines that you can follow to help you distinguish between necessary and unnecessary adjective clauses.

1. When a *noun has modifiers* preceding it, these modifiers are usually enough to identify the noun so that the adjective clause after it is not necessary. Notice the modifiers in the following sentences.

   a. My grammar book, **which is at home,** was not very expensive.
   b. The first grammar test, **which was on the tenses,** was difficult for me.
   c. When the teacher returned my test, she gave me a disappointed look, **which made me feel very uncomfortable.**

The nouns "book," "test," and "look" are fully identified without the adjective clause. The clauses only provide additional information.

2. The name of a *specific place* does not usually require a necessary adjective clause.

   Denver, **which is a beautiful city,** has two universities.

3. The *name of a person* (especially when the person is well known) does not usually require a necessary adjective clause.

   a. Muhammed Ali, **who has retired from boxing,** is a millionaire.
   b. Dr. Hurst, **who is our dentist,** is a big fan of Muhammed Ali.

4. A *specific name or geographical location* does not usually require a necessary adjective clause.

   The Arctic Ocean, **which is a polar ocean,** occupies about 5,440,000 square miles between North America and Greenland.

REMEMBER:

An adjective clause is used to give information about a noun. Sometimes the information is necessary because the noun has not been identified.

If the noun has already been identified by adequate modifiers, or if *which* person, thing, or place we are talking about is clear, then the information in an adjective clause is not necessary for identification. The information may be interesting, but it is not necessary.

In your compositions and free writing exercises, your decision to use commas to indicate that a clause is unnecessary depends not only on the four points given but also on the context and the information you have already given. A noun in sentence 10 of your composition may not need a necessary adjective clause because of information you gave in sentence 2.

Exercise 1:   Necessary versus unnecessary adjective clauses. First, underline the adjective clauses in the following sentences. Second, circle the noun that each clause identifies. Third, punctuate the unnecessary clauses. Finally, explain why a clause is necessary or unnecessary.

1. Our grammar class which meets at nine in the morning is very interesting.
2. In the class, we don't have any students who are from China.
3. My best friend Carlos whose ability to speak English is very good is from Mexico.
4. The students who entered the class late are having a little trouble.
5. The grammar teacher dislikes students who are intelligent but lazy.
6. Sedig Kenous who is an excellent student is from Libya.
7. His parents live in Tripoli whose ancient name was Tripolis.
8. His father who is very tall is an engineer in Libya.
9. His parents whom he spoke to last night are going to visit him during the next break.
10. They are planning to spend a week in Puerto Rico which is a beautiful island.
11. Sedig's birthday which is in February is only two weeks away.
12. We are planning to give him a surprise birthday party which will be at my apartment.
13. The party that we had last week was for another student who has to return home.
14. The place where we had the party last week was too small.
15. I don't enjoy parties where everyone is crowded into one small room.

Prepositional Phrases after a Noun

We have said that it is important to put the adjective clause next to the noun it modifies. However, sometimes a short prepositional phrase occurs next to a noun and also modifies it. It is best to keep the prepositional phrase after the noun.

   a. He lives in an area *of Colorado*. This area is a famous ski resort.
                    (prep. phrase)
    He lives in an area *of Colorado* **that is a famous ski resort.**

   b. I'm waiting for the ski instructor *in red*. He will be my teacher.
                    (prep. phrase)
    I'm waiting for the ski instructor *in red* **who will be my teacher.**

   c. This book *about Olympic skiers* is excellent. You will enjoy reading it.
                    (prep. phrase)
    This book *about Olympic skiers*, **which you will enjoy reading,** is excellent.

Subjective Complements

Very often the noun before the verb "be" and the noun after the verb "be" refer to the same person.

> My **brother** is a **doctor.**
>
> **Mr. Ray** has been our substitute **teacher** for one week.

The words "brother" and "doctor" refer to the same person. The words "Mr. Ray" and substitute "teacher" refer to the same person. "Doctor" and "teacher" are called subjective complements.

The adjective clause should be placed *after the noun subject.*

> d. My brother is a doctor. My brother lives in Texas.
>
> My *brother* **who lives in Texas** is a doctor.
>
> e. Mr. Ray has been our substitute teacher for one week. He has just gotten married.
>
> *Mr. Ray,* **who has just gotten married,** has been our substitute teacher for a week.

Grammatical Functions of Relative Pronouns

The relative pronouns *who, whom, which, that,* and *whose* have a grammatical function *within the adjective clauses* of which they are a part.

Relative Pronoun as Subject of the Clause: Who, Which, That

> I have a *friend.* **He** has many beautiful classical records.
> (subject)
>
> I have a friend who has many beautiful classical records.
>
> I really enjoy the *symphony.* **The symphony** is by Beethoven.
> (subject)
>
> I really enjoy the symphony which is by Beethoven.
>
> Here is a beautiful *recording.* **It** was made by the Boston Pops Orchestra.
> (subject)
>
> Here is a beautiful recording that was made by the Boston Pops Orchestra.

NOTE: As subject of the clause, "that" may replace "who" or "which." But "that" can only be used in necessary (restrictive) adjective clauses.

Exercise 2:   Oral. Combine the following sentences with *who, which,* or *that.* Identify each clause as necessary or unnecessary.

1. The author was a Frenchman. He wrote this book.

2. He comes from an area in France. This area is famous for its white wine.

3. He married a beautiful woman. This woman was also an author.

4. Do you remember the name of his novel? The novel won the Pulitzer Prize.

5. They had only one son. He became an artist in the style of impressionism.

6. That is the editor. He publishes most of their works.

7. The apartment is now a famous tourist attraction. The apartment is used as an art studio by their son.

8. The painting is one of my favorites. The painting is hanging over the fireplace.

9. A friend purchased the painting for me last year. This friend is a successful art dealer in New York.

10. The painting depicts a café scene. The scene was very common during the nineteenth century.

Exercise 3:   Written. Combine the following sentences with who, which, or that. Be careful of punctuation.

1. The professor is a famous chemist. He wrote the book on synthetic fuels.

   _____

2. His book is in the library. The book is for graduate students.

   _____

3. Chemistry can be enjoyable. Chemistry is a difficult subject.

   _____

4. The chemistry students have worked hard this quarter. The students have Dr. Smith.

   _____

   _____

5. Dr. Smith is going to go to Spain next semester. Dr. Smith has already taught in several European countries.

   _____

   _____

6. He will lecture at the University of Madrid. The University of Madrid is a well-known university in Spain.

_____

_____

7. My roommate has been accepted into Harvard for next year. He received a scholarship.

_____

_____

8. Harvard has always been a prestigious American university. It is in Massachusetts.

_____

9. Many politicians are high government officials. They graduated from Harvard.

_____

10. John F. Kennedy was a graduate of Harvard. He was the thirty-fifth president of the United States.

_____

_____

Relative Pronoun as Object of the Clause: Whom, Which, That

He is the friend. I visited **him** last week.
　　　　(object)
He is the friend **whom** I visited last week.

He has many beautiful classical records. He bought **the records** in Vienna.
　　　　　　　　　　　　　　　　(object)
He has many beautiful classical records **which** he bought in Vienna.

I am looking for the symphony. He bought **it** last week.
　　　　　　　　　　　(object)
I am looking for the symphony **that** he bought last week.

NOTES:

1. "That" may replace "whom" or "which" as object of the clause.

　　He is the friend **whom/that** I visited last week.

　　I am looking for the records **which/that** he bought in Germany.

2. When using a relative pronoun as the object of the clause, notice that the relative pronoun *whom* is placed in front of a subject–verb combination.

The man whom **I met** was a famous conductor.

Notice the position of **who** as subject of the clause.

He is a man **who enjoys** beautiful music.

Exercise 4:   Whom, which, that as object. Oral practice. Combine the following sentences. Explain why a clause is necessary or unnecessary.

1. I have just spoken with a friend. I met this friend in Michigan last year.
2. He is currently finishing a Ph.D. degree. I haven't even started a Ph.D. yet.
3. He is really a very intelligent student. All his professors respect him.
4. Last quarter, he wrote a paper. His economics professor urged him to send the paper to a business journal for publication.
5. Another professor often used him as an assistant. He had this professor for a marketing course.
6. He recently scored 95 on an economics test. The other students failed the test.
7. Here is the score. I received this score on the test.
8. I failed parts 1 and 2 of the test. I didn't understand these parts very well.
9. The final grade will probably be very low. I will get this grade in economics.
10. In addition to being a very good student, my friend is a nice person. All his classmates like him.

Exercise 5:   Whom, which, that as object. Written practice. Combine the following sentences. Use commas to punctuate the unnecessary clauses.

1. A T.V. set may be more dangerous than the kitchen stove. Most Americans own a T.V. set.
2. Not all the programs are desirable. We watch these programs.
3. A top CBS executive was trying to defend the network's choice of children's programs. A newscaster was interviewing this executive.
4. There are many television critics. I have heard these critics express negative opinions about most of the programs on television.
5. The chief objections are that television has raised the crime rate among young people and has caused students' test scores to go down. The critics of television present these objections.
6. Many parents believe there is too much sex and violence on the shows. The networks put these shows on early in the evening.

7. The majority of the shows were full of fighting and killing. I watched these shows last night.

8. Many people also criticize T.V. commercials. The stations show these commercials when children's programs are on.

9. Some parents feel that these commercials do not teach the children good eating habits. Their children believe the commercials.

10. Mrs. Jones said that her young son refused to eat anything but candy and sugar-coated cereals. I know him.

11. The programs must represent a higher quality of entertainment than sex and violence. The networks offer these programs night after night.

12. Viewers must learn to choose the programs. They will let these programs into their homes each night.

Exercise 6: Relative pronouns as subject or object of the clause. Combine the following sentences. Sometimes the relative pronoun will be the subject of the clause; sometimes it will be the object.

1. The adverb clause test was easy. The test was last Friday.

2. I enjoy taking grammar tests. The tests are easy for me.

3. Our grammar teacher didn't tell us the test would take two hours. She surprised everyone.

4. I had reviewed the practice exam. I understood it very well.

5. The test will be on adjective clauses. We will take this test next.

6. This quarter is almost over. It started approximately six weeks ago.

7. The students in this class will be studying in a partial academic program next quarter. The students receive an average of 70 in their classes this quarter.

8. When I enter the university, I'll study economics. I have always liked this subject.

9. Before I begin my academic work, I'm going to take a short vacation. I need a vacation.

10. My parents are planning to visit the United States at this time. I really want to see them.

11. My sister isn't coming with them. I haven't seen her in two years.

12. My sister is going to have a baby soon, so I'll be an uncle. She was married last year.

13. When I talked to her on the phone last week, she told me that her husband was really a nice person, so I'm anxious to meet him. I have never seen her husband.

14. Her husband has a good job with the government. He has a masters degree in economics.

Relative Pronoun as Modifier of a Noun: Whose

Whose replaces a possessive expression for

1. people

    He is a conductor. This conductor's orchestra is well known.

    He is a conductor **whose orchestra is well known.**

2. things

    The house needs a lot of repair work. The roof **of the house** is very old.

    The house **whose roof is very old** needs a lot of repair work.

NOTE: Although "whose" may express a possessive relationship for things, many native speakers sometimes use a "with" phrase.

    The house **with the old roof** needs a lot of repair work.

    Notice that in the "with" phrase, the adjective is in front of the noun.

3. groups of people

    The crowd of soccer fans shouted loudly. **Their** excitement was evident.

    The crowd of soccer fans, **whose excitement was evident,** shouted loudly.

    The angry mob ran toward the White House. **Its** size had increased.

    The angry mob, **whose size had increased,** ran toward the White House.

    I agree with the students. **Their** decision is to cancel all final exams.

    I agree with the students, **whose decision is to cancel all final exams.**

4. animals

    They had to shoot the horse. **His** leg was broken.

    They had to shoot the horse **whose leg was broken.**

Exercise 7:   Whose as modifier of a noun. Oral practice. Combine the following sentences with "whose." Explain why a clause is necessary or unnecessary.

1. Elvis Presley was a legendary American singer. His records made him a millionaire.
2. His fans still buy his records. Their memories of him have not died.
3. He was a man. His generosity was felt by many people.
4. Elvis Presley entertained all over the world. His career began as a singer in a church choir in Tennessee.
5. He also made many movies. The success of these movies was also tremendous.

130

6. At the beginning of his acting career, many movie critics said he didn't have any talent. They said his pictures were terrible.

7. Many people will remember him as a musical giant. His music gave enjoyment to millions of people all over the globe.

8. After he died, many of his fans visited the Presley mansion in Nashville, Tennessee. Their grief over his death was deep.

9. His career was magical and successful. The life of his career was cut short.

10. He was a man. His talent will always be remembered.

Exercise 8: Whose as modifier of a noun. Written practice. Combine the following sentences with "whose." Be careful of punctuation.

1. The Red Cross is helping the family. The family's home was damaged by the storm.

2. Their house was almost destroyed. The roof of the house was blown off.

3. Their little boy has been crying for a week. His dog was killed.

4. The families lost everything in the storm. Their homes and cars were completely destroyed.

5. The department stores were heavily damaged. The windows of the stores were shattered.

6. The business executives will not be able to start new businesses. Their property was demolished.

7. Mr. Smith was very lucky. His furniture store was not damaged.

8. Public agencies will have to find temporary homes for all children. These children's parents were seriously injured.

Relative Pronoun as Object *of the Preposition:* Whom, Which, That

Sometimes a preposition is used with a relative pronoun, for example, *with which, for which, to whom.*

The preposition is a part of the adjective clause, and it is determined by the verb and the meaning you want to communicate.

Example: speak *to,* speak *with,* speak *for*

The man had just arrived in the United States. We spoke **to** him.
spoke **with** him.
spoke **for** him.

The man **to whom we spoke** had just arrived in the United States.
with whom
for whom

Positions of the Preposition

1. In the following examples, the prepositions are placed **in front of** the relative pronouns.

    The composer is Brahms. I am listening **to him.**
    The composer **to whom** I am listening is Brahms.

    The country is Germany. Brahms was born **in this country.**
    The country **in which** Brahms was born is Germany.

2. Prepositions may also be separated from the relative pronoun and placed **at the end** of the adjective clause.

    The composer **whom** I am listening **to** is Brahms.
    The country **which** he was born **in** is Germany.

    Mrs. Parks is the music teacher **whom** I studied **with** for many years.

3. When "that" is used as object of the preposition, the preposition can *never* be placed in front of the relative pronoun.

    incorrect: The concert about that I told you was last night.

    correct: The concert **that** I told you **about** was last night.

4. If the adjective clause is long, it is best to keep the preposition and relative pronoun together.

    incorrect: Mrs. Parks is the music teacher **whom I studied in Denver two years ago with.**

    correct: Mrs. Parks is the music teacher **with whom** I studied in Denver two years ago.

Summary of Positions of the Preposition

a. in front of the relative pronoun:	Professor Ray is the man **about whom** I told you. That is the house **in which** he lives.
b. at the end of the adjective clause:	He is the man **whom** I told you **about.** He is the man **that** I told you **about.** That is the house **which** he lives **in.** Here is the house **that** he lives **in.**

Exercise 9:   Whom, which, that as object of the preposition. Combine the following sentences in the two ways discussed. Remember, "that" can only be used in necessary clauses.

1. Dr. Jones is the man. I have talked about him many times.
2. This is the hospital. He has worked in this hospital for several years.

3. He has performed many difficult operations. He has received much acclaim for them.

4. Many people are grateful to him. He performed successful operations on them.

5. The surgeon is still alive. Dr. Jones studied with this surgeon.

6. Dr. Jones is a very modest man. The Nobel Prize in medicine was awarded to him.

7. This award is greatly valued by people around the world. He worked hard for it.

8. Alfred Bernhard Nobel was a Swedish chemist and inventor. The Nobel Prize was named after him.

9. Medicine is one of six fields. The Nobel Foundation presents awards in these fields.

10. Dr. Jones is undoubtedly a great man. I have much respect for him.

11. He is the physician. My doctor studied under him when he was in medical school.

12. His hospital staff is planning a celebration. Dr. Jones will be the guest of honor at this celebration.

Exercise 10: When, where, why to introduce adjective clauses. Combine the following sentences with "when," "where," "why." Be careful of punctuation.

A. Oral Practice

1. Sue met Dick during the summer quarter. She was studying in New York then.

2. They got married a year later. He finished his degree in marketing at that time.

3. Dick didn't give an explanation. He changed from psychology to marketing.

4. They are now living in Houston, Texas. Dick's company is located there.

5. They didn't give a reason. Dick wanted to leave Texas.

6. Next year, they will move to Boston. Dick will become the executive in charge of marketing for his company's new East Coast office.

7. They will not move until June. The weather is nice for driving long distances at this time of year.

8. Sue has not given an explanation. They decided to drive instead of fly.

B. Written Practice

1. I can't give you an explanation . . .

2. This is the park . . .

3. Could you please give me a reason . . .

4. Christmas is the time of year . . .

5. Could you please direct us to a hotel . . .

6. Can you remember the time . . .
7. New York is the city . . .
8. Three o'clock in the afternoon is the time of day . . .
9. That is the corner . . .
10. My friend got married at a time . . .

Leaving Out the Relative Pronoun

You now know that the relative pronouns who, whom, which, and that have a grammatical function in the adjective clauses they introduce. Let's review these functions.

1. Who, that, which may function as the subject of the clause.
2. Whom, that, which may function as the object of the clause.
3. Whom, that, which may also function as object of the preposition.

In speaking and writing, speakers of English often leave out the relative pronoun that introduces the adjective clause when the pronoun functions as *direct object* or *object of the preposition* (when the preposition is at the end of the adjective clause.)

Relative Pronoun as Direct Object

a. She is the teacher (whom) **I had** last quarter.
b. This is the book (that) **we used.**
c. Here is a copy of the first test (which) **she gave.**

NOTE: It is *easy* to recognize when the relative pronoun can be left out if you look for a subject–verb combination right after the noun.

Relative Pronoun as Object of the Preposition

a. This is the book (that) I am interested **in.**
b. Here is a copy of the first test (which) I told you **about.**

NOTE: In these sentences, the prepositions "in" and "about" are at the *end* of the adjective clause, so the relative pronoun can be left out.

In the following sentence, the preposition "for" is not at the end of the adjective clause, so the relative pronoun cannot be left out.

c. She is the teacher **for** whom I worked so hard.

Exercise 11: Omitting the relative pronoun. Write "who," "whom," "which," or "that" only in the sentences that need a pronoun.

1. John Wayne, _____ was a famous American cowboy actor, died in 1979.

2. Most of his movies, _____ have been seen all over the world, were Westerns.

3. Westerns were the movies _____ he loved most of all.

4. The Hollywood director with _____ John Wayne enjoyed working was John Ford.

5. The ranch _____ the Wayne family owns is in California.

6. John Wayne lived in California, but the state _____ he was born in was Iowa.

7. His father was a druggist _____ moved his family to California early in John Wayne's life.

8. The film _____ we saw last week was his last movie.

9. John Wayne also produced several of the movies _____ he starred in.

10. The *Alamo* is the name of one of the films _____ he produced.

11. The film for _____ he received an Academy Award was *True Grit*.

12. Many movie critics _____ constantly gave his movies bad reviews didn't believe he was a good actor.

13. However, it was the ordinary moviegoer to _____ John Wayne owed his success.

14. Isn't that the movie studio in _____ he made many of his films?

15. John Wayne had three wives by _____ he had a total of seven children.

16. Cowboy fans, _____ are all over the world, will miss him greatly.

Unnecessary Adjective Clauses Referring to the Complete Sentence

Sometimes an adjective clause comes after the entire sentence and refers to the entire sentence instead of to a noun in the sentence.

John made high grades on his exams, **which made his parents happy.**

John's parents were not happy because of the "exams"; they were happy because *John made high grades on his exams.* The adjective clause modifies the entire idea expressed in the sentence.

This type of adjective clause is very common in speaking. When you write it, however, you must be careful not to leave out the comma. If the comma is left out, the adjective clause becomes a necessary clause and will modify only the noun in front if it. This can sometimes make the entire sentence sound "funny."

Jim tried to sing at the party which made everyone laugh.

The party didn't make everyone laugh. *Jim's singing at the party* made everyone laugh. The sentence needs a comma after party.

Exercise 12: Restate the following sentences so that an adjective clause modifies the entire statement.

1. The little boy brought his pet frog to class. This surprised the teacher.
2. The frog escaped from its basket, and this caused all the little girls to scream.
3. The frog jumped on top of a bookcase. This made it difficult to reach.
4. The students finally recaptured the frog, but it wasn't an easy job.
5. While the children were trying to catch the frog, they were screaming and yelling. All this disturbed the class next door.
6. The principal of the school sent the little boy home. This action made his parents punish him.
7. The little boy had to stay in his room, and this punishment made him sad.
8. He promised never to take the frog to school again. His parents were thankful for this.

Exercise 13: Review. Complete the following sentences with adjective clauses. Be careful of prepositions. They will determine the verbs that can be used after them. *All* sentences must relate to the topic of discussion.

A. Topic of Discussion:
Preparing to enter a university

1. Here is the letter of recommendation . . .
2. I really would like to enter a university . . .
3. I'm planning to major in economics . . .
4. There are many good schools, but I want a place . . .
5. I've already started reading some economic books . . .
6. There is the professor . . .
7. He is the man about . . .

8. He received his Ph.D. in 1960 . . .

9. He is a man for . . .

10. I could major in the field of science, but I've always enjoyed subjects . . .

11. I really do not know the reason . . .

12. The University of Pennsylvania has a good business school . . .

13. I have already sent for an application . . .

14. I also wrote a letter to Dr. Ray . . .

15. Pennsylvania is a state in . . .

B. Topic of Discussion: Telephoning an embassy to get information on scholarships

1. My government will not give a scholarship to a student . . .

2. I only have a partial scholarship . . .

3. Yesterday afternoon, I called my embassy . . .

4. I spoke with Dr. Wilson . . .

5. I asked him many questions . . .

6. He is a very nice person . . .

7. I understood all the answers . . .

8. He is responsible for all the students . . .

9. The first time I called, he was busy. I had called at a time . . .

10. He explained the reasons . . .

Exercise 14: Rewrite the following paragraph using adjective clauses to connect the sentences.

Coffee is a rich, aromatic drink. Coffee has been a popular beverage for over a thousand years. Though many people drink coffee, it contains a stimulant. This stimulant affects the nervous system. The effect it has depends on each person's individual system, the amount of caffeine a person consumes, and the amount of coffee an individual usually drinks every day. One or two cups of brewed coffee contains only mild doses of caffeine. These mild doses make you more alert and less tired. The person may experience headaches, nervousness, and irritability. This person habitually drinks three to six cups of brewed coffee. This amount contains heavy doses of caffeine. It is interesting to note that large doses of caffeine affect heavy coffee drinkers differently than light coffee drinkers. The person becomes less nervous and has fewer headaches with large doses of caffeine. This person is a heavy drinker. On the other hand, the people feel nervous and have upset stomachs with increased doses of caffeine. These people are light coffee drinkers. Morning is the time. At this time, the heavy drinker must have a cup of coffee to wake up and begin the day's activities. Because this drink is a stimulant, it is not good for children. These children are normally overactive.

Reduction of Adjective Clauses

Adjective clauses can often be reduced to phrases which will modify a noun without changing the meaning of the sentence. Study the following examples.

Full Clauses	*Reduced Phrases*
a. The student **who is talking to the teacher** is from China.	b. The student **talking to the teacher** is from China.
c. Last night he gave a lecture **which was on technological developments in his country.**	d. Last night he gave a lecture **on technological developments in his country.**
e. Anyone **that is interested in this country** should plan to attend another lecture tonight.	f. Anyone **interested in this country** should plan to attend another lecture tonight.

NOTE: Only adjective clauses having *who, which,* or *that* as the *subject of the clause* can be reduced to a phrase modifying a noun.

If the adjective clause needs commas, the adjective phrase will also require commas.

There are three common ways to reduce an adjective clause beginning with *who, which,* or *that* (used as SUBJECT OF THE CLAUSE) to a phrase.

1. Omit the *relative pronoun* and the *be* form of the verb.

    g. The man **who is** wearing the grey suit is my uncle.

    h. The man   wearing the grey suit is my uncle.

    i. He is the person **who is** most concerned about my success.

    j. He is the person   most concerned about my success.

    k. The essays **that are** written in this book are very interesting.

    l. The essays   written in this book are very interesting.

    m. The book **which is** on my desk also contains many interesting essays.

    n. The book   on my desk also contains many interesting essays.

2. In adjective clauses that do not contain a form of *be* it is often possible to omit the relative pronoun and change the verb to its *-ing* form.

    o. Anyone **who has** a library card may check out books.

    p. Anyone **having** a library card may check out books.

    q. This library does not contain any studies **which deal** with the psychological effects of the Civil War.

    r. This library does not contain any studies **dealing** with the psychological effects of the Civil War.

3. Some adjective clauses can be reduced to *appositive phrases.* An appositive phrase is a noun or pronoun with modifiers that is placed after another noun or pronoun to explain it.

    s. History, *which is my favorite subject,* has always fascinated me.

    t. History, **my favorite subject,** has always fascinated me.

    u. Mrs. Bryson, *who is the head librarian,* has a degree in history.

    v. Mrs. Bryson, **the head librarian,** has a degree in history.

    w. Boston, *which is an interesting city,* has many historical points of interest.

    x. Boston, **an interesting city,** has many historical points of interest.

NOTE: Because an appositive phrase only adds "extra, unnecessary" information, it is always set off from the rest of the sentence by commas.

By using adjective and appositive phrases as well as adjective clauses in your written work, you add variety to your sentence structure and make your work more interesting to read.

Exercise 15:   Oral. Change the adjective clauses to **adjective phrases** or **appositive phrases.**

    Example: Dr. Smith is the professor *who is teaching chemistry 101 this semester.*

                    Dr. Smith is the professor **teaching chemistry 101 this semester.**

1. Chemistry, *which is a difficult subject,* can be enjoyable.

2. Nevertheless, the students *who are taking Dr. Smith's class this semester* are enjoying it.

3. Dr. Smith has written several chemistry books, *which are used in universities around* the world.

4. He has just completed an important government report, *which is on reserve in the library.*

5. Bill Smith, *who was the top graduate student in Dr. Smith's advanced chemistry course last semester,* helped with the research for this report.

6. The students *that have been in his classes* consider it a privilege to study with him.

7. He has also written several articles *which comment on the effects of chemicals in our food.*

8. These articles, *which were written several years ago*, have been published in several popular magazines.

9. He believes that we should avoid all foods *which contain chemical preservatives.*

10. I heard that his wife, *who is a very nice person*, is writing a book *which is on cooking with only natural ingredients.*

11. By the way, the girl *who is behind you* is his daughter.

12. You are fortunate to be in a class *which is taught by such a respected scholar.*

Exercise 16: Written. Change the adjective clauses to **adjective** and **appositive phrases.**

1. Dr. William F. Fry Jr., *who is a Stanford University professor of psychiatry*, is an authority on laughter.

2. He notes that of all the major psychological studies *which were done on human emotions between 1877 and 1962* only 31 percent were concerned with pleasant reactions such as laughter.

3. Many members of the medical profession now believe that laughter, *which is a common element of everyday life*, has valuable therapeutic effects on the human body.

4. Patients *who suffer with heart disease, which is the major illness that exists in the Western world today*, can benefit from laughter.

5. Science has demonstrated that the healthy effects *that are provided by laughter* are the activation of the muscles, the increase of heart rate, and the amplification of respiration.

6. Sudden and intense anger is an emotion *which is often responsible for starting a heart attack* in people *who have heart trouble.*

7. Dr. Fry, *who is a respected authority on this subject*, believes that laughter can save many lives.

8. He also believes that for individuals *who lean toward aggressive behavior*, laughter and humor may offer alternatives to violence.

Exercise 17: Written. Combine the following sentences using **adjective** and **appositive phrases.**

1. The violence has upset many people around the world. It exists in every country today.

2. It has become almost impossible to protect prominent people. They hold public offices.

3. It seems as though any person can find an opportune moment to harm a public figure. The person has a personal motive.

4. Even private citizens may be the innocent victims of violence. They are engaged in their everyday activities.

5. Public personalities have a better chance of escaping violence. They are guarded by security officers.

6. Nightly television news programs usually contain at least one report of incidents. These incidents involve private citizens. These citizens are on their way to work or at their places of business.

7. One of my neighbors is even afraid to walk to the park by herself during the day time. My neighbor is a seventy year old woman.

8. Unfortunately, there are numerous international terrorist organizations. They operate around the world.

9. International law enforcement organizations have been able to realize some degree of success in identifying the organizations and their leaders. The law enforcement organizations have been concerned with the problem of controlling these groups' activities.

10. Unfortunately for all of us, violence is all too prevalent. It is a common element in our society today.

Exercise 18:   The following paragraphs on the American author, Alex Haley, contain short and sometimes awkward sentences. Rewrite the paragraphs connecting the sentences with adjective clauses, adjective phrases, and appositive phrases.

Alex Haley has become a famous author. Alex Haley wrote the book *Roots*. *Roots* is the history of one black American family. Alex Haley was born in Henning, Tennessee. In Henning, Tennessee he first heard stories about the African slaves in his family's history. These stories had been passed from generation to generation. His grandmother told him these stories. Mr. Haley first became interested in his family's history at a time. During this time he was in London. In London he was on a writing assignment. Mr. Haley's research eventually took him to Gambia in Africa. Here he was able to learn about a young African boy. The young African boy's name was Kunta Kinte. As a child, Mr. Haley had often heard this name, and he was happy to learn that Kunta Kinte was a real person. Slave traders had stolen Kunta Kinte from his family and brought him to the United States.

The book *Roots* is more than a book about one black American family. *Roots* was the number one nonfiction bestseller in 1977. *Roots* is an important book. It tells much about the early history of the United States. Mr. Haley wrote another book. This book was published in the spring of 1980. The title of this book is *Search*. This book is about how he wrote *Roots*.

LESSON NINE: PRACTICE EXAM

Rewrite the following paragraphs connecting the sentences with adjective clauses, adjective phrases, and appositive phrases.

When we hear the word pollution, most people think of air pollution. However, there is another kind of pollution. It is called noise pollution. We are constantly surrounded by sounds. These sounds awake us, put us to sleep, entertain us, and annoy us. Most people have become accustomed to the noise. These individuals live in big cities. This noise surrounds them night and day. The fact is that their ears are immune to the racket around them. This fact surprises me. Indeed, I am always surprised when I see teenagers. They are wearing radio earphones. Loud rock music bombards their eardrums from these radio earphones.

I remember the time. I was visiting my friend, Reza, in New York at this time. Reza was a student at New York University. His apartment was on Fifth Avenue. Fifth Avenue is one of the busiest streets in Manhattan. Nevertheless, he slept like a baby every night in spite of the ambulance and police sirens at 3:00 in the morning. Even his dog never woke up. His dog slept beside his bed.

I enjoyed visiting New York City. New York City is a fascinating place. However, I prefer a small town. In a small town at night, only the soft sounds of crickets can be heard.

LESSON TEN

NOUN CLAUSES

A noun clause is used in the same way as a single-word noun. Single-word nouns have many different functions in sentences; therefore, noun clauses have many different functions.

In this lesson, we will not study all the ways noun clauses are used in sentences. We will concentrate on the four most common uses: (1) *subject* of a sentence, (2) *object* of a sentence, (3) *object* of the preposition, and (4) *complement* of the adjective.

The following words called *subordinating conjunctions* introduce noun clauses.

who	whatever	whenever	how much
whoever	which	why	how many
whom	whichever	whether (or not)	how long, often,
whomever	where	that	soon, and so on
whose	wherever	how	
what	when	however	

Word Order of Noun Clauses

| | Noun Clause | | |
	SUBORDINATOR	SUBJECT	VERB	REMAINDER OF SENTENCE
I don't know	where	Bob	went	last night.
I can't understand	why	she	has left	the children alone.
I don't believe	what	they	said	about you yesterday.

NOTE: The subordinator introduces the noun clause that has its own subject (Bob) and verb (went).

Sometimes the subordinator is used as the subject of the verb in the noun clause. Only *who, whoever, what, whatever, which, whichever* can be used as the subject of the verb in the noun clause. Look at the following noun clauses.

	Subordinator Subject	*Verb*	*Remainder of Sentence*
I know	who	borrowed	my book.
She doesn't understand	what	happened.	
Nobody knows	which	came	first, chicken or eggs.

Noun Clause as Subject of a Sentence

Single-Word Noun	*Noun Clause*
His **house** is beautiful.	**Where he lives** is beautiful.
Our **discussion** was private.	**What we talked about** was private.
Her **speech** was excellent.	**What she said** was excellent.
Her **reasons** for being angry surprised me.	**Why she was angry** surprised me.

Additional Examples

Noun Clause Subjects	*Verbs + Complements*
a. **Who(m) you are dating**	is none of my business.
b. **Where he goes every night**	bothers me.
c. **What they have done**	does not concern me.

   d. **Why she is angry**   has not worried me.
   e. **How they choose to live**   is up to them.

Oral Drill A: Provide noun clause subjects for the following verbs + complements.

1. . . . does not concern us.

2. . . . is none of our business.

3. . . . is a private matter.

4. . . . has not worried me.

Noun Clause as Object of a Sentence

Single-Word Noun	*Noun Clause*
I don't know the **answer**.	I don't know **what the answer is**.
I don't know **him**.	I don't know **who he is**.
I like her **house**.	I like **where she lives**.
We didn't hear their **discussion**.	We didn't hear **what they were talking about**.

Additional Examples

Noun Clause Objects

   a. Linda's parents felt   that she was too young to get married.
   b. I don't understand   why they feel this way.
   c. Linda didn't tell me   what she was going to do.
   d. She has not decided   when she will tell Bob.

Oral Drill B: Complete the following sentences with noun clause objects.

1. I really don't know . . .

2. The teacher didn't tell us . . .

3. None of the students understood . . .

4. Bob does not have to explain . . .

5. Bob and Linda didn't say . . .

6. The weatherman predicted . . .

Noun Clause as Object of the Preposition

Single-Word Noun	Noun Clause Objects of the Preposition
She was looking at my **painting**.	She was looking at **what I had painted**.
I was worried about his **health**.	I was worried about **how sick he was**.
The teacher was not interested in his **excuses**.	She was not interested in **why he was late**.
Nobody can depend on Jim's **promises**.	Nobody can depend on **what Jim promises**.

Additional Examples

a.	Everyone believes in	**whatever John says.**
b.	I never think about	**how I will pay my bills.**
c.	They were looking at	**what the police were doing.**
d.	I cannot rely on	**what you tell me.**

Oral Drill C: Complete the following sentences with noun clauses as objects of the preposition.

1. I am really not interested **in** . . .
2. Nobody cares **about** . . .
3. Everybody was looking **at** . . .
4. Some parents do not approve **of** . . .
5. Be quiet. I cannot concentrate **on** . . .
6. I cannot agree **with** . . .

NOTE: **WHO** versus **WHOM** *Whom* is used if the verb in the noun clause already has a subject.

  Example: I never pay attention **to whom** *my roommate* telephones.

  I never pay attention to **who** telephones my roommate.

In conversational English, **who** and **whoever** are often used instead of **whom** and **whomever.** In formal speech or writing, **whom** and **whomever** are preferred.

Noun Clause as Adjective Complement

As an adjective complement, the noun clause completes the meaning started by the adjective. *That* is the most commonly used subordinator in this pattern; however, it can be omitted from the sentence. Study the following examples.

a. He will succeed. I'm sure.	I'm **sure that** he will succeed. I'm **sure** he will succeed.
b. She is unhappy. I'm convinced.	I'm **convinced that** she is unhappy. I'm **convinced** she is unhappy.

Oral Drill D: Combine the following sentences. Make the first sentence a noun clause used after the adjective.

1. John cheats on every exam. I'm convinced.
2. He always denies it. We are aware.
3. He doesn't think anybody sees him. I'm sure.
4. He has never studied for an exam. His roommate is certain.
5. Cheating doesn't bother John. We are all convinced.
6. He doesn't have a conscience. I'm positive.
7. The instructor will never find out. John is confident.
8. He thinks cheating is acceptable. I'm sure.
9. He'll get caught one day. Everyone is certain.
10. He is going to be very surprised. I'm afraid.
11. He will ever stop cheating. I'm not certain.

-Ever Words in Noun Clauses

WHOEVER **WHOMEVER**	mean any person.	**WHICHEVER** **WHATEVER**	mean any thing.
WHEREVER	means any place.	**WHENEVER**	means any time.
HOWEVER	means any way (manner).		

However used to introduce a noun clause is not the same as the conjunctive adverb. Compare the following sentences.

However (any way) you cook this meat is all right with me.

I'll help you to cook it; **however** (but), I don't like rare meat.

Oral Drill E: One student ask the question. Another student complete the response.

Example: Student A: What should I do about my problem?

Student B: Do <u>whatever</u> seems best.

Student C: Can I leave now?

Student D: <u>Whenever</u> you want to leave is fine with me.

1. A: I'm getting tired of this party. Are you ready to go?

   B: I'm having a good time, but _____ you are ready is fine with me.

2. A: What should I tell our hostess?

   B: Tell her _____ you think is best.

3. A: I'm hungry. Do you want a hamburger or some chicken?

   B: I don't care. We can get _____ you prefer.

4. A: Tell me. Should we go to Burger King or to Kentucky Fried Chicken?

   B: It really doesn't matter to me. Let's go to _____ you like best.

5. A: What's the matter with you tonight? Can't you make a decision?

   B: Nothing is the matter. _____ you want to go is all right with me.

6. A: How do you want your hamburger, with or without onions?

   B: _____ she prepares it is all right with me.

7. A: Whom should we invite to our party next week?

   B: I don't know. _____ you invite will have fun.

8. A: By the way, who called at 12:00 last night?

   B: I don't know because _____ called hung up before I reached the phone.

9. A: It's really late, and I'm getting tired. Let's not get any dessert.

   B: O.K. _____ you say.

10. A: Are you angry because I wanted to leave the party early?

    B: Angry? Of course not. It's your car, so you can do _____ you like. Just don't ask me to go anywhere with you again.

Noun Clauses Beginning with "That"

THAT can often be omitted when it introduces a noun clause used as object of the verb.

   a. We assumed **our son was sick.**
   b. I could not believe **he had lied to us.**
   c. I hope **he will tell the truth soon.**
   d. Do you imagine **he knows our feelings?**

  e. He doesn't understand **we love him.**

  f. He thinks **his father and I will never forgive him.**

  g. We realize **he is beginning to feel sorry about the lie.**

THAT cannot be omitted when it introduces a noun clause used as subject of the verb.

  h. **That he had lied to us** was unbelievable.

  i. **That we accepted his apology** made him feel better.

  j. **That small boys sometimes lie** should not surprise anyone.

Oral Drill F: Follow the examples and combine the following sentences.

  Examples: He told us the truth.
              This made us happy.
              That he told us the truth made us happy.

              John failed the course.
              This surprised me.
              That John failed the course surprised me.

  1. Muhammed Ali has become a millionaire. This doesn't surprise anyone.
  2. He is known all over the world. This is a fact.
  3. He loved to compose poems about his opponents. This is known by everyone.
  4. He avoided the military draft a few years ago. This angered some people.
  5. Muhammed Ali has done some T.V. commercials. This is not strange.
  6. Many companies use famous people to sell their products on T.V. This is not unusual.
  7. He had a very successful boxing career. This cannot be denied.
  8. He was a hero to many young boys. This is true.
  9. He earned a reputation for being a bragger. This cannot be denied.
  10. He won more than fifty fights. This is on record.
  11. His fights always attracted thousands of spectators. This is a well known fact.

Using "It" as Subject of the Sentence

The use of a noun clause beginning with "that" is very formal. In conversation, speakers of English often use the word "it" as subject of the sentence and place the noun clause at the end of the sentence. In this pattern, a noun clause may follow a noun, pronoun or an adjective.

Examples: a) **That the world is facing a food shortage** is a fact.

It is a fact **that the world is facing a food shortage.**

b) **That many people are starving** is true.

It is true **that many people are starving.**

Oral Drill G: Restate the sentences in Oral Drill F using "it" at the beginning of the sentence.

Example: Muhammed Ali has become a millionaire. This doesn't surprise anyone.

It doesn't surprise anyone **that Muhammed Ali has become a millionaire.**

Exercise 1:   Noun clause as *subject* of the sentence. Answer the following questions using a noun clause as the subject of the sentence.

Example: What did the instructor tell Bob about cheating?

What she told him is none of my business.

1.   Who reported Bob's activities?

_____ does not concern me.

2.   Where is Bob now?

_____ is none of my business.

3.   When is he going to talk to the director?

_____ is not my concern.

4.   Why was he copying from Bill?

_____ is a mystery to me.

5.   Has he been cheating all quarter?

_____ does not really matter at this point.

6.   What will happen to him?

_____ depends on the director.

7. How many times has he met with the director this quarter?

    _____

    is none of our business.

8. What did the director tell him during their last meeting?

    _____

    is not our concern.

9. Will the director notify his parents?

    _____ probably

    depends on Bob's attitude.

10. Bob is very intelligent. Why does he get into so much trouble?

    _____ has always

    puzzled me.

Exercise 2: Noun clause as *subject* of the sentence. Restate the following sentences using a noun clause as the subject.

> **Example:**   The **date** of Sue's marriage is a secret.
>
> **When Sue is getting married** is a secret.

Notice that the tense of the verb in the noun clause must show a logical relationship to the main verb of the completed sentence.

a. When Sue is going to be married

b. When Sue is going to get married

                                            is a secret.

c. When Sue will be married

d. When Sue was married

In sentences a, b, and c, Sue has not been married yet. In sentence d, she has been married, but *the date is still a secret.*

The tense of the verb in the noun clause also depends on the "meaning" of the verb. Why is the following sentence incorrect?

    incorrect: When Sue has been married is a secret.

Restate the following sentences using a noun clause as the subject. The underlined words will help you to decide which of the subordinators on page 142 to use.

1. The president's <u>destination</u> was a secret.

    _____

2. The <u>time</u> of his departure was also a secret.

_____

3. His <u>ignorance of world affairs</u> has surprised everyone in Washington.

_____

_____

4. His <u>reason for taking this trip</u> has been worrying his advisors.

_____

_____

5. The president decided not to take his wife with him. This surprised everyone.

_____

6. The <u>number of days</u> he will stay is confidential.

_____

7. The <u>leaders</u> he will meet with makes everyone nervous.

_____

8. His <u>decision to go alone</u> concerns the members of his cabinet.

_____

9. He did not tell anyone about this sudden trip. This made everyone curious.

_____

10. His <u>strange behavior</u> has upset many people.

_____

11. His <u>future actions</u> will certainly be of interest to everyone.

_____

Exercise 3: Noun clause as *object* of the sentence. Answer the following questions using noun clauses as the object of each sentence.

Examples: How cold was it last night? I don't know **how cold it was.**
(Remember: introductory verb present, no tense change.)

Where did your roommate go last night? I didn't ask him **where he had gone last night.**
(Remember: introductory verb past, change the tense in the noun clause.)

1. Who had a party last night?
I don't know . . .

2. Where was it?
   I have no idea . . .

3. When did it start?
   I can't tell you . . .

4. When was it over?
   I can't say . . .

5. How did Reza get home?
   I don't know . . .

6. Whose car did he borrow?
   He didn't say . . .

7. Do you know whether or not he enjoyed the party?
   He didn't tell me . . .

8. Did he know about the party before last night?
   I really don't know . . .

9. Why didn't he invite you to go with him?
   I didn't ask him . . .

10. Where is he now?
    I have no idea . . .

11. How long will he be gone?
    He didn't tell me . . .

Exercise 4: Noun clause as *object* of the sentence. Complete the following sentences with a noun clause object. Be careful of meaning and tense changes.

1. Three weeks ago, a police officer stopped me and my roommate and wanted to know *where* . . .

2. Since I was driving, he asked me *why* . . .

3. I was so nervous that I began speaking in my native language, so he asked *if* . . .

4. I began to speak English and explained *that* . . .

5. He wanted to know *how long* . . .

6. He also wanted to know *what* . . .

7. Then the officer asked to see my driver's license, but I didn't know *where* . . .

8. My roommate, who was sitting quietly, couldn't believe *what* . . .

9. The officer wanted to know *whether* . . . *or not*

10. Finally, he gave me a ticket and said *that* . . .

11. As we drove away, my roommate promised me *that* . . .

Exercise 5: Noun clause as *adjective complement.* Complete the following sentences with a noun clause to complement the adjective. Be careful of tense and meaning.

> Example: Muna has been a good student all quarter, so she is confident . . .
>
> Muna has been a good student all quarter, so she is **confident that** she **will pass this level.**

1. The final exam in grammar will cover every lesson, so I am **sure** _____

   _____

2. Because our grammar teacher has emphasized the tenses all quarter, I am

   positive _____

3. However, she may not give us a long exam; in fact, we are **convinced** _____

   _____

4. I am really not worried about the exam; on the contrary, I am **certain** _____

   _____

5. The clauses are important; therefore, I am **sure** _____

   _____

6. For some reason, Ryoji believes that our teacher doesn't like him, so he is **con-**

   vinced _____

7. Concerning the conversation final, I am **positive** _____

   _____

8. When I talked with the conversation teacher, he seemed **certain** _____

   _____

9. All of the students are **confident** _____

   _____

10. We are all **sure** _____

Using More Than One Noun Clause in a Sentence

Native speakers of English often reply to a question using more than one noun clause in different functions.

> **Example:** Question: Is Maria dating Jose?
>
> Reply: I don't know **if she's dating him,** but **whether or not she is** is none of our business.

NOTE: The statement after "but" uses the verb "be" as the verb of the noun clause subject and as the main verb of the statement.

> Question: Why was Mirko in the director's office all day?
>
> Reply: I'm not sure **why he was there all day;** besides, **why he was** is a private matter.

Tense Changes after an Introductory Verb

In the replies given, the verbs that introduce the noun clause objects are in the simple present tense: "don't know," "am not sure." Therefore, the verbs in the noun clauses do not change: "if she's dating him," "why he was there all day."

However, if the introductory verb is in the simple past, the verb in the *noun clause object* must change.

> Question: Why was Mirko in the director's office all day?
>
> Reply: He didn't tell me **why he had been there all day;** besides, **why he was** is a private matter.

Notice that the verb in the noun clause subject does not change.

To introduce the noun clause as object of the sentence or complement of the adjective, the following expressions are often used.

1. I don't know
2. He/she/they/Ana didn't say
3. I didn't ask her/him/them
4. He/she/they didn't explain
5. I am not sure/certain
6. I have no idea why/when/where . . .
7. I can't tell you if/what/why . . .
8. He/she/they didn't tell me
9. He/she/they (hasn't/haven't) told anyone

To complete the noun clause subject, use any verb + complement combination that is *appropriate* to the situation you are discussing.

1. ... does not concern me/us/them
2. ... is none of his/our/her business
3. ... depends on several things
4. ... is up to him/her/them
5. ... is a private matter
6. ... has not worried me

Exercise 6: Using *more than one noun clause* in a sentence.

Student 1: Ask the question.
Student 2: Answer the question as shown on page 154.

1. Why is Jamal returning to his country?
2. Did his parents tell him to go home?
3. Is he going to return to finish his studies?
4. How long will he stay?
5. Has he received an acceptance letter to a university yet?
6. Is his family having financial problems?
7. Was he packing last night?
8. What is he going to do with his new car?
9. Will he work or continue to study at home?
10. When does he have to leave?
11. Had he been expecting this to happen?
12. Are his cousins going home, too?
13. Why haven't they been to class?
14. What was Jamal telling the director about this situation?
15. What did the director say to him?
16. Is he going to pay his phone bill before he leaves?

Simple Form of the Verb in Noun Clauses

When certain verbs have a noun clause as direct object, they require the simple form of the verb. The simple form is used regardless of the tense of the main verb or the subject in the noun clause. The use of the simple form stresses the urgency or importance of the statement.

The simple form of the verb is used after the following verbs:

advise	**demand**	**insist**	**prefer**	**recommend**	**require**
command	**desire**	**order**	**propose**	**request**	**suggest**
					urge

Examples:

	Noun Clause Object
1. The doctor advised	that **Bob remain** in the hospital.
2. The nurse had insisted	that **we leave** his room.
3. She recommended	that **we return** in the morning.
4. The doctor will require	that **Bob rest** in the evenings.
5. Bob's wife desires	that **he get** the best care.
6. I have suggested	that **we send** him a card.
7. Bob requests	that **he be** moved to a single room.
8. His surgeon demands	that **he have** the operation soon.

The negative is formed by putting *not* before the verb in the noun clause.

The doctor advised that Bob **not** remain in the hospital.

The nurse recommended that we **not** stay too long.

In informal usage, the auxiliary *"should"* is sometimes used with the verb in the noun clause, but *"should"* is not used with the verbs *command* and *demand*.

The nurse **recommended** that we should return in the morning.

The doctor **advised** that Bob should remain in the hospital.

Exercise 7:   Use the above verbs to introduce noun clauses containing the following information. Provide an appropriate subject the teacher, my father etc.

Example: speak to the director   The teacher **advised that I speak to the director.**

1. move to another city
2. buy a new car
3. learn to type
4. take only three courses
5. get married
6. study in my own country
7. be on time
8. wear a suit
9. not come to class late
10. not write in pencil
11. not smoke in the hospital
12. drive carefully
13. not talk so loudly in the restaurant

Exercise 8: Underline the noun clauses in the following paragraph and tell how each noun clause is used: subject, object, object of preposition, complement of the adjective.

Why some very good students often fail exams was recently studied by a professor of psychology at New York University. Professor Iris Fodor conducted research on the anxiety of some students before taking exams. Professor Fodor stated that many students fail exams because they become extremely nervous and cannot think logically. Furthermore, although they have studied, they are afraid of whatever is on the exam. Extremely nervous students forget everything they have studied, and some even become sick before a test. Dr. Fodor says how a student feels before a test is very important. She worked with fifty students and taught them how they could reduce their test anxiety and perform well on their exams. She reported that the students in the program felt better able to cope with their anxieties. What she told them to do before a test was the following:

1. Breathe deeply and slowly to relax.
2. Speak to yourself about positive and happy subjects and get rid of any negative thinking.
3. Be realistic. Don't think your life will end if you fail.
4. Don't be too hard on yourself. If you know you have studied, do your best.

By following these simple suggestions, Professor Fodor is certain that many unusually nervous students can perform better in test situations.

Exercise 9: Noun clauses versus adjective clauses. Underline the clauses in the following sentences and tell if they are used as *nouns* or *adjectives.* Remember that the noun clause follows the verb or indirect object; the adjective clause follows the noun.

Example: _____N_____ I like **what you like.**

_____A_____ Do you know the woman **who speaks French?**

1. _____ The announcer reported whose name was mentioned as a possible candidate for the presidency.

2. _____ Ted Kennedy was the man whose name was given.

3. _____ The TV announcer said that most Democrats were in favor of Senator Kennedy.

4. _____ Can you recall what the reporter's name was?

5. _____ I believe Walter Cronkite was the reporter who made the announcement.

6. _____ He is a man whom many people admire.

7. _____ Do you know when Dr. Smith will give the next chemistry exam?

8. _____ No, I don't. But the exam will cover Chapter 10, which is very difficult.

9. _____ Did he say how much time we would have for the exam?

10. _____ There is the building where most of my classes are.

11. _____ Where the new chemistry lab will be has not been decided yet.

12. _____ I heard that you received good grades on the last two exams.

13. _____ That they were fairly easy helped quite a bit.

14. _____ Why didn't you tell me the reason why you were upset with your last grade?

15. _____ There is Sedig Kenous, with whom I study before every exam.

16. _____ He is an excellent student who understands whatever the in-
_____ structor says.

17. _____ Isn't he from Libya, which is on the continent of Africa?

18. _____ I don't know the answer to the question you asked.
_____

Exercise 10: Review of clauses. Underline the clauses in the following sentences. Then, identify each clause: N = noun, Adv = adverb, Adj = adjective.

1. _____ Yesterday, many students didn't understand what we were talking about.

2. _____ Yesterday, many students didn't understand the lesson which was on clauses.

3. _____ Yesterday, many students didn't understand the lesson because it was on subordination.

4. _____ Dr. Larson, who is our director, visited our class.

5. _____ When he came in, Behrooz looked at him.

6. _____ What Dr. Larson said about the class was very complimentary.

7. _____ Although Behrooz had eaten a big breakfast, he was still hungry during the class.

8. _____ Ahmed enjoyed what he had eaten for breakfast.

9. _____ He had had a breakfast that was good and nutritious.

10. _____ This class understood what the instructor had said about the past perfect.

11. _____ When the instructor explained the past perfect, everyone understood.

12. _____ The past perfect was one of the tenses that everyone understood.

13. _____ Ali went to the library and asked for the book that was on reserve.

14. _____ The librarian, however, didn't know which book he wanted.

15. _____ Before he could get the book, he had to show her the title of it.

Exercise 11: Review of clauses. Combine the following sentences with the indicated clause or clauses.

> **Example:** We complete this chapter. We will have a test. The test will include everything in this lesson.
>
> **When (after) we complete this chapter,** we will have a test, **which**
> (adv. clause)
>
> **will include everything in this lesson.**
> (adj. clause)

1. Yesterday, we had a review of clauses. Everyone understood the review. (adj. clause)

2. We had had the review. Everyone told the teacher this. They felt much better about the clauses. (adv. clause, noun clause/object)

3. The class was finished. All the students looked happier. We had all done very well. (adv. clause, adv. clause)

4. Some students went into the lounge. They relaxed or did homework there. (adj. clause)

5. The grammar teacher gave Mihoko copies of an additional exercise. She had forgotten to give the exercises to the students. They left the grammar class. (adj. clause, adv. clause)

6. Mihoko had given everybody a copy of the exercise. They went to their reading class. (adv. clause)

7. The students felt more secure in using the clauses. This greatly pleased our teacher. (combine this sentence in *two* ways: adj. clause, noun clause/subject)

8. Every student understood the review. This made the teacher happy.   (noun clause/subject)

9. José said this. He had always had trouble with the clauses. He was studying in his country.   (noun clause/object, adv. clause)

10. The teacher wanted to know this. What had been his problem?   (noun clause/object)

11. Now José understands very well. This makes him feel more confident.   (noun clause/subject)

12. Using the clauses correctly and spontaneously is not easy to do. Nevertheless, everyone did well on the review.   (adv. clause)

13. I am not worried about this. How well will I do on the test on this chapter? (noun clause/object of prep.)

Exercise 12:   Review of clauses. Combine the following sentences using *noun, adverb, adjective* clauses. Arrange your sentences in paragraph form. Use the coordinating conjunctions and conjunctive adverbs in Unit Two. Remember not to over connect.

1. The grammar final was difficult. I took it last quarter.

2. I entered the room. I was a little nervous.

3. I didn't feel very confident. I had studied diligently.

4. The teacher gave us some directions before the exam. Her directions were poor.

5. I asked her a question. She answered the question very poorly.

6. I was supposed to do something. I didn't understand what.

7. Her explanation was so poor. I didn't know what to do.

8. I do not like teachers. Their directions are not clear.

9. Everyone else had finished the exam. I completed it.

10. I went to her desk. She was correcting exams from an earlier class there.

11. She took my paper. She didn't even look up.

12. She didn't like me all quarter. I don't know why.

13. My grade will be high or low. I'm not certain.

LESSON TEN: PRACTICE EXAM

A. *Underline* and *identify* the noun clauses in the following sentences.

a. subject of the sentence
b. object of the sentence
c. adjective complement
d. object of a preposition

1. _____   Although I'm going to be an engineering student, I have always been interested in how people learn languages.

2. _____ I don't know why this subject has always fascinated me.

3. _____ That speaking a language always precedes writing it is obvious because

_____ children understand what their parents say before they learn to write.

4. _____ Nevertheless, I am always surprised at how many words a one-year-old child knows.

5. _____ Language learning research reports that all languages have a lot in common.

6. _____ For example, I am certain that every language has a way to express time.

7. _____ I really don't remember when I spoke my first word.

8. _____ However, I am sure that I said something very interesting.

B. *Restate* the following sentences using a *noun clause as subject* of the sentence.

1. My first word as a child was probably mama.

_____

2. The reason most children learn this word first is obvious.

_____

3. The way most small children pronounce the words of their language is always amusing.

_____

4. The age at which a child speaks his or her first words is very important.

_____

5. Einstein didn't speak until he was three years old. This surprises me.

_____

C. *Answer* the following questions using a *noun clause subject* and a *noun clause object*.

1. Why was our teacher's little boy in class yesterday?

_____

_____

2. How long has she been married?

_____

_____

3. Does her husband have a good job?

_____

_____

4. Is she going to have more children?

_____

_____

D.   Rewrite the following sentences in the form of a paragraph. Use *noun, adjective,* and *adverb* clauses.

1. Einstein didn't speak until he was three years old. This surprises everyone. He grew up to be a genius.
2. I know the reason. He hated school.
3. He had a rebellious attitude toward his teachers. This caused him to behave disrespectfully in class.
4. I have a little cousin. He also has poor behavior in school.
5. We hope this. He will grow up to be another Einstein.
6. His parents have always been certain of this. He has a high I.Q.

E.   Complete the following sentences with –EVER words.

1. _____ you decide to dress your children is up to you.

2. However, they simply cannot wear _____ they want to wear, in most private schools.

3. _____ wants more information on public versus private schools should visit each type of school.

4. _____ type of school you choose, public or private, should provide your children with a good education.

5. My parents moved a lot when I was a child, but I enjoyed _____ I was.

6. Furthermore, I made friends with _____ I met.

UNIT 5

Passive Voice

To the Student Read before you begin this unit.

The term "voice" refers to the relationship between the verb (or action) and the subject of a sentence. *In an active voice sentence,* we place the subject before the verb because we want to emphasize who or what performs the action. We want to emphasize the *doer* of the action.

In a passive voice sentence, we want to emphasize the *the action, what happened* rather than who or what performs the action. The subject is placed after the verb or is omitted from the sentence.

Examples: ACTIVE VOICE: *The mechanic* discovered the problem.
PASSIVE VOICE: The problem was discovered by *the mechanic.*

ACTIVE VOICE: *The mechanic* repaired the brakes.
PASSIVE VOICE: The brakes were repaired.

As you study this unit, remember the following points.

1. Not every verb can be changed into the passive voice. Only those verbs which have an object can be changed. For example, the following sentences cannot be written in the passive voice because they do not contain objects.

    Examples: She seems tired.   He ate quickly.

    Verbs followed by reflexive pronouns cannot be changed to the passive voice, as in "She picked herself up."

2. The passive voice is used more frequently in written than in spoken English. It is usually found in textbooks, scientific, business, technical reports, government reports, and in newspapers. However, in the spoken language it is used quite frequently in television and radio news reports and in commercials.

3. The *doer* in a passive voice sentence is often not mentioned; therefore, a passive sentence often sounds *impersonal* and *objective*.

4. A sentence in the active voice is usually preferable to a sentence in the passive voice because an active voice sentence is shorter, stronger, and more direct.

In spite of the "don'ts," the passive voice is important in English, and there are several very important instances when we use it. However, you must not *overuse* it. *You should always have a specific reason for using the passive voice.* As you study this unit, pay attention to the passive voice in other texts you are using this quarter and in newspapers as well as in the spoken English of native speakers. In this way, you will feel more and more at ease with this point of grammar.

LESSON ELEVEN

FORMING THE PASSIVE

Form: be + past participle   or   auxiliary + be + past participle

Study the following chart. Notice that the form of *be* for the continuous tenses is *being;* for the future tenses and for the present infinitive, *be;* for the perfect tenses, *been.*

	Active Voice	**Passive Voice**
Simple Present	Many older citizens **use** the library.	The library **is used** by many older citizens.
Simple Past	Many children **used** the library last summer.	The library **was used** by many children last summer.
Present Continuous	Workmen **are painting** the third floor.	The third floor **is being painted.**
Past Continuous	Last week, they **were painting** the children's room.	Last week, the children's room **was being painted.**
Future	The library **will offer** many new programs next year.	Many new programs **will be offered** next year.
	A local author **is going to organize** a story hour for children.	A story hour for children **is going to be organized** by a local author.
Present Perfect	The director **has ordered** a lot of new equipment.	A lot of new equipment **has been ordered.**

	Active Voice	**Passive Voice**
Past Perfect	Workmen **had** already **installed** the new computer when I was there last week.	The new computer **had** already **been installed** when I was there last week.
Future Perfect	The library **will have started** the children's story hour by the end of next month.	The children's story hour **will have been started** by the end of next month.
Present Infinitive	I have **to renew** my library card.	My library card **has to be renewed.**

NOTE: The present perfect continuous, past perfect continuous, future continuous and future perfect continuous tenses are not used in the passive voice.

Note: The modal + verb also uses the forms *be* and *been.*

Examples: You **must finish** this work before two o'clock today.

This work **must be finished** before two o'clock today.

You **should have finished** it two weeks ago.

It **should have been finished** two weeks ago.

Oral Drill A: Rapidly change the following active verbs to their passive forms.

Examples: do = is done   did = was done   is doing = is being done

1. tell	11. should write	21. is fixing
2. is telling	12. to write	22. will finish
3. told	13. will write	23. sent
4. was telling	14. had written	24. is giving
5. has told	15. has written	25. does
6. had told	16. was writing	26. has seen
7. will tell	17. wrote	27. was correcting
8. to tell	18. is writing	28. is taking
9. will have told	19. writes	29. will have finished
10. must tell	20. will have written	30. is going to fix

USING THE PASSIVE VOICE AND USING "BY"

The passive voice is used in English in the following instances:

1. It is more interesting or important *to emphasize what happened* rather than who or what performed the action.

   Example: There was a terrible storm last night. Hundreds of houses **were destroyed.**

   "By" is unnecessary.

2. The *doer* of the action is *unknown.* The subjects of such sentences in the active voice are words such as "they," "people," "someone," "somebody," etc.

   Example: Someone stole my car last night. My car **was stolen** last night.

   "By" cannot be used because the doer is unknown.

3. The *doer* of the action is *known,* but *the speaker or writer does not want to* name the person who made a statement or did something wrong.

   Example: The teacher ruined the top of this desk accidentally.

   The top of this desk **was ruined** accidentally.

   "By" is unnecessary.

   Note: Sometimes the doer of the action is necessary to complete the meaning of the sentence.

   Example: The police officer **is seen** as an enemy **by some; looked to** for aid and protection **by others,** and taken for granted **by most.**

   Notice that the auxiliary "is" is used only one time.

   Example: The holiday weekend traffic death toll climbed above the lower limit which **was predicted by the National Safety Council.**

4. The *doers* of the action represent a *large group of different individuals.*

   Example: A lot of coffee **is grown** in Brazil.

   "By" is unnecessary.

5. The *doer* of the action is *obvious.*

   Example: This letter **will be picked up** after 1:00. (The mailman will pick it up.)

   Our tests **have** already **been corrected.** (The teacher corrected them.)

   "By" is unnecessary.

Note: Very often "by" is used in an early statement but not in the statements which follow because the doer of the action has already been mentioned and is, therefore, obvious.

> **Example:** Who gets a scholarship will be decided **by the scholarship committee.** Students **are judged** on grade point average, community activities and financial need. All scholarship recipients **will have been announced** by the time classes begin next quarter.

After *are judged* and *will have been announced*, it is not necessary to identify the doer (the scholarship committee). The committee was identified in the first sentence.

Oral Drill B: Change the following sentences to the passive voice. Decide when to use "by."

Group 1

1. A hurricane *destroyed* the small town.
2. The hurricane *has left* many people homeless.
3. The Red Cross *is feeding* the homeless victims.
4. The president *is going to sign* an emergency relief bill.
5. The citizens of the town *have* already *organized* clean up crews.

Group 2

1. Someone *broke* the pay phone on the third floor of my dormitory.
2. The dorm director *had to notify* the phone company immediately.
3. I hope the phone company *will repair* it soon.
4. Both the students on the second and the third floors *use* it.
5. Phone company officials *were interviewing* all the students last night.

Sentences with Direct and Indirect Objects

Some sentences contain both a direct and an indirect object.

> **Example:** Someone gave **him a thousand dollars.**

Either the indirect or direct object can become the subject of the passive sentence.

> **Example:** **He** was given a thousand dollars.
>
> **A thousand dollars** were given to him.

When the direct object becomes the subject of the passive sentence, sometimes the sentence may need a *preposition* to make the sentence sound more natural.

> **Example:**   The salesclerk gave me a pen. A pen was given **to** me by the salesclerk.
>
> The waiter found us a table. A table was found **for** us by the waiter.

Oral Drill C: Change the following sentences to the passive voice in the two ways discussed above.

> **Example:**   The teacher gave **Sue a perfect score** on her composition.
>
> **Sue** was given a perfect score on her composition.
>
> **A perfect score** was given **to** Sue on her composition.

1. A local art club recently awarded *Steve a four-year scholarship* to study art.
2. Many different organizations have presented *him awards for his artistic ability*.
3. Steve will give *a group of children art lessons* next week.
4. The children's parents are paying *him a lot of money*.
5. They have already sent *him their checks*.
6. Steve is going to provide *the children the necessary supplies*.
7. Several department stores have offered *him jobs*.
8. Undoubtedly, some company will offer *him a good job* after graduation from art school.

Note: Remember that a *noun clause* may be the direct object of a sentence. The rules for changing the verb forms are the same. However, while the introductory verb which introduces the noun clause must be changed, the verb in the noun clause may be changed, or it may remain in the active voice.

> **Example:**   Active Voice: Everyone applauded **what Bob said.**
>
> Passive Voice: What Bob **said was applauded** by everyone.
>
> or
>
> What **was said** by Bob **was applauded** by everyone.

VERB + PREPOSITION COMBINATIONS

When a verb + preposition is put into the passive voice, the preposition remains *immediately after the verb*.

> **Example:**   Active: We **must put out** the fire. The thief **locked** us **in** the closet.
>
> Passive: The fire **must be put out.** We **were locked** in the closet.

Oral Drill D: Change the sentences to the passive voice.

1. In Professor Smith's political science class, you must *write down* everything.
2. Furthermore, you have to *turn in* every assignment on time.
3. He *turned down* my request for a make-up exam.
4. He *called* me *into* his office for a conference.
5. He *pointed out* all my mistakes on the exam.
6. For one thing, I had not *filled in* all the blanks on page 2 of the exam.
7. Nevertheless, he told me that I could not *do* it *over*.
8. Before you give him a paper, you should *check* it *over* carefully.

Exercise 1:   Oral practice. Change the following sentences to the passive voice. Decide when "by" is necessary. Keep all modifiers next to the word they modify.

Homework

Examples: adjective clauses: the man who . . .
prepositional phrases: the top of the desk

1. The police **have caught** the man who broke into the office last night.
2. The thief **had** completely **destroyed** some very important files.
3. They **are holding** him in the city jail until he **can contact** his lawyer.
4. They **are going to schedule** his trial for next month.
5. Officer Smith, chief of security, **is studying** the report of the break in.
6. Because of the incident, the president of the company **canceled** the stockholder's meeting.
7. His secretary **will send** notices of the next meeting to everyone.
8. She **typed** the notices yesterday afternoon.
9. The company's security force **is** currently **revising** all security procedures.
10. The force **is holding** its meeting in Room 432 at the moment.
11. The chief of security **was making** some recommendations a few minutes ago.
12. By the end of next week, they **will have revised** all security procedures.
13. Since last year, people **have burglarized** the building five times.
14. Two months ago, someone **locked** a secretary, who had been working late, in a closet for eight hours.
15. They **must maintain** the safety of the employees working in the building.
16. The security force **will present** the new plan before the end of next week.

Exercise 2: Change the following sentences to the passive voice. Decide when "by" is necessary.

1. One of the hospital's top surgeons **is operating on** John at the moment.

   _____

   _____

2. The hospital **will send** his wife the bill next week.

   _____

   _____

3. Fortunately, their insurance company **is going to pay** 70 percent of the bill.

   _____

   _____

4. The hospital **admits** visitors from seven to nine each evening.

   _____

5. However, you **must notify** the receptionist of your visit.

   _____

6. Last night, John had a slight fever, so the nurse **had to take** his temperature every hour.

   _____

   _____

7. A few minutes ago, someone **was paging** John's surgeon. I hope everything is all right.

   _____

   _____

8. The doctor **will have released** John from the hospital by the time his parents arrive in Denver.

   _____

   _____

9. This hospital staff **has provided** John with excellent care.

   _____

10. John's wife **had already packed** his clothes when the doctor signed John's release papers.

   _____

   _____

FORMING QUESTIONS IN THE PASSIVE VOICE

	Active Voice	*Passive Voice*
Simple Present	Do many older citizens use the library?	**Is** the library **used** by many older citizens?
Simple Past	Did many children use the library last summer?	**Was** the library **used** by many children last summer?
Present Continuous	Are workmen painting the third floor?	**Is** the third floor **being painted?**
Past Continuous	Were they painting the children's room last week?	**Was** the children's room **being painted** last week?
Future	Will the library offer many new programs next year?	**Will** many new programs **be offered** next year?
	Is a local author going to organize a children's story hour?	**Is** a children's story hour **going to be organized?**
Present Perfect	Has the director ordered a lot of new equipment?	**Has** a lot of new equipment **been ordered?**
Past Perfect	Had workmen already installed the new computer when you were there last week?	**Had** the new computer already **been installed** when you were there last week?
Future Perfect	Will the library have started the children's story hour by the end of next month?	**Will** the children's story hour **have been started** by the end of next month?
Present Infinitive	Do you have to renew your library card?	**Does** your library card **have to be** renewed?

Exercise 3: Oral practice. Asking and answering questions in the passive voice. *Change* the following passive sentences to passive questions.

Example: This radio can be fixed.   **Can this radio be fixed?**

1. The dean of studies was told about John's cheating.
2. All his test papers have been reviewed by his professors.
3. His term papers were also reread.
4. Most of his term papers had been plagiarized.
5. He has already been expelled from his psychology class.

171

6. His parents were notified last night.
7. Cheating, in any form, is detested by all professors.
8. Dishonest students are dealt with severely.
9. John will be dismissed from the university.
10. He is being consoled by his roommate.

Making Passive Sentences Negative

To make a verb in the passive voice negative, place *not* after the first auxiliary.

is being painted = is **not** being painted
has been painted = has **not** been painted
is used   = is **not** used

The present infinitive uses the auxiliary *do* to form the negative.

I have *to renew* my library card.   My library card **does not** have to be renewed.

Exercise 4:   Answer the following yes/no questions in the passive voice. Answer first in the affirmative, then in the negative.

Example: Do many people use public transportation?
Yes, it's **used** by the majority of the people.
No, it **isn't used** by many people.

Do, Does or Did never use with passive voice.

Group 1

1. Had motorists reported over twenty accidents by 10:00 last night?
2. Are the police recording all accident reports?
3. Have the police given out many tickets?
4. Did the police write over 350 tickets last year?
5. When I saw you last night, was the police officer giving you a ticket?
6. Did a judge suspend your driver's license for thirty days last year?
7. Does someone report every accident?   *(drunk)*
8. Will intoxicated drivers kill many innocent people this year?
9. Are the police going to punish careless drivers severely? *strongly*
10. Can anyone find good drivers?
11. Will the garage have repaired your car by the time classes begin?

Group 2

1. Do many students use the university library?

2. Did the university recently fire the director?
3. Is the university concealing the reason why he was fired?
4. Has the university found another director?
5. Will the university hire a woman?
6. Is the university going to hire an experienced person?
7. Has the hiring committee received any applications from highly qualified individuals?
8. Were they interviewing applicants yesterday afternoon?
9. Had they chosen anyone when the interviews were finished?

Exercise 5:   Review the uses of the passive voice and when to use *by*. Decide which of the following sentences should be used in the passive voice and which should remain in the active voice. Then, write the sentences in the form of a *paragraph*.

REMEMBER:

You should always have a specific reason for using the passive voice. *Do not overuse it.*

1. This is Ed Scott, your reporter for the 6:00 news.
2. I'm at the airport waiting for the Denver Broncos football team to arrive.
3. Hundreds of fans meet the team's plane every time it returns to Denver.
4. Everyone knows that the fans in Denver are the most enthusiastic in the country.
5. Some T.V. sportscasters have even called them fanatics.
6. An unusually large number of people greeted the Broncos last weekend.
7. I see that their plane has just landed.
8. The police are pushing the crowd back.
9. Somebody has just lost a little boy in this mass of people.
10. I can hear his parents calling his name.
11. In the past, the pushing and shoving has hurt many people.
12. These fans must learn the rules of politeness and safety.
13. The Broncos have just gotten off their plane, and they're entering the airport now.
14. The ecstatic fans are shouting their congratulations.
15. The Broncos, as you know, defeated the mighty Dallas Cowboys last night.
16. They will play the championship team of Oakland next week.
17. After that important game, undoubtedly thousands will crowd the airport.

Exercise 6:   Combine the following sentences into one paragraph. Use the passive voice *when appropriate.* Use the methods of coordination and subordination when you can, but *do not over connect.*

Situation: Ray is standing in a phone booth on the corner of University Blvd. and Evans St. He's talking to a friend and telling her about an accident that has just occurred.

1. A speeding car has just hit a student riding a bicycle.
2. The girl was crossing the street.
3. A large crowd is surrounding the car and the student.
4. A very tall police officer is inspecting the injured student.
5. A short police officer is ordering the crowd to move back.
6. I am certain that this officer will call an ambulance after he has inspected her.
7. He is calling for an ambulance on his car radio now.
8. I know that the officers are going to question the driver of the car.
9. I can see that the driver is extremely nervous.
10. The officers have asked a few people if they would testify in court.
11. About ten people witnessed the accident.
12. The ambulance will be here in a minute. I can hear its siren.
13. The ambulance driver will probably give the student oxygen and cover her with a blanket.
14. Now the man who hit the student is getting into the police car.
15. The short officer is locking the driver's car doors.
16. They are undoubtedly going to take him to the police station.
17. The state legislature should pass stricter laws to punish careless drivers.
18. We must eliminate reckless driving.

UNIT FIVE: PRACTICE EXAM

Write about a *true* event in your life. Use the passive voice when you think it is appropriate.

The following paragraphs were written during the winter quarter of 1979.

Jabria A. Jassim, Iraq

On my wedding day, we had a small party at which our parents, relatives, and some of our friends were present and from whom we received many presents. After the marriage ceremony, my husband and I decided to leave on our honeymoon to

London. The tickets **had been bought** for us by his parents; moreover, the journey **had been arranged** very well by my husband's friend, who drove us to the airport.

We took the airplane from Baghdad to London. When we got on the plane, we **were directed** to our seats by the stewardess, and as the plane was ready to fly, all the passengers **were asked** to fasten their seat belts and to stop smoking. Furthermore, we **were given** some advice on what to do in case of an emergency. After that we **were served** a delicious cocktail and **shown** an old English movie about the Second World War. Later on, dinner **was served** to all the passengers while newspapers and magazines **were being distributed.**

When the plane landed, we **were met** by some friends of my husband who drove us to a very nice hotel. Although we stayed in London for only ten days, we lived very happily, and we felt as if we had just bought the whole world; hence, we still remember those days. We returned home to our new home, parents, and friends, hoping to live happily forever.

UNIT 6

Modal Auxiliaries

To the Student   Read before you begin this unit.

TENSE, MEANING, TIME

In Unit Three (indirect speech) you learned that, after an introductory verb in the past tense, the past tense form of a modal must be used as in the sentence, He *said* he *could go*. When expressing statements in indirect speech, it is helpful to think of the modals as having the following present and past forms.

Present	*Past*
can	could
will	would
may	might
shall	should

However, it is important to know that these past tense forms do not always indicate past time. Sometimes the past forms indicate present time:

We **could leave** right now.

John **might be** upstairs.

Sometimes the past tense forms indicate future time.

You **should study** before the exam next week.

Would you **like** for me to study with you?

Concerning time, it is *not only* the modal but other elements in the sentence that give us the time of an action. The modals often indicate time, but their main job is to denote different shades of *meaning*. Look at the following sentences. The grammatical construction of each sentence is the same. Are the meanings the same?

I **will go** with you.

I **might go** with you.

I **can go** with you.

I **should go** with you.

I **must go** with you.

As the speaker or writer, only *you* know the meaning you want to express based on a particular situation, your knowledge about it, and your feelings toward it.

As students learning to speak English, you must learn the many different *meanings* that the modals express. In some instances the differences in meaning are easy to understand; in other instances the differences in meaning are very subtle. Nevertheless, it is important for you to learn these meanings because they will enable you to express what you are thinking and feeling more precisely. They will help you to communicate what *you* mean.

LESSON TWELVE

CAN

Meaning 1: *Ability (am, is, are able to)*

Example: Bill **can speak** five languages fluently.

time references: present, at any time

Meaning 2: *Strong Possibility*

In this use, *can* indicates that something is highly capable of happening as a *certain result* of another action.

Example: Don't light a match in this chemical factory!
The fire **can cause** an explosion.

time references: present, at any time.

Meaning 3: *Suggestion*

REMEMBER:

To make a suggestion is to give someone an idea that the person can think about and decide to use or forget.

Example: Bob: I don't understand this physics problem.

                Sam: John's very good in physics.
                       You **can ask** him to help you.

time references: present, at any time

NOTE: The expressions *why don't you . . .* and *let's + two simple verb forms* also express suggestion.

Sam: **Why don't you ask** John when he returns. He's good in physics.

Sam: I'm not good in physics, but **let's go ask** John. He's in his room now.

Notice that *let's . . .* always includes the person making the suggestion (let *us*).

Meaning 4:   Permission

Can is used both to ask for and to give permission.

Example: **Can I borrow** your eraser for a minute?
                Sure. You **can use** it.

time reference: present

Example: **Can I use** your car next Saturday?
                Of course, you **can use** it.

time reference: future

COULD

Meaning 1:   Past Ability (was, were able to)

To express past ability, *could* is used with a past adverbial phrase or clause.

Example: Two years ago, **I could play** tennis like a professional.

                When my brother was in high school, he **could beat** anyone at chess.

time reference: past

Meaning 2:   Ability Based on Certain Conditions

Example: We **could leave** now if we want to.

                I could be a good chess player if I wanted to. (But I'm not that interested in the game.)

time reference: present, future

Meaning 3: Strong Possibility

See explanation under "can," meaning 2.

Example:	Don't drive so fast! We **could have** an accident.
time reference:	present, at any time

Meaning 4: Permission

To ask for permission, "could" is more polite than "can."

Example:	**Could I borrow** your eraser for a minute?
	Could I use your car next Saturday?
time references:	present, future

Meaning 5: Polite Request

Example:	**Could** you **hold** my books until I find my door key?
time reference:	present
Example:	**Could** you **explain** this to me again after class?
time reference:	future

NOTE: When asking for permission, the speaker wants to do something, as in
"Could **I** close the window?"

When making a request, the speaker wants someone else to do something, as in
"Could **you** close the window?"

Meaning 6: Suggestion

This use is the same as suggestion with *can.*

Example:	Tom:	I don't have any money.
	Sue:	You **could call** your father and **ask** him for some.
	Jim:	You **could borrow** some from your roommate.
	Bob:	You **could stop** giving parties every weekend.
time references:	present, future	

REMEMBER:

"Could" is the past of "can" in indirect speech.

Expressing past time: **could + have + past participle**

Could + have + past participle is used to express

a. *Ability* that was *not used* in the past.

   I **could have gotten** an A in grammar last quarter, but I didn't like the instructor.

b. A *suggestion* that was *not taken* about a past situation

   You **could have asked** the director to put you in a different grammar class, but you didn't.

Exercise 1: Listen as your instructor reads the following sentences. Indicate which meaning is expressed.

a. past ability   c. suggestion   e. strong possibility

b. permission   d. polite request   f. ability based on certain conditions

_____ 1. **Can I borrow** your books on strange life forms on other planets?

_____ 2. My books are outdated, but you **could call** the planetarium and ask for the titles of some recently published books.

_____ 3. When I was in high school, **I could name** all the planets from memory.

_____ 4. You **could do** it again if you reviewed them.

_____ 5. **Could** you **give** me the number at the planetarium?

_____ 6. Instead of calling the planetarium, we **can drive** out there tomorrow. I haven't been there for a long time.

_____ 7. That's a good idea, but look at the sky; we **could have** a big snowstorm.

_____ 8. **Could I turn** on your television and **watch** the weather report?

_____ 9. Sure. I was just thinking about my grandfather. When he was alive, he **could predict** the weather.

_____ 10. **Could** he **predict** the weather accurately?

_____ 11. He **could do** it when and if his big toe began to hurt.

_____ 12. I think something's wrong with your television. Everybody has green faces. Your picture tube **could be** loose. I'll check it.

_____ 13. Be careful! Don't touch anything inside the television with wet hands. You **can get** electrocuted.

Exercise 2: Oral practice. Can, could: Suggestion (time reference: future). Listen as your instructor reads the following paragraph.

Over the past few years, marriage ceremonies in the United States have become less and less traditional. Newspapers frequently report about couples who have said their marriage vows while riding motorcycles, deep-sea diving, dancing, or jumping out of airplanes. Nevertheless, many marriages are still taking place in the more traditional settings of the church or the home, but there are still a few couples who prefer to be somewhere in between. They neither want to get married while under the sea nor do they want a formal church ceremony.

What suggestions would you give an American friend who made the following statements concerning his upcoming marriage?

1. I don't want to get married in a formal church ceremony because large, expensive weddings are a waste of money.
2. My fiancée and I have decided not to send out expensive wedding invitations, but we want our friends and relatives to know that we are getting married.
3. We do not feel that it is necessary to go on an expensive honeymoon, but we would like to go somewhere and be alone for a week. We both enjoy the outdoors.
4. Neither my fiancée nor I want the word "obey" in our ceremony.
5. We really do not want our friends and relatives to give us expensive gifts that we will never use.
6. My future wife doesn't want me to give her a "diamond" engagement ring.
7. We really do not know what to serve during the party after the wedding, but we want to keep the menu simple.
8. I think our parents are going to ignore our desires and plan a big wedding for us.
9. My fiancée's cousin wants to sing at our wedding, but she has a terrible voice.
10. You know, I'm not really sure that I am ready for marriage.

Exercise 3: Could + have + past participle: Suggestion (time reference: the past). Unfortunately, your friend's marriage lasted for only six months. After his divorce, he made the following statements to you. Respond to each statement using could + have + past participle.

> **Example:** My wife didn't want to live in a small apartment, but we couldn't afford to buy a house.
>
> You **could have rented** a house.

1. My wife didn't want me to spend so much time away from her with my single friends. I didn't know what to do because I wanted to be with her and them.
2. She complained about my snoring and talking in my sleep.

3. She didn't like my coming home at 7:30 some evenings when she had dinner ready by 6:00.

4. She was angry because only my name was on the checks.

5. I didn't like her spending so much time on the phone because I often received business calls in the evenings.

6. Because she had a full-time job too, she always complained about being too tired to do housework, so the apartment was always a mess.

7. I didn't like the way she ironed my shirts.

8. She didn't approve of my watching television in bed.

9. I didn't like the way she cooked.

10. I didn't like spending every weekend with her parents, although I like them.

MAY

Meaning 1:   Permission

May is more formal than *can* or *could* and indicates a recognition of an individual's authority or respect for an individual's position.

Examples:	a. Jim to police officer:	**May** I use your pen?
	b. Jim to stranger in a bank:	**Could** I use your pen?
	c. Jim to roommate:	**Can** I use your pen?
time references:	present, future	

Meaning 2:   Weak Possibility

a. referring to a *future action*

Example:	It **may snow** tomorrow. (I haven't listened to the weather report yet, but the air feels cold, and the sky looks the way it always looks before it snows.)
time reference:	future

b. referring to a *present condition*

Example:	John **may be** sick. (He didn't tell me he was sick, but his eyes look strange.)
time reference:	present

MIGHT

Meaning 1: Weak Possibility

a. referring to a *future action*

b. referring to a *present condition*

NOTE: In this use, might is the same as may; however, many grammarians believe that might expresses possibility that is much weaker than that of may.

Examples: It **might snow** tomorrow.   (but probably won't)

John **might be** sick.   (but probably isn't)

REMEMBER:

"Might" is used as the past of may in indirect speech.

John says, "We may get married soon." He **said** they **might** get married soon.

Expressing past time: **may/might + have + past participle**

May/might + have + past participle expresses *weak possibility* about past actions or conditions.

He **may/might have passed** the exam two days ago.   **(But I doubt it.)**

It **may/might have snowed** in the mountains last night.   (I see that there are snow clouds over the mountains, but the weathercaster didn't say anything about snow.)

John **may/might have been** sick yesterday.   (His eyes were red although he didn't act sick.)

Expressing *Possibility:* Could versus May/Might

Although "could," "may," and "might" all express possibility, remember that *could expresses possibility with a stronger degree of certainty* than does either may or might.

Compare the following sentences.

Student A: We **could have** a vocabulary quiz tomorrow. We have just finished the lesson, and we usually have a quiz after each lesson.

Student B: We **might have** a vocabulary quiz tomorrow, but I don't think we will.

Both might and could can be used in either of the sentences given with very little noticeable difference in meaning; however, student A seems to be a little more certain. Student A even offers some reasoning to support the opinion expressed.

REMEMBER:

The degree of certainty is determined by the situation, meaning, and the attitude of you the speaker.

Are you fairly certain about something?   (Use "could.")

Are you less certain?   (Use "might.")

Exercise 4:   Could versus **May/Might.** Listen as different students take turns reading the following. Choose a. or b. *EXPLAIN* your choice for each sentence.

a. weak possibility   b. strong possibility

_____ 1. Jamal: This quarter is almost finished, and this **could be** the last time we will see each other since your family doesn't have enough money.

_____ 2. Reza: **I might be able** to continue my academic studies at this university, if my father can convince the bank to give him a loan.

_____ 3. Jamal: You have been an excellent student here in the English program. You **could get** a partial scholarship for academic work.

_____ 4. Reza: I asked our grammar instructor about it, and she said she would talk to the director of the foreign student aid department. She **could be having** some luck. She thinks I'm a good student.

_____ 5. Jamal: You *are* a good student, but the amount of money in the scholarship fund **might be** very low. I saw our grammar teacher yesterday. She was walking across campus with the director of the student aid department, and she looked a little depressed. She **could have tried** to get you a scholarship without any luck.

_____ 6. Reza: I read in the student newspaper that someone just gave the university a million dollars for its student aid program, so you **could be** wrong.

_____ 7. Jamal: You **may have** a good point.

_____ 8. Reza: **I might go** to the student aid department tomorrow afternoon and ask about the availability of aid.

_____ 9. Jamal: I passed their building yesterday, and the place was full of painters, so their office **could be** closed tomorrow.

_____10. Reza: I know, but their office is small, and the painters work quickly, so they **could already have finished** their work.

VERB TENSES AFTER THE MODAL

Before we continue our review of the modals, let's take a few minutes to study the various tenses of the main verb that may follow a modal auxiliary.

1. modal + simple form	**could take**
2. modal + have + past participle	**could have taken**
3. modal + be + present participle	**could be taking**
4. modal + have + been + present participle	**could have been taking**

1. The forms *could take* and *could be taking* refer to present or future time. The use of time words or expressions help to make the time reference clear.

> You **could take** your make-up test *now*.   (if you are ready)
>
> You **could take** it *tomorrow*.   (if you want to)
>
> I **could be taking** it *now*.   (But I'm not ready.)
>
> I **could be leaving** for home *tomorrow*.   (if I didn't have to take a make-up test)

2. The forms *could have taken* and *could have been taking* always refer to past time.

> I **could have taken** my make-up test *yesterday*.   (But I wasn't ready.)
>
> I **could have been getting** ready to go home *last night*.   (Instead of doing this, I was studying for my make-up test.)

Rapid oral practice: verb tenses after a modal

A.   Answer the following questions in complete sentences.

1. What are you doing right now? What **could you be doing** if you were not in class?
2. You went to a terrible movie last night. What **could you have done** instead?
3. This afternoon you have to study for tomorrow's grammar test. If you didn't have a test tomorrow, what **could you be doing** this afternoon?
4. Which student **could have been** in class yesterday? Where was he?
5. What **could you have been doing** last night if your television had not been in the repair shop?
6. **Could you take** a test on this lesson tomorrow and pass it with a high grade?
7. Which mode of transportation **could you have used** to come to the United States instead of the airplane?

B.   Change the following statements to the questions indicated.

1. Maria **could save** more money if she didn't make so many long-distance phone calls every night.
   a. who subject
   b. yes/no question
   c. what object

2. She **could be talking** to her family now.
   a. whom object
   b. what + do
   c. yes/no question

3. Her younger sister **could have come** here to study also, but she didn't want to.
   a. who subject
   b. where
   c. yes/no question
   d. what + do

4. Maria's parents **could have been trying** to convince her to come.
   a. who subject
   b. what + do
   c. yes/no question

REMEMBER:

Modals can also be followed by the passive construction.

    active: You **can finish** this assignment tomorrow.
    passive: This assignment **can be finished** tomorrow.

    active: You **should have written** your composition last week.
    passive: Your composition **should have been written** last week.

Exercise 5:   Verb forms after "could." Complete the following dialogue with the correct form of the verb after could. Pay attention to the time words and expressions.

Bob: Where's Pete? He wanted me to give him a ride home.

Sue: I don't know for sure, but he wanted to talk to Professor Ray about his

grades so far, so he _____could be talking_____ (talk) to her right now.

Bob: You're probably right. He's probably talking about his lateness, too.

Sue: I know. He doesn't have to come to class late every morning. He

_____ (come) to class on time if he tried.

Bob: Why was he late this morning?

Sue: Don't ask me. He _____ (stay) up late last night to study.

Bob: Or, he _____ (go) to a party.

Sue: He has passed only one test so far this quarter. He

_____ (fail) this course if he doesn't get serious.

Bob: Professor Ray _____ (tell) him that right now.

Sue: You're his best friend. You _____ (talk) with him and see if he has any big problems.

Bob: That's a good suggestion. Pete _____ (have) trouble with his girlfriend this quarter.

Sue: That's right. They _____ (have) an argument last night.

Bob: They _____ (plan) to break up soon.

Sue: They _____ (discuss) this all last night.

Bob: Well, whatever the problem is, I'll talk to him.

Sue: Good. Who knows? Just your concern _____ (make) him feel better.

Bob: I _____ (say) something to him earlier, but I have been so busy during the past few weeks.

Sue: Well, better late than never.

SHOULD

Meaning 1:   Obligation

Obligations are *duties* or *responsibilities* that a person, organization, and the like has, although they do not necessarily meet their responsibilities all the time.

Examples: A restaurant's kitchen **should be** clean at all times.   (But some aren't.)

A teacher **should be** well prepared for every class.   (But some aren't.)

A student **shouldn't waste** his parents' money.   (But many do.)

time reference: all the time

Meaning 2: Expectation

An expectation refers to an *action* that we are sure will happen because of our familiarity with or previous knowledge about a situation, a person, and so on.

Examples:	We **should reach** the airport in about twenty minutes. (The traffic is not heavy. The streets are dry. I only live eight miles from the airport. I've made this trip many times.)
	Ali **should get** an A in grammar. (He has received high grades on all his tests, attends all classes, and completes all homework assignments thoroughly.)
time reference:	future

An expectation can also refer to a *condition* that we are sure will result.

Example:	Bob **should be** sick tomorrow. (He ate four big pizzas and drank two six packs of beer before going to bed.)
time reference:	future

An expectation can also refer to present time.

My roommate **should be** home now.

Meaning 3: Advice

When giving advice, the speaker is expressing *an opinion* as to what to do or what not to do.

Examples:	You **should study** more. You **should study** tonight.
	You **should be working** now.
	You **shouldn't drink** alcohol.
time references:	present, future, at any time

REMEMBER:

In indirect speech, should does not change.

obligation:	She says, "All eligible citizens should vote." She said that all eligible citizens **should** vote.
expectation:	He says, "We should arrive at the airport in twenty minutes." He told me that we **should** arrive at the airport in twenty minutes.
advice:	She says, "You should study more." She told me that I **should** study more.

188

Expressing past time with should + have + past participle

obligation: You **should have voted** in the election.
expectation: We **should have arrived** at the airport twenty minutes ago.
advice: You **should have studied** harder last semester.

Rapid oral practice: Change the following statements to the questions indicated.

1. My roommate **should be** in the library now.
   a. who subject
   b. where
   c. yes/no question

2. He **should be studying** vocabulary words because he has a quiz tomorrow.
   a. what + do
   b. what object
   c. why
   d. yes/no question

3. He **should have gotten** an A on the quiz last week since he really studied for it.
   a. yes/no question
   b. what object
   c. why

4. I **should have been helping** him all quarter because he has a lot of trouble learning vocabulary words.
   a. who subject
   b. yes/no question
   c. why
   d. when

Exercise 6:   *Should.* Obligation versus advice. Students sometimes confuse these two meanings of should; however, it is not difficult to distinguish between the two if you think about the meaning of the idea you want to express.

Example: A father is **obligated** to send his children to school in the United States. But he is not obligated to send them to Disneyland every summer.

Read the following groups of sentences and indicate if advice (A) is expressed or obligation (O) is expressed.

1. _____ A father should take care of his family.

   _____ Mr. Smith, you should buy your son a new bicycle.

2. _____ Parents should teach their children right from wrong.

_____ Bob, you should ask your father to help you with your problem.

3. _____ A student should be on time for class.

_____ Tom was late for every class last quarter. He should have bought an alarm clock.

4. _____ You really should stop driving so fast.

_____ Every driver should obey the traffic laws.

5. _____ Jim, you should call your grandfather tonight.

_____ Every society should take care of its senior citizens.

6. _____ You should have told your doctor about the pain in your back.

_____ Hospitals should hire only well-qualified doctors and nurses.

7. _____ A used-car dealer should give customers correct information about every car.

_____ I should not have bought such an expensive car.

8. _____ A teacher should treat all students equally.

_____ You should think about becoming a teacher. You're good with children.

9. _____ Should we report our loud neighbors to the police?

_____ The apartment manager should make sure that all residents respect the rights of others.

10. _____ All citizens should pay their taxes.

_____ You should ask someone to help you fill out your tax forms.

11. _____ A newspaper should report the truth.

_____ You should read *The New York Times*.

Exercise 7:   *Should.* Advice versus expectation. Read the following sentences and decide if the underlined verbs indicate advice (A) or expectation (E).

1. _____ Get my cigarettes for me. They <u>should be</u> on my dresser in the bed-room.

2. _____ Your cough is getting worse. You really <u>should stop</u> smoking.

3. _____ Your doctor <u>should be able</u> to tell you about the current research on cancer.

4. _____ Because of your cough, you <u>should have made</u> an appointment with your doctor weeks ago.

5. _____ You <u>should be discussing</u> the dangers of smoking with your children.

6. _____ They are in junior high school now, so they <u>should understand</u> what you say.

7. _____ When you stop smoking, you <u>should be able</u> to save money.

8. _____ Cigarette prices have risen in the past, and they <u>should be going up</u> again.

9. _____ You really <u>should heed</u> the warning on the pack and at least cut down a little.

10. _____ If you can't stop completely, you <u>should use</u> a filter.

11. _____ A filter <u>shouldn't cost</u> too much.

12. _____ Shouldn't you seriously <u>be considering</u> all that I have said?

13. _____ Your cough <u>should cease</u> if you think about what I've been saying.

14. _____ You <u>should have</u> your lungs checked as soon as possible.

15. _____ Your doctor <u>should have</u> the necessary equipment in his office.

Assignment: Choose *one* situation (topic of discussion) and write five statements of advice and five statements of expectation.

MUST

Meaning 1: Necessity (have to)

Example: A soldier **must obey** army regulations.   (He has no choice.)

time references: future, at any time

Example: Teacher: The time is up. You **must give** me your papers.
              Student: I haven't finished Part III yet.
              Teacher: I'm sorry. You **must stop.** Your paper please.

time reference: present

Expressing necessity in the past: **had to**
had to not "must" expresses necessity in the past.

When I was in the army, we **had to obey** all regulations.   (We had no choice.)
Student: I had not finished Part II of the exam, but I **had to turn in** my test.

NOTE: The phrase *have to* also expresses a *rejection of necessity.*

Mother: You **must go** to bed now.
Child: **I don't have to go** now. Daddy said I could stay up late tonight.

Meaning 2:   Assumption

In this use, must expresses a strong belief that something is true based on available facts, strong evidence, or familiarity with a situation. But the facts or evidence may not be totally complete.

Example: She **must have** the flu. (She has a fever and a runny nose.)

They **must live** close to the university. (They walk to class every day.)

Expressing assumption in the past: must + have + past participle

She **must have had** the flu. That's why she had a fever and a runny nose.
They **must have lived** close to the university last quarter. That's why they walked every day.

Meaning 3:   Prohibition

A prohibition is an order or a law against doing something. In this use, must is usually used in the negative.

Examples: You **must not walk** on the grass.
You **must not smoke** in class.

time reference: at any time

Exercise 8: *Must.* Assumption. Use must + simple form of the verb, must + be + present participle, or must + have + past participle to complete the following sentences.

Example: John looked depressed after the exam; it (be) **must have been** difficult.

1. Richard Nixon was the second American president to have been threatened

   with impeachment. Today he _____ (regret) some
   of the decisions he had made.

2. At the time he made those decisions, however, he

   _____ (believe) that he was right.

3. Since he left the presidency, he has been isolated from political life. Today,

   he _____ (feel) very lonely.

4. Some people say that he _____ (be) power hungry
   to have permitted such activities on the part of his staff.

192

5. During the Senate investigations, many of his staff members lied. They
   _____ (think) that the American people would
   never learn the truth.
6. So far, Nixon has refused to let his presidential papers be made public. The
   papers _____ (contain) damaging evidence.
7. During the Watergate investigations in 1972, Nixon criticized the press
   severely. Many people still feel that he _____
   (try) to cover up any evidence that would have harmed him.
8. The members of his family _____ (still, be) sad
   about the turn of events in their lives.
9. When Nixon had to leave the White House, he _____
   (feel) disgraced.
10. He _____ (know) that he could not get away with
    his activities.
11. It _____ (be) terrible to know that the entire world
    knows about your disgrace.
12. I am certain that every newspaper in the world
    _____ (print) the news of his downfall.

Exercise 9: *Must.* Assumption (present and past time). The rules of grammar tell us
how to form the present and the past of the modals; however, the rules do not dictate
which tense we must use. This choice belongs to the speaker and what he wants to
say.

> **Example:**   Speaker 1:   My brother was a star soccer player in high school.
>
> Speaker 2:   He **must still be** a good player.   (present)
>
> (or)
>
> Speaker 2:   He **must have started** playing when he was very
> young.   (past)

Respond to the following sentences as indicated.

1. Two 747 airplanes crashed last week, and two hundred people died.

   present: Their families _____

   past: The pilots _____
2. The men in the controller's tower were responsible for the crash.

   present: Today, those men _____

   past: At the time of the accident, they _____

3. My friend's parents were aboard the plane, but they survived.

   present: Today they _____

   past: When the accident occurred, they _____

4. My sister who is a stewardess was supposed to work that flight, but she was sick, so another flight attendant substituted for her.

   present: Your sister _____

   past: When your sister heard about the crash, _____

5. The two captains were not aware of each other on their radar screens; nevertheless, both of them survived the crash.

   present: Now, every time they fly, they _____

   past: Their equipment _____

Exercise 10: *Must.* Necessity versus assumption. Read the following sentences and decide if the underlined verbs indicate necessity or assumption.

> **Example:** The instructor looks very tired. She **must have stayed up** late last night correcting our compositions. <u>assumption</u>

1. The city of Denver does not have a good system of public transportation. A visitor from New York <u>must be surprised</u> by having to wait for an hour to catch a

   bus. _____

2. To cut down on the amount of pollution, the city <u>must improve</u> the public transportation system so that fewer people will drive their cars.

   _____

3. In fact, something has already been started. During the morning and afternoon rush hours, cars <u>must avoid</u> driving in the specially marked bus lanes.

   _____

4. My friend Al, who returned to Denver after this law was passed, <u>must have been</u> very surprised when he received a ticket for having been driving in a bus

   lane. _____

5. When people receive citations for traffic violations, however, they <u>must pay</u> them immediately or appear in court and defend

   themselves. _____

6. The police officer who gave Al the ticket <u>must have gotten</u> angry when Al adamantly informed him that he would not pay the

   fine. _____

7. Al is generally a calm person, but he <u>must have</u> really <u>been</u> angry to have spoken to a police officer that way. _____

8. Nevertheless, he <u>must obey</u> the traffic laws like everyone else.

_____

9. Right after the bus lane law was passed, the police <u>must have written</u> hundreds of tickets a day. _____

10. This is only one law, but when driving the motorist <u>must be</u> aware of every law.

_____

11. If one does not know the traffic laws, one <u>must learn</u> them. Ignorance of the laws is no excuse. _____

Should for Expectation versus Must for Assumption

Present and Past Time

1. Both "must for assumption" and "should for expectation" involve making an "intelligent guess."

2. In sentences that refer to present or past time or a present or past condition either one or the other is often possible. However, *must* expresses a greater degree of certainty.

    My wallet **should be** on the dresser.   (I **usually** put it there.)
    My wallet **must be** on the dresser.   (I **always** put it there.)

    My wallet **should have been** on the dresser.   (I **usually** put it there.)
    My wallet **must have been** on the dresser.   (Did you look carefully?)

REMEMBER:

The grammatical rules of a language do not tell you *what to think* or *say*. The rules tell you *how to express your own individual* ideas about and reactions to a situation.

In sentences where either "must for assumption" or "should for expectation" is possible, the choice to use one or the other depends upon the degree of certainty *you* wish to convey.

Study the following sentences where either "should" or "must" is possible.

1. Speaker 1:   My roommate left Denver for Colorado Springs at 6:00. It's 7:00 now, and it only takes one hour to drive from Denver to Colorado Springs.

    Speaker 2:   He **should be** in Colorado Springs now.
    Speaker 3:   He **must be** in Colorado Springs now.

2. Speaker 1:   Jim studied for six straight hours last night. That's a long time to study without a break.

   Speaker 2:   He **must have been** tired when he went to bed.
   Speaker 3:   He **should have been** tired when he went to bed.

3. Speaker 1:   During the summer months, it gets dark after 8:30 P.M.

   Speaker 2:   It **should be** around 9:00 now because it's almost dark outside.
   Speaker 3:   It **must be** around 9:00 now because it is dark outside.

4. Speaker 1:   The telephone is ringing.

   Speaker 2:   My parents said they would call me tonight around 8:00, and it's 8:10 now, so I'll get the phone because it **must be/should be** my parents calling.

5. Speaker 1:   Bob studied in France for three years. He has always enjoyed learning languages, and he learns them easily.

   Speaker 2:   He **must speak** French very well.
   Speaker 3:   He **should speak** French very well.

Future Time

1. When making "an intelligent guess" about the future, only "should" can be used.
2. "Must" has a different meaning when it refers to future time. It means *necessity*.

   The check from my parents **must arrive** tomorrow.   (**I really need some money.**)

Study the following sentences. Note carefully the expressed or implied time references. Note also the different reactions of each speaker. These reactions lead each speaker to make different comments about the situation expressed by the first speaker.

Speaker 1:   Bob has already drunk six beers and eaten five hamburgers and four pieces of cherry pie.

Speaker 2:   Reaction: Nobody can eat and drink that much without getting sick.

   Response: He **should be** sick tomorrow morning.

Speaker 3:   Reaction: Nobody eats like that unless they haven't eaten for a while, and they are really hungry.

   Response: He **must be** very hungry.   *or*   He **must not have eaten** for a couple of days.

Speaker 4:   Reaction: He has eaten and drunk a lot, but after all he *is* a big man.

   Response: He **must need** a lot of food.

REMEMBER:

Your response to a situation will reflect the reaction you have in your mind. You may or may not express your reaction verbally.

Exercise 11: *Should,* Expectation, versus *Must,* Assumption. Complete the following statements with should or must. Each speaker's reaction is included in the response. Be careful of the time reference.

1. Speaker 1: I haven't eaten any sweets for two weeks.

   Speaker 2: You _____ be on a diet, or you would not be giving up sweets.

   Speaker 3: You _____ lose a lot of weight because sweets contain many calories.

2. Speaker 1: I took two aspirins a half hour ago.

   Speaker 2: Then your headache _____ go away soon because that brand of aspirin is very effective.

   Speaker 3: (A half hour later) You _____ need something else beside aspirin because you are still in pain.

3. Speaker 1: Look at the sky tonight. It's full of stars.

   Speaker 2: We _____ have a beautiful day tomorrow because it's clear tonight.

4. Speaker 1: Mansour is trying to sell his Trans Am.

   Speaker 2: He _____ get a lot of money for it because it's in excellent condition.

   Speaker 3: It _____ be giving him a lot of trouble.

   Speaker 4: He _____ seen another car that he liked better than the Trans Am.

5. Speaker 1: Pierre was elected president of the International Student's Organization.

   Speaker 2: He _____ know a lot of people at the university because he received the largest number of votes.

   Speaker 3: He _____ make a good president because he's very intelligent; also, he understands the concerns of foreign students.

   Speaker 4: He _____ be an excellent student, too, because you have to have an "A" average to enter the election.

6. Speaker 1: I haven't received my parent's check for next quarter's tuition.

Speaker 2:   Don't worry. It _____ arrive soon. Your parents have never been late with your tuition money.

Speaker 3:   Your parents _____ have a lot of money. My parents don't, so I have to work and pay my own tuition.

7. Speaker 1:   I've been trying to solve this statistics problem for four hours.

Speaker 2:   It_____ be very complicated; otherwise, it would not take so long to solve.

Speaker 3:   The answer _____ be in the back of the book. Some statistics books contain the answers to the exercises.

Speaker 4:   It_____ be in the back of the book. All statistics books contain the answers to the exercises.

8. Speaker 1:   Ali's best friend is a German student who doesn't speak English or Arabic, and Ali doesn't speak German.

Speaker 2:   You're kidding! Then both of them _____ speak another language; otherwise, they couldn't communicate with one another.

Exercise 12:   Complete the following statements with either *must* or *should*. In some sentences either is possible. In other sentences, only one or the other can be used.

A. 1.   We have only two more weeks of classes. The students_____ be very happy.

2.   We will have a two-hour grammar final. The final _____ be difficult.

3.   A few students failed the grammar test last quarter, so that final

_____ been difficult.

4.   Our teacher has already written the final, but she wouldn't leave it at

school, so she _____ taken it home.

5.   Part I of the test is true/false, so it _____ be very easy.

6.   Maria has gotten an A on every test so far. She _____ get an A on the final.

7.   All the students understand adjective clauses now; therefore, everyone

_____ do well on that part of the test.

8.   Our teacher likes long tests, so our final _____ be at least five pages long.

B.   Speaker 1:   It is 9:20, and our teacher has not arrived yet.

Speaker 2: I'm a little worried. She is never late. She _____ have had an accident.

Speaker 3: Stop worrying. She _____ be here in a few minutes.

Speaker 4: She was sick yesterday afternoon, so she _____ have decided to stay home today.

C. Speaker 1: A fire engine is stopping in front of our building.

Speaker 2: I smell smoke. There _____ be a fire somewhere in the building.

Speaker 3: Don't worry. These firefighters are experienced. They

_____ have everything under control in a little while.

Speaker 4: The smoke is coming from the third floor. The fire

_____ have started there.

Speaker 5: Our grammar teacher _____ be worried about our modal test. She put the test papers in her desk this morning.

WILL

Meaning 1:   Simple Future

Example: The meeting **will begin** at eight o'clock.
time reference: future

Meaning 2:   A Promise

Example: Don't worry. **I'll be** at the meeting on time.
time reference: future

Meaning 3:   Determination

Example: At the meeting, we **will solve** our financial problems if it takes all night.
time reference: future

NOTE: The speaker's *intonation* is very important in distinguishing the simple future from the other two meanings. Ask your teacher to read the three sentences given.

SHALL

The most common use of "shall" in American English is when it is used to make an offer to do something for someone.

Shall I put these papers on your desk?   (Do you want me to put these papers . . .)

Shall is *sometimes* used in first-person questions asking for *agreement*.

Shall we leave now?

WOULD

Meaning 1:   Polite Request
Example: **Would** you please **close** the door?
time reference: present
Example: **Would** you **complete** this assignment for Tuesday?
time reference: future

Meaning 2:
An inquiry as to someone's willingness to do something
Examples: **Would** you **help** me review for the chemistry exam?
                  Sure. **I would be** happy to help you review for it.
time references: present, future

Meaning 3:   Habitual Action in the Past
Example: When I was in elementary school, we **would sing** every afternoon, and I **would sing** as loudly as I could.
time reference: past

Meaning 4:   Past of Will in Indirect Speech
Example: Tim says, "I'll see you later."
           Tim said he **would see** us later.

Meaning 5:   Result of a Condition
Would expresses the result of a condition in conditional sentences.

200

Examples: *Condition*   *Result*

Condition	Result
If I were rich,	I would take a long vacation.
If I had had enough money,	I would have taken a long vacation.

This use of would will be studied in Unit Seven under conditional sentences.

ADDITIONAL MODAL EXPRESSIONS

Auxiliary	*Meaning*	*Example*
1. **Would rather** **Would sooner**	a. preference	I **would rather** stay home than go out tonight.
2. **Had better**	a. consequence	She **had better** stop speeding (or risk losing her license).
3. **Have to (must)**	a. necessity	I **have to** go now. I'm already an hour late for my appointment.
4. **Used to (would)**	a. past habitual action	I **used to eat** a lot of candy.
5. **Ought to (should)**	a. obligation	You **ought to work** harder.
	b. expectation	The instructor **ought to be** in her office now.
	c. advice	You **ought to leave** that job. It's making you nervous.

1. *Would rather* expresses a choice or a preference.

> **I would rather** go to a movie   (instead of going bowling).   **Sue would rather** go bowling   (instead of going to a movie).

Would sooner expresses preference and is interchangeable with would rather.

> **I would sooner** eat beef than pork. He **would rather** eat beef, too.

Expressing preference in the past: **would rather + have + past participle**

I **would rather** have gone to a movie. (But we went bowling.)

Expressing preference in the past: **would sooner + have + past participle**

We **would sooner** have eaten beef. (But they didn't have any.)

---

2. *Had better* indicates that a consequence (usually bad) will follow if something is *not done*.

> *You* **had better hurry** or you will miss your flight.
>
> You'**d better not talk** during the final, or the instructor will give you a zero.

3. *Have to* like must expresses necessity. *Have to* requires an auxiliary verb (do, does, did) to form the interrogative and the negative.

> **Do** you **have to leave** right now? No. **I don't have to.** I can stay a little longer.

4. *Used to* like would expresses habitual action in the past.

> **I used to** smoke two packs of cigarettes every day.

NOTE: Used to changes to *use to* (without the "d") in the interrogative and negative.

> Did you **use to** drink also?
>
> She **didn't use to** bother me, but now she does.

5. *Ought to* like should expresses

> obligation: You **ought to help** your grandfather. He's an old man.
>
> expectation: The check from my parents **ought to arrive** today.
>
> advice: You're gaining weight. You **ought to exercise** more.

Referring to past time: ought to + have + past participle

Now your grandfather is in the hospital. You **ought to have helped** him with the heavy work around the house.

I'm really worried. The check from my parents **ought to have arrived** two days ago.

Now you have to go on a strict diet. You **ought to have exercised** more.

LESSON TWELVE: REVIEW EXERCISES

A.   Indicate the meaning expressed by each modal in the following sentences.

a. advice	e. assumption	i. willingness
b. expectation	f. necessity	j. present ability
c. suggestion	g. prohibition	k. preference
d. promise	h. strong possibility	

_____ 1. You **should dress** warmly when it's cold.

_____ 2. You **must dress** warmly if you want to stay well.

_____ 3. Your eyes are red. You **must be catching** a cold.

_____ 4. You **could put** some drops in your eyes to get out the redness.

_____ 5. Your eyes **should be** clearer in a little while.

_____ 6. Your voice sounds funny. You **must have** a sore throat.

_____ 7. You really look sick. You **must call** a doctor now.

_____ 8. My doctor **should not be** very busy today. Call him.

_____ 9. If he is busy, you **can call** the health center.

_____10. You really **should see** a doctor soon.

_____11. Your forehead is wet, too. You **must have** a fever.

_____12. That does it. You **must leave** the class immediately.

_____13. In fact, you **should go** home.

_____14. Since you have to wait for your ride home, you **could go** into the student lounge and lie down.

_____15. Because you have a slight fever, the doctor **could put** you in the hospital overnight.

_____16. I know you **would rather be** at home now instead of at school.

_____17. You really **should have stayed** in bed today.

_____18. You **must have felt** bad last night.

_____19. If you felt bad, you **could have called** me.

_____20. I **would have been** happy to come over and stay with you.

_____21. I don't know why your friend is late. I'm finished for today. **I can drive** you home.

_____22. Go to bed when you get home. You **could feel** better by tomorrow.

_____23. I **will do** all I can for you. Don't worry.

_____24. You **must not go** anywhere tonight. Stay in bed and rest.

_____25. I **would be** glad to come over to your apartment and fix dinner for you.

_____26. You **could get** worse if you do not take it easy.

B.   Respond to the following statements according to the meanings indicated.

Example: *The sky is very dark.*

State a *weak possibility*   It **might rain** this afternoon.
about a future action:

Give some *advice:*   You **should roll up** your car windows.

Make a *suggestion:*   We **could go** to the museum instead of the park.

1. The director doesn't seem to be in a good mood this morning.

   a. State a strong possibility.
   b. Make an assumption about the past.
   c. Give another student some advice.

2. The leader of any country has many responsibilities.

   a. State an obligation.
   b. State a necessity.
   c. Make an assumption.

3. Tetsuo is over six feet tall.

   a. Make an assumption about Tetsuo when he was in high school.
   b. Give Tetsuo some advice.
   c. State a weak possibility about his future.
   d. State an ability based on certain conditions.

4. Rosa's brother has just entered the Army for three years.

   a. State an obligation.
   b. State an expectation.
   c. Make an assumption.
   d. Give some advice for Rosa's brother.

5. Bob suddenly decided not to finish his Masters degree.

   a. State a weak possibility about a present condition.
   b. State a weak possibility about a future action.
   c. State an expectation.
   d. Make an assumption.

C.   In one paragraph, tell about a *correct* decision you made in the past. Tell some things you **could have done,** and then tell *why you did not do them.*

In a separate paragraph, tell about a decision you made in the past that you now regret. Tell **what you should have done** instead.

Read the following student paragraphs before you begin.

   1. In 1969, I graduated from high school. I decided to register at the College of Engineering. I **could have registered** at the Medical College, but I like the subjects that depend on mathematics. The first two years I took general engineering courses. In the beginning of the third year, I **could have studied** electrical engineering, but I preferred mechanical engineering because I like thermodynamics and the strength of material subjects. In the summer of 1972, I worked with the Royal Saudi Air Force, and I **could have worked** there the next summer, but I worked with an oil company to get different knowledge.

   After graduation, I **could have worked** at a research center in Saudi Arabia, but I worked at the University of Riyadh because they give students a chance to continue studying after graduation. I **could have gone** to England for my Masters and Ph.D., but I preferred American universities because they are on the credited course system. **I could have gone** to Oklahoma to study English, but I came to Denver because it is a nice place.

2. Last Friday night, I went to the movies with my friend. I think we **should have gone** to the movies in the afternoon instead of at night. Because neither I nor my friend had a car, we had to take a bus to go to and return from the theater. After we had waited twenty minutes, the bus came. We **should have known** the bus schedule before we left. When we reached the theater, the movie had started. We **should have had** time to spare. The movie was over at 11:30, and it was snowing outside. It was too cold to stand at the bus stop; so we dropped into a coffee shop and drank a cup of coffee. We **should not have taken** that break. After we had waited thirty minutes, we started to walk home. It took about thirty minutes, and I caught a cold. Now, my friend and I are talking about last Friday. We agree that we **should not have gone** to the movies at night, and we **should have known** the bus schedule before we left.

D.   Verb forms after the modal. Complete the following dialogue with the appropriate form of the main verb after each modal.

modal + simple form	modal + have + past participle
modal + be + present participle	modal + have + been + present participle

Ray: This quarter is almost finished, and I'm really disgusted with myself.

Linda: Why do you say that?

Ray: I _____ (could, study) much harder than I did.

Linda: I agree. You really _____ (should, pass) the last two tests.

Ray: I don't know what happened to me this quarter. I just

_____ (could, study, negative).

Linda: You _____ (must, feel) very bad right now about all the time you wasted.

Ray: I do feel bad. I _____ (should, look forward to) the break right now, like everyone else. Instead, I'm worrying about my grades.

Linda: Don't give up yet. Who knows? You _____

(might, pass) all your courses. All the professors _____ (will, give) reviews in their classes all next week.

Ray: I _____ (should, attend) all the review classes.

Linda: SHOULD? You _____ (must, attend) all the review lectures. That's your only hope.

Ray: You _____ (would, review) chemistry with me this afternoon?

Linda: I can't this afternoon, I'll be busy. But I _____ (will, study) with my roommate tonight from 6:00 to 12:00. You are welcome to study with us.

Ray: That's impossible tonight. I have a date.

Linda: You have a WHAT! You _____ (must, be) crazy.

Ray: Why do you say that?

Linda: You _____ (should, think about, negative) dates right now.

You _____ (should, plan) to use your time for studying.

Ray: I _____ (would, get) better grades on the last two tests if the chemistry professor liked me.

Linda: That's a poor excuse. You were always late, and you never studied before a test. For example, three weeks ago you _____ (must, be) crazy to come to the test thirty-five minutes late.

Ray: I'll tell you what happened on that day.

Linda: Don't bother. I'm going to the library now. See you later.

CHART OF MODAL AUXILIARIES

Modal	Meanings	Examples
1. **Can**	a. ability	Bob **can ski** very well.
	b. strong possibility	Don't stop your car suddenly. You **can cause** an accident.
	c. suggestion	Sue: My roommate is a nuisance. Bob: You **can get** a single room.
	d. permission	Jim: **Can I see** you again? Pat: Yes, I would like that.

Modal	*Meanings*	*Examples*
2. **Could**	a. past ability	When I was ten years old, **I could pat** my head and rub my stomach at the same time.
	b. ability based on certain conditions	You **could be** a good pianist if you practiced more.
	c. strong possibility	Be careful with those matches! You **could start** a fire.
	d. permission	**Could I use** your eraser?
	e. polite request	**Could** you please **be** quiet?
	f. suggestion	You **could get** your father a pen for his birthday.
	g. past of can in indirect speech	Gail said she **could drive** us to the airport.
3. **May**	a. permission	Dr. Smith, **may I borrow** your lecture notes?
	b. weak possibility	
	(1) about a future action	I **may go** home during the next break.
	(2) about a present condition	Jim **may be** homesick. He has been very depressed for two weeks.
4. **Might**	a. weak possibility	
	(1) about a future action	I **might go** home during the next break.
	(2) about a present condition	Jim **might be** homesick.
	b. past of indirect speech	He said he **might go** home before the break is over.
5. **Should**	a. obligation	A teacher **should have** patience.
	b. expectation	That police officer **should know** where the downtown area is.

	c. advice	You really **should read** more.
6. **Must**	a. necessity	You **must get** to work on time.
	b. assumption	He **must be** a good writer because he has won so many awards.
	c. prohibition	You **must not smoke** in this section of the hospital.
7. **Will**	a. simple future	**I'll see** you tomorrow.
	b. promise	**I will be** there on time. (Intonation distinguishes between a future tense and a promise.)
	c. determination	**I will get** an A in this course if it kills me. (Intonation distinguishes between a future tense and determination.)
8. **Shall**	a. an offer to do something for someone	**Shall I put** these papers on your desk?
	b. first-person question asking for agreement	**Shall** we **leave** now? (Are you ready to leave now?)
9. **Would**	a. polite request	**Would** you **hold** my books for a moment?
	b. willingness to do something	**Would** you **like** to eat out tonight?
	c. past habitual action	My last roommate **would play** the stereo until 3:00 in the morning.
	d. past of "will" in indirect speech	She said Bob **would help** me.
	e. result of a condition	If I had time, **I would meet** with you.

LESSON TWELVE: PRACTICE EXAM

Part I: Complete the following dialogue with the appropriate modals.

Son: Dad, _Can/may/~~should~~ could_ I use the car tonight?

Father: I don't know. I _may/might_ let you use it. I'm not sure. I'll have to think about it for a minute. Last week, the police gave you a ticket for speeding.

Son: I ~~should~~ _will_ drive more carefully this time. I promise. I realize now that I _should have_ driven more carefully last week.

Father: Last week? You _must/have to/should_ drive carefully *every* week, *every* day, and *every* minute. A car is not a toy. Do you understand?

Son: Yes, sir. I do.

Father: All right, you _can/may_ use the car tonight, but if anything happens, you _have to/will/must_ walk until you _can/are able to_ buy your own car. Now leave before I change my mind.

Son: Thanks, Dad. Oh, excuse me Dad, _would/could_ you please give me the car keys? And some money for gas?

Father: I don't have my wallet with me. It _must/should/might_ be in the bedroom on the dresser. Get it and bring it to me.

Son: Here it is.

Father: Here is ten dollars. I expect you to pay me back next week.

Son: But Dad, I lost my part-time job, so I _won't/~~can't~~_ be able to pay you back next week.

Father: Then take a bus tonight instead of the car. It's a beautiful evening. The stars _must/might_ look like diamonds.

Son: My date _will_ be angry if I tell her that we _have to/must_ ride the bus tonight.

Father: That's not my problem. You _should have_ thought about that before you lost your job. A car doesn't run on soda pop, you know. It uses gas, and gas costs money.

30 JAN 89

Part II: Indicate the *meaning* expressed by the modals in the following sentences.

a. necessity   c. advice   e. expectation   g. weak
b. suggestion   d. assumption   f. preference   possibility

1. _____ You **should have put** snow tires on your car last week.

2. _____ Snow tires aren't cheap, but they **shouldn't be** very expensive.

3. _____ If new tires are very expensive, and you don't have enough money, you **could buy** a set of used tires.

4. _____ I saw several accidents on the freeway yesterday. Many people **must not have had** snow tires on their cars.

5. _____ My next-door neighbor is coming over in a few minutes to help me put on my new snow tires. Someone's at the door now. It **must be** my neighbor.

6. _____ Driving in the snow is very dangerous. You **must get** some new snow tires before the next storm.

7. _____ You **should buy** your tires at the discount store. It has good tires that are not very expensive.

8. _____ That store **might be having** a sale on tires now.

9. _____ You **could call** to see if it is having a sale.

10. _____ I **would rather see** you spend money on tires instead of on a hospital bill.

Part III: Respond to the following situation as indicated for each student.

Student 1:   Our teacher is twenty-five minutes late this morning.

Student 2:   Make a statement of **assumption about the past.**

_____

Student 3:   Make a statement of **expectation.**

_____

Student 4:   Make a statement of **strong possibility about the past.**

_____

Student 5:   Make a **polite request** to the director.

_____

Student 6:   Make a **suggestion** to the other students.

_____

UNIT 7

Conditional Sentences

To the Student   Read before you begin this unit.

Native speakers of English use conditional sentences for many different purposes. A few of them are listed here.

Conditional sentences enable the speaker or writer to

1. Make predictions

   A prediction is a statement that tells what we believe will happen in the future, based on other actions (conditions).

   If I study hard this quarter, I will get A's in every class.

2. Discuss mistakes in the past

   If I had studied more last quarter, I would not have failed reading.

3. Express dreams

   I wish I had a million dollars.

   I wish my parents were rich.

   If I were rich, I would travel around the world.

4. Give advice

   If I were you, I would save money instead of wasting it.

   If I were you, I would not take the TOEFL test this quarter.

5. Make apologies

   If I had known you were waiting for a call, I would not have stayed on the phone so long. (I'm sorry.)

As advanced students, you know that there are several ways in which to express the sentiments illustrated. In this unit you will practice the conditional, which will give you still another method for saying what you want to say.

LESSON THIRTEEN

English conditional sentences contain two clauses:

Dependent (Subordinate) Clause	*Independent (Main) Clause*
If I have any free time,	I will meet with you.
If I had any free time,	I would meet with you.
If I had had any free time,	I would have met with you.

As the examples indicate, there are three types of conditional sentences in English, and each type

1. expresses a different meaning
2. refers to a different time
3. uses a different combination of tenses

PRESENT REAL

Type I: Present Real (Future Possible)

Meaning: Refers to a situation that may or may not happen in the future.

I may have some free time, but I am not sure; however, if I **have** any I **will meet** with you.

Time Reference: The future

Tense Combinations:

Dependent (Subordinate) Clause	*Independent (Main) Clause*
simple present present continuous present perfect present perfect continuous modals: can, have to, must, should + main verb	will, can, should, may, might, ought to + main verb
If John studies	he will pass the test.
If John is studying,	he can pass the test.
If John has studied,	he should pass the test.
If John has been studying,	he might pass the test.
If John can study,	he ought to pass the test.

NOTE: The tense you choose depends on the specific time to which you are referring.

If he is studying (right now) . . .

If he has been studying (since the last exam) . . .

The modal you choose depends on the specific *meaning you want to communicate.*

. . . he will pass the test. (There is no doubt in my mind.)

. . . he might pass the test. (I'm not sure, but I think he will.)

. . . he should pass the test. (I expect him to do very well on the test.)

PRESENT UNREAL

Type II: Present Unreal

Meaning: Refers to a situation that does not exist (is not real) at the present time.

I'm sorry. **I do not have** any free time. But if I **had** any, I **would meet** with you.

Time Reference: The present

Tense Combinations:

Dependent (Subordinate) Clause	*Independent (Main) Clause*
simple past	would, could, might, should
past continuous	+ main verb.
modals: could, had to + main verb	
*would	
If John studied,	he would pass the test.
If John were studying,	he might pass the test.
If John could study,	he could pass the test.
* If John would study,	he could pass the test.

---

* Note: Neither *will* nor *would* can be used in the "if" clause when they are used with a future meaning. They can be used in the *if* clause only when the meaning is "don't mind."

If you will have a seat = If you don't mind sitting down

correct: If you will have a seat, I'll see if the doctor is ready for you.
                   If you would take time to study, you could be an excellent student.

incorrect: If you will go next week, I'll go with you.

In this type of conditional sentence, the subjunctive "were" is used for all persons.

If **I** were rich, I would . . . ,   If **he** were . . . ,   If **they** were, . . .

Be careful. Several past tenses are used in the if clause, but remember that the time reference is *present.*

PUNCTUATION:

In writing, a comma follows an "if" clause when it is at the beginning of a sentence. Do not use a comma when the "if" clause follows the independent clause.

> If I had any free time, I would meet with you.
>
> I would meet with you if I had any free time.

Many students have trouble with type II conditional sentences. Just remember that this type of conditional sentence refers to present time and present truths although the verbs in the dependent (if) clause are in a past tense, and the modals in the independent clause are in the forms they take in indirect speech. Compare the following sentences.

Present Truths (Realities)	*Type II Conditional Restatement*
1. I **don't have** (right now) any money, so I **am not able** to lend you any.	If I **had** some money (right now), I **could lend** you a few dollars.
2. My roommate **isn't** here (now), so you **can't talk** with her.	If she **were** here (now), you **could talk** with her.
3. I'm **not concentrating** (at the moment), so this page **is** difficult to understand.	If I **were concentrating** (at the moment), I **would understand** this page.
4. I **don't like** beer, so I'm really **not enjoying** this party.	If I **liked** beer (or) if I **did**, I **might be enjoying** this party.
5. Bob **can't pass** the driver's examination, so he **will not have** his license anytime soon.	If he **could**, he **would have** his license now.
6. I **have** a cold, so I **can't go** out tonight.	If I **didn't have** a cold, I **could go** out.

NOTE: In sentences 1, 2, 3, 4, and 5 on the left, all the statements are negative, but the restatement of the ideas in the conditional sentences on the right is in the affirmative.

Sentence 6 is in the affirmative, but the conditional restatement is in the negative.

---

1. don't have	had
2. isn't	were
3. am not concentrating	were concentrating
4. don't like	liked

5. can't pass	could (pass)
6. have	didn't have

While native speakers of English usually follow the pattern given, it is not always necessary. The most important thing is to *keep the meaning* you want to express, and this may be done by making the verbs affirmative or negative.

Compare the following sentences.

1. I am not hungry.	affirmative:	If I were hungry, . . .
	negative:	If I weren't so full, . . .
2. Bob isn't home.	affirmative:	If he were home,
	negative:	If he weren't out, . . .
3. I am afraid.	affirmative:	If I were brave, . . .
	affirmative:	If I had more courage, . . .
	negative:	If I weren't afraid, . . .

Exercise 1: Restate each of the following statements in a type II conditional sentence.

Group 1

1. The weather is terrible today, so we can't have the party in the park.
2. It is raining, so the grass in the park is wet.
3. We can't have the party in my apartment because it is too small.
4. The university will not permit us to have the party in the dorm; otherwise, we could have it downstairs in the recreation room.
5. None of our friends is renting a house this quarter. Let's forget about the party.

Group 2

1. I don't know how to ski, so I am not going to go to Colorado during the break.
2. You aren't an experienced skier, so you are not able to teach me.
3. Besides, I don't have any money, so I can't go.
4. I have to finish a term paper during the break, so I won't have a real vacation anyway.
5. My roommate is gone, so I will have plenty of peace and quiet.

PAST UNREAL

Type III: Past Unreal

Meaning: Refers to a situation that did not happen.

> I'm sorry that I **did not have** any free time to talk with you.
> If I **had had** any free time, I **would** gladly **have met** with you.

Time Reference: The past

Tense Combinations:

Dependent (Subordinate) Clause	Independent (Main) Clause
past perfect	would
past perfect continuous	could + have + past participle
passive: had + been + past participle	might
	should
If John had studied,	he would have passed the exam.
If John had been studying,	he could have passed the exam.
If John had been told about the exam,	he might have studied for it.

Additional Notes

Omitting "if"

The word "if" may be omitted when it is followed by an auxiliary verb such as should, had, were. Notice the position of the auxiliary when "if" is omitted.

If I **should** see him today, I'll tell him to call you.
Should I see him today, I'll tell him to call you.

If he **were** home now, you could call him.
Were he home now, you could call him.

If I **had** known you wanted to talk with him, I would have told him yesterday.
Had I known you wanted to talk with him, I would have told him yesterday.

Wish

Because "wish" indicates a situation that is unreal, it is always followed by a past tense to indicate present time (type II) and a past perfect to indicate past time (type III).

I wish I **knew** how to drive. (But I don't.)   (present time)

I wish **I had learned** when I was in high school. (But I didn't.)   (past time)

Exercise 2:   Complete the following sentences.

A.   *Type I: Present Real*

1. If it snows, _____

2. If the streets are icy, _____

3. If I have to wait for the bus in the cold weather, _____
   _____

4. If you can drive tomorrow, _____

5. If it has stopped snowing by morning, _____

6. If the highway department is sanding the roads now, _____
   _____

7. If the landlord doesn't turn on the heat in my apartment, _____
   _____

8. If he has already turned the heat on, _____
   _____

9. If it is snowing when our class is over this afternoon, _____
   _____

10. If I wear my boots tomorrow, _____

B.   *Type II: Present Unreal*

1. If I could drive, _____

2. If I had a car, _____

3. If I were rich, _____

4. If I knew where to buy a good used car, _____
   _____

5. If my parents were here, _____

6. If my roommate had a car, _____

7. If this city had a good system of public transportation, _____
   _____

8. If I lived closer to the university, _____

9. If I didn't live so far from the university, _____

_____

10. If I could get a single room in the dorm, _____

_____

C.   Type III: Past Unreal

1. If Bob had studied, _____

2. If he had known all the answers to Part III, _____

_____

3. If the instructor had given us more time, _____

_____

4. If I had not been late for the exam, _____

5. If the test had been easier, _____

6. If Tom had not missed so many classes before the test, _____

_____

7. If I had remembered to wear my eye glasses, _____

_____

8. If you had not talked to me during the test, _____

_____

9. If the instructor had believed me when I said I had not been talking, _____

_____

10. If I had gone to bed earlier on the night before the test, _____

_____

Exercise 3:   Meaning.

A.   Add an explanation to explain the meaning of the following sentences.

Examples: **If he has time, he'll meet with you.**
Maybe he will and maybe he won't have time. I'm not sure.
If he had time, he could meet with you.
I'm sorry. He doesn't have any time, so he can't meet with you.
If he had had time, he could have met with you.
But he didn't have any free time, so he could not meet with you.

1. If I see your roommate, I'll tell him to buy a six pack of soda.
2. Had I known you wanted some soda, I could have bought it for you.
3. If you lived closer to the supermarket, you could walk there and get a six pack yourself.
4. If the price of gas goes down, I'll buy a bigger car.
5. My father would have sold his large car if he had believed that gas would be so expensive.
6. If someone wants to buy my car in a few weeks, I'll sell it.
7. If my parents come to the States this summer, I'll have a party for them.
8. They could come sooner if my mother were not afraid to fly.
9. If they decide to come by ship, the trip will take three weeks.
10. She might have agreed to fly last year if there had not been so many airplane accidents.

B. Restate the following sentences using an "if" construction.

Examples: I did not hear the phone, so I didn't answer it.
If I had heard it, I would have answered it.

I do not know her number, so I can't give it to you.
If I knew it, I would give it to you.

I don't think I will have time to call you tomorrow.
But if I have time, I'll call.

1. I didn't take a vacation last summer because I didn't have enough money.
2. I hope I'll have enough money to take a vacation next summer.
3. I don't even have enough money to go home next month during the spring break.
4. I didn't know you were going to visit Colorado, so I didn't invite you to stay at my house.
5. I won't get an opportunity to take a vacation next year, so you're welcome to stay with me instead of in a hotel.
6. I don't have a very big house, so your friends will have to stay in a hotel. I'm sorry.
7. Another friend might come to Colorado next year, and I think she'll like it very much.
8. My roommate's cousin was in Denver last year, but he didn't write and tell us he was coming, so when he arrived we were out of town.
9. We learned later that he had lost our address and telephone number, so he couldn't notify us of his visit.

10. I don't know his last name, so I can't tell you what it is.

11. I don't think I'll have time to help you with your statistics problems tonight.

Exercise 4:   Supply the correct forms of the verbs in parentheses.

1. If the final exam _____ (be) easy, I might get an A in grammar.

2. I will certainly get a B if I _____ (review) all the lessons.

3. Of course, if I _____ (have) a quiet roommate, I could study more.

4. During finals, I'll go to the library if my roommate _____ (continue) to make a lot of noise.

5. If I _____ (can) move to a single room, I would.

6. I _____ (apply) to Harvard University for the fall quarter if I get a score of 600 on the TOEFL exam.

7. I might have worked harder at the beginning of this quarter if I

_____ (not, be) so homesick.

8. If I had received more money from home, I _____ (get) an apartment.

9. After this quarter ends, I'm going to go to Canada if I

_____ (have) enough money for a ticket.

10. I would drive to Canada if I _____ (own) a car.

11. I wish I _____ (have) a car.

12. If I had saved my money last year, I _____ (buy) a new car at the beginning of this quarter.

13. I would buy a used car if I _____ (trust) used cars.

14. If my parents _____ (be) rich, I wouldn't be worrying about all of this.

15. My roommate has a car, so if he decides to go to Canada, I

_____ (not, have) any problems.

Replacing "if"

"If" may be replaced by the following words.

1. *Unless*

unless + affirmative verb = if + negative verb

Unless you hurry, we're going to miss the movie.

If you don't hurry, we're going to miss the movie.

2. *Provided (that)*

Provided (that) can replace "if" when the idea of restriction is very strong.

I will lend you fifty dollars **provided that** you repay me as soon as your check arrives.

I will lend you fifty dollars **if you promise** to repay me as soon as your check arrives.

3. *Suppose/supposing*

Suppose/supposing = what will/would happen if . . .? or what would have happened if?

Suppose you fail the final exam?   (What will happen if you fail the final exam?)

Supposing you had failed the final exam?   (What would have happened if you had failed the final exam?)

4. *In case*

"In case" usually appears in type I conditional sentences.

In case it snows, we'll have the picnic inside.
If it snows, we'll have the picnic inside.

I'll plan to drive **in case** you have trouble with your car.
I'll plan to drive **if** you have trouble with your car.

Exercise 5:   Restate the following sentences with *unless, provided that, suppose,* or *in case.*

1. The energy shortage will get worse if everyone doesn't begin to conserve fuel.
2. I'll be happy to drive you to Mexico if you promise to help me pay for gas.
3. What will happen if we run out of fuel in the middle of the desert?
4. Don't worry. If we run out of fuel, I'll have some extra gas in the trunk of my car.
5. If you don't remember to put an extra can of gas in the trunk, we could be stranded in the middle of nowhere.
6. Stop worrying. If that happens, we can call for help on my CB radio.
7. That's a good idea if someone is around to hear our call.
8. What would have happened if we had not had the CB last year on our way to Alaska?
9. If you don't stop worrying, I'll cancel the whole trip.

10. All right, but if you discover that your car can't make such a long trip, I'm going to find out about the bus schedule.

11. If Tom decides to go with us, we should agree on what to charge him for gas.

12. He can go with us if he promises to leave his dog at home.

13. You know that he won't leave his dog if he can't find a responsible person to take care of him.

14. That's not our problem. We will simply tell him that he can't go with us if he insists on taking his dog.

PASSIVE CONSTRUCTION IN CONDITIONAL SENTENCES

You may use the passive construction in either the dependent (*if*) clause or in the independent clause.

If I **had mailed** my application on time, I could have taken the TOEFL test last week.

If my application **had been mailed** on time, I could have taken the TOEFL test last week.

Exercise 6:   Change the underlined verbs to the passive voice. Don't forget to make the other necessary changes in each sentence. Use "by" when necessary.

1. If the garage had repaired my car correctly, I would not be taking the bus everywhere.

2. Bob would not be riding the bus either if someone had not stolen his car.

3. If Bob had reported the theft right after it happened, the police might have found his car.

4. The thief might not have taken the car if Bob had locked it.

5. If someone had seen the thief, he might not have gotten away.

6. Bob still might get his car back if some garage is not painting it a different color.

7. If the police can catch the thief, he will certainly spend time in jail.

8. If every citizen reported car thefts promptly, we could solve this problem.

9. We would discourage many criminals if some people were not afraid to report crimes.

10. If the police patrolled more neighborhoods regularly, we would see less crimes.

11. If Bob has to buy a new car, I believe that his insurance company will pay for it.

12. If I ever see anyone doing anything illegal, I will make a report immediately.

Communicating Your Own Thoughts: Mixing the Types

Remember that the grammar of a language tells you *how* to say something correctly. The grammar of a language does not tell you *what* to say.

In responding to a statement made in a conversational situation or in responding to a statement in writing, two or more individuals may respond in a number of different ways. For example, one person may use a type I conditional sentence, another a type II sentence, and another a type III sentence. Furthermore, a fourth person may respond in a sentence that *mixes* type II and type III.

Which person is making a correct response? All are because they are communicating what they are thinking about. They are communicating their own thoughts.

Study the following example. It is Thursday night and six friends are talking about their plans for the coming weekend. Notice how five of the individuals respond to the first speaker's statement.

Jim:	Last night (Wednesday), the weatherman said that the temperature was going to be in the 90s this coming weekend.
Bob: (type I)	If it **is** that hot, I'll spend Sunday afternoon in the park.
Sue: (type II)	I **would go** to the mountains this weekend if I **didn't have** an exam on Monday. (But she has an exam, so she can't go to the mountains.)
Gail: (type III)	If I **had heard** the weather report last night (Wednesday), I **would not have promised** (last night) to help my roommate with her chemistry assignment on Saturday. (But she didn't hear the weather report, so she promised to help her roommate.)
Tom: (type II + type III)	Jim, I **would plan** to play soccer with you in the park this weekend if I **had already completed** my composition, which is due on Monday.
Rita: (type II + type III)	I don't believe everything the weatherman says anymore. If I **had not listened** to him *last weekend*, I **would not have** this terrible cold *now*.

Exercise 7:   Respond to the following situations using as many of the different types of conditional responses *as possible*. Be careful of meaning and time reference. Sometimes only one type may be possible.

1. You have a friend who wants to work in Spain next year, but he doesn't speak Spanish. What would you say to him?

2. Your alarm didn't go off, so you got up late and missed your final exam in grammar. What would you say to your teacher?

3. You were invited to Ali's party, but you stayed home. Three days later a friend tells you that it was really a good party. What would you say to him?

4. You are going to go to a party with a friend next Saturday night. He wants you to introduce him to some girls when you get there. However, you do not know for certain if you will see anybody you know. What would you tell him?

   You arrive at the party, and you discover that you don't know anyone at the party, but your friend is still begging you to introduce him to some of the girls. What would you tell him?

   The party is over. You are on your way home. Your friend is angry with you because you did not introduce him to any girls. What would you tell him?

5. The dealer who sold you your used car was not honest, so you went back to the used-car lot to tell the salesperson that you were going to make a report to the police, but the salesperson had quit. What would you say?

6. Two of your friends were driving at 85 miles per hour and had a terrible accident. They are now in the hospital. What would you say?

7. The tuition at the university you are attending has risen three times in the last year. What would you say?

8. You need a book to use as resource material for your Masters Thesis, but

   a. you can't afford to buy the book right now.

   b. the book is difficult to find.

   c. you found a copy of the book, but it is written in a language you don't know.

LESSON THIRTEEN: PRACTICE EXAM

Part I: Complete the following sentences.

1. If the airline pilots go on strike, _____

   _____

2. If the airplanes had more modern equipment, _____

   _____

3. If I had known they were planning to strike at this time, _____

   _____

4. If the pilots get the changes they are asking for, _____

   _____

5. Had the public been notified of the possibility of a strike, _____

   _____

6. If the trains were dependable, _____

_____

Part II: Restate the following sentences using a conditional construction.

Example: I really don't understand economics, so I can't explain why inflation is so high.

If I could understand (If I understood) economics, I could explain (would be able to explain) why inflation is so high.

1. Saleh didn't get to the cleaners before it closed, so he couldn't pick up his suit.

_____

_____

2. I don't think I will have time this afternoon to help you review the work that you missed yesterday, but I might.

_____

_____

3. I won't have time to help you review the work you missed. I'm sorry.

_____

4. Rafael has not been taking the medicine his doctor prescribed, so he's going to have to spend a few days in the hospital.

_____

_____

5. You were speeding again, so naturally the police officer gave you a ticket.

_____

_____

6. I might have a party next weekend, but I'm not sure. My roommate hasn't agreed to the idea yet.

_____

_____

Part III: Restate the following sentences using *unless, provided that, suppose,* or *in case.*

1. If the cost of new houses doesn't go down, we'll have to stay in our apartment.

_____

_____

2. We might be able to buy a house if we can get a large down payment.

_____

_____

3. What will happen if the landlord raises our rent?

_____

4. We'll start looking for a smaller apartment if that happens.

_____

5. If I get a good raise next year, we might be able to afford a small house.

_____

6. However, we had better start saving more money if I don't get a large enough raise.

_____

_____

Part IV: Read the following situation and write the type of conditional response indicated for each speaker.

All the students are sitting in class waiting for the grammar teacher to arrive with the tests. However, the director walks in and announces that the teacher is very sick and will not be able to come to class and give the test. He tells the students that they cannot leave the class, but they may use the time for additional study before their next class begins.

Student 1:   (Type I Response) _____

_____

Student 2:   (Type II Response) _____

_____

Student 3:   (Type III Response) _____

_____

Student 4:   (Mixed Response, Types II and III) _____

_____

_____

UNIT 8

Verbals

To the Student   Read before you begin this unit.

In English a verb form may sometimes function in a sentence as another part of speech. Verb forms that are used as other parts of speech are called *verbals*. The infinitive and gerund forms of a verb are two examples of verbals. Look at the following sentences.

a. **To smoke** is bad for your health.

b. **Smoking** is bad for your health.

c. Some people really like **to smoke.**

d. Some people really enjoy **smoking.**

In the sentences given, the infinitive and gerund forms are used as nouns. In sentence a, the infinitive is the subject of the sentence. In sentence b, the gerund is the subject of the sentence. In sentences c and d, the infinitive and gerund forms are used as the direct objects of the statements. In addition to functioning as a noun, the infinitive may also be used as an adjective or an adverb.

In this unit, we will study infinitive and gerund constructions and the ways they are used in English sentences.

LESSON FOURTEEN

INFINITIVES

The Simple Infinitive

"To" + the simple form of a verb makes up the simple infinitive.

Most people want **to work.**

We stopped our work **to rest.**

To succeed is difficult.

227

The verbs *help, have, let, make* and verbs of sense such as *feel, see, hear* are followed by nouns and object pronouns and the simple form of the verb, *without* "to."

The instructor **helped** us *organize* our outlines.

But he **had** the students *write* the compositions in class.

He **let** us *use* our dictionaries.

He **saw** me *open* my dictionary several times.

I **made** myself *write* as neatly as I could.

The Infinitive Phrase

An infinitive, however, may have its own subject or object or both.

My father wants **me to succeed.**	me = subject of infinitive
I have always liked **to study business.**	business = object of infinitive
He advised **my brother to take economics.**	my brother = subject of infinitive economics = object of infinitive

In addition to a subject and/or object, an infinitive may also take modifiers.

Many people like to live **dangerously.**   (The infinitive "to live" is modified by "dangerously.")

Professor Smith is the person to see **about student scholarships.**   (The infinitive "to see" is modified by "about student scholarships.")

The infinitive with its subject, object, and modifiers makes up the infinitive phrase.

Functions of the Infinitive and Infinitive Phrase

In a sentence, the infinitive or infinitive phrase may function as a noun, adjective, adjective complement, or adverb.

Noun

Subject of the Sentence

To study takes a lot of time.

To learn another language is not easy.

To be a student is a difficult job.

Subject Complement

A subject complement renames or refers to the subject of a sentence.

My **goal** is **to get good grades.**

His **desire** has been **to enter graduate school.**

Her **job** last summer was **to answer the phone.**

Object of the Verb

I like **to travel.**

I have always liked **to study languages.**

They are planning **to live in Europe next year.**

Adjective

modifies the noun "work"	I have a lot of work **to do.**
modifies the noun "problems"	Dr. Ray gave us five problems **to solve.**
modifies the noun "assignment"	The assignment **to do for tonight** is on page 83.
modifies the noun "time"	I won't have time **to go anywhere tonight.**

Adjective Complement

As complement of an adjective, the infinitive/infinitive phrase completes the meaning started by the adjective.

complements the adjective "difficult"	This problem is difficult **to do.**
complements the adjective "glad"	I'm glad **to see you in class today.**
complements the adjective "eager"	We were eager **to hear about his trip.**

Adverb

As an adverb, the infinitive/infinitive phrase modifies a verb or an entire sentence.

modifies the verb "came"	We came here **to work.**
modifies the verb "am leaving"	I'm leaving now **to get to class on time.**
modifies the verb "should buy"	**To keep warm at night,** you should buy an electric blanket.

229

modifies the entire sentence	**To be honest,** I hate the cold weather.
modifies the entire sentence	**To tell the truth,** I miss the beautiful weather in my country.
modifies the entire sentence	**To be frank,** snow has never excited me.

Making Infinitives Negative

Read the following two sentences. In sentence a, the verb is negative. In sentence b, the infinitive is negative. Notice the difference in meaning.

    a. Bob **did not agree** to help me.

    b. Bob agreed **not to help** me.

In sentence a, Bob did not make any agreement. The main verb "agree" is negative. In sentence b, Bob made an agreement. He agreed that he is not going to help me. The infinitive is negative.

In some sentences, the meaning would be the same.

    I didn't want to take the test.

    I wanted not to take the test.

To make an infinitive negative, "not" is placed immediately before the infinitive. However, not all infinitives can be made negative. It depends on the *meaning* of the verb that precedes the infinitive.

Exercise 1:   Student 1:   Complete the question with not + infinitive phrase.
                 Student 2:   Answer the question with not + infinitive phrase

   Example: Student 1:   Did your roommate agree **not to play the stereo loudly?**
                   Student 2:   Yes, he agreed **not to play it so loudly.**

1. Because of the bad weather, did you decide . . .?

2. After your car accident last week, have you promised yourself . . .?

3. Has your little boy finally learned . . .?

4. In the face of danger, do you usually pretend . . .?

5. Please, in class, will you try . . .?

6. Since you apologized to your landlord for the loud party last night, has he been persuaded . . .?

7. Because airline tickets are so expensive, have you chosen . . .?

8. You haven't turned in any assignments for two weeks, are you going to continue . . .?

9. Since the grades on the last test were so low, has the teacher agreed . . .?

10. Did our conversation teacher tell you . . .?

Infinitive/Infinitive Phrase as Subject

An infinitive or infinitive phrase can be used as the subject of the sentence. However, the English language often (1) uses the word "it" as the *false subject* of the sentence and (2) places the *true subject* after the verb. Look at the following sentences. The true subjects are underlined.

a. To save is not easy. It is not easy to save.

b. To read is fun. It is fun to read.

c. To read a good mystery story is fun. It is fun to read a good mystery story.

In the examples, the infinitive structures follow adjectives, but they may also follow nouns.

d. To buy a house takes a lot of money. It takes a lot of money to buy a house.

e. To furnish our new home took a lot of time. It took a lot of time to furnish our new home.

Exercise 2: Answer the questions that follow using "it" as the *false subject* of the sentence.

Example: When someone is studying for a driver's license, what usually takes a lot of time?

It usually takes a lot of time **to learn the rules in the driver's manual.**

1. When a person is taking the road test, what is sometimes difficult?

2. After you had been driving for a while, what was easy?

3. When driving, what is against the law?

4. Before taking a long trip by car, what is important?

5. If you were on a long trip by yourself, what would be necessary?

6. When taking a long trip by car, what is enjoyable?

7. If a traffic light is yellow, what can be dangerous?

8. If you are behind an inexperienced driver, what is very frustrating?

9. Before turning a corner, what is necessary?

10. When driving in an unfamiliar city, what takes a lot of time?

11. Concerning the care of a car, what is essential?

12. Before buying a new car, what is advisable?

"For" + Noun/Pronoun + Infinitive

Sometimes the *false subject* "it" is followed by "for" + noun/pronoun + infinitive. Look at the following sentences. The *true subjects* are underlined.

a. For me to learn a second language is difficult.

It is difficult for me to learn a second language.

b. For Ana to pass this class will be easy.

It will be easy for Ana to pass this class.

Exercise 3:   Student 1:   Complete each question with for + noun/pronoun + infinitive or infinitive phrase.

Student 2:   Answer each question in a complete sentence.

Example: Student 1:   Yuko, when you first came to the States, was it difficult **for you to make new friends?**

Student 2:   Yes (no) it was (wasn't) difficult **for me to make new friends** when I first came here.

1. When you were at home in your country, was it fun . . .?

2. When you were in high school, did it take much time . . .?

3. On the weekends, is it relaxing . . .?

4. Before the next test, will it be necessary . . .?

5. Concerning the international party next weekend, is it taking a lot of time . . .?

6. I would like to go to Mexico during the break. Would it cost much money . . .?

7. Since your cousin has been visiting you, has it been exciting . . .?

8. When you go to a restaurant for the first time, is it difficult . . .?

9. When you are watching American television, is it sometimes hard . . .?

10. Because you are living with a roommate this quarter, has it been almost impossible . . .?

"Of" + Noun/Pronoun + Infinitive/Infinitive Phrase

In sentences where "it" is used as the false subject, certain adjectives may be followed by the preposition "of" + noun/pronoun + infinitive construction.

It was **nice of you** to visit me in the hospital.

It was **foolish of me** to ski without any lessons.

It was **considerate of the class** to send me flowers.

With some adjectives, "for" is also possible.

It was foolish **for** me to ski without any lessons.

Exercise 4: Complete the following sentences with "of" as shown in the examples.

1. It was really foolish _____

2. It was very smart _____

3. It is generous _____

4. It was very kind _____

5. It was extremely disrespectful _____

6. It is rude _____

7. Actually, it was stupid _____

8. It is very impolite _____

9. It was friendly _____

10. It is deceitful _____

11. It is wise _____

12. It was intelligent _____

13. It is very nice _____

14. It was wrong _____

15. It is inconsiderate_____

Infinitive/Infinitive Phrase as Subject Complement

Exercise 5: Complete each of the following sentences with an infinitive phrase that renames the underlined subjects.

   Example: My goal is **to be a lawyer.**

1. When I graduated from high school, my ambition was . . .

2. Before I return to my country, my plan is . . .

3. A medical doctor's highest purpose should be . . .

4. In every country in the world, the police officer's <u>main job</u> is . . .
5. My father believes that his <u>responsibility</u> has always been . . .
6. Before I can pass this level, my <u>problem</u> will be . . .
7. Our grammar teacher's main <u>goal</u> is . . .
8. Before Ana gets married, her one <u>desire</u> is . . .
9. In the library, the information clerk's <u>duty</u> is . . .
10. When I was a child, my <u>dream</u> was . . .
11. The reading teacher said that the <u>assignment</u> for tomorrow was . . .
12. Since my brother was a small child, his <u>hobby</u> has always been . . .
13. The <u>purpose</u> of this exercise has been . . .

Infinitive/Infinitive Phrase as Direct Object

Group I:	Verbs followed immediately by an infinitive or an infinitive phrase

Pattern: subject + verb + infinitive phrase
 I   hesitated to answer the question.

* afford	come	happen	offer	remember
agree	consent	hesitate	* plan	seem
appear	decide	hope	prepare	struggle
arrange	demand	intend	pretend	swear
be (am, is, are)	deserve	learn	proceed	tend
care	endeavor	manage	prove	threaten
choose (prefer)	fail	mean	refuse	volunteer
claim	forget	neglect	regret	wait

* The verb afford is always used with a form of *can or be able to:* They **can** afford to buy a new house, but they **aren't able to** afford to get a new car, too.
The verb plan indicates future time when used in the simple present tense: We **plan** to leave soon.

To add additional information, several words may separate the main verb and the infinitive *but do not* separate the infinitive.

correct: **to work** carefully
incorrect: **to carefully work**   *MV*   *Infinitive*
additional information: I did not come **to this country as a student** to waste
time.   (additional information)

Study the following sentences in which the infinitive phrase is the object of a verb.

1. I must get a roommate; otherwise, I *can't afford* **to rent** an apartment.
2. My cousin *has agreed* **to live** with me.

3. She *appears* **to be happy** about our decision.
4. We *have arranged* **to share** the cooking and the cleaning.
5. I *am* **to be** the one who will cook.
6. I don't mind cooking, but I *don't care* **to clean.**
7. My cousin and I *are hoping* **to have** a really nice apartment.
8. My parents *decided* **to visit** us last year.
9. Before they came, our landlord *consented*, after much begging, **to paint** the bathroom.

Note that the main verbs of the sentences given are in several different tenses.

Exercise 6: Complete the following sentences with an infinitive or infinitive phrase that will *appropriately complete the meaning* of the sentence. In some sentences, there may be more than one correct answer.

1. Although the hitchhiker **seemed** _____ to be _____ cold and tired, we

   hesitated _____, so we **pretended** not

   _____ him. Before we began our trip, we **had decided** not

   _____ any strangers along the road.

2. There are good universities in every part of the world; however, many

   students **choose** _____ in another country because they

   hope _____ another language in addition to studying in
   their particular major. After I complete my studies, I **am preparing**

   _____ to my country where I **intend**

   _____.

3. My roommate, Ana, and I **had forgotten** _____ our door
   before we left our apartment, so when we returned, the door was open and
   we heard noises inside. Ana, who is afraid of everything, **hesitated**

   _____ the apartment first, and I **agreed**

   _____. I **was pretending** not _____

   afraid, but I was very nervous. Finally, I **volunteered** _____ the
   apartment. Turning on the hall light, I looked around but saw no-one.

   Whoever was there **refused** _____, so I quickly returned

   outside into the hall where Ana **was waiting** _____ what
   had happened. We heard a loud noise, which came from the living room, and

   both of us **proceeded** _____ down the hall as quickly as we could to the manager's office. We **endeavored** _____ to him why we were knocking so loudly on his door, but we weren't speaking very calmly.

Finally he **consented** _____ to our apartment with us. As we entered the apartment, the lights came on, and twenty of our friends shouted "HAPPY BIRTHDAY, ANA!"

4. *Advisor:*   You were an excellent undergraduate student. **Do** you **intend**

_____ graduate school?

Student: My parents _____ **afford**

_____ .

Advisor: I have been aware of your financial troubles, so I **managed**

_____ you a scholarship for the entire four years of study.

Student: I don't know how to thank you.

Advisor: Don't worry about it. You **have proven** yourself

_____ a serious young man, so you **deserve**

_____ some help.

Student: **I don't mean** _____ a problem, but how will I pay for books and other supplies?

Advisor: Don't worry about that either. The department **has arranged** for

you _____ as a lab assistant three days a week.

Student: Thank you, but will I make enough to pay for an apartment?

Advisor: **I failed** _____ you that my wife and I would like you to live with us. We have plenty of room.

Student: I can't thank you enough for your kindness.

Infinitive/Infinitive Phrase as Direct Object

Group II:	Verbs followed by a noun or pronoun plus infinitive
Pattern:	subject + verb + object + infinitive phrase
	The doctor advised Bill to take a long vacation.
	me

The following verbs must be followed by an object then the infinitive. These verbs are never used with an infinitive alone *except when the main verb is in the passive voice.*

Bill and I **were advised to take** a long vacation.

advise	direct	instruct	request
allow	enable	invite	require
appoint	encourage	motivate	show . . . how
cause	forbid	oblige	teach
caution	force	order	tell
challenge	get	permit	tempt
command	*help	persuade	urge
compel	hire	remind	warn
convince	implore		

Study the following verb + object + infinitive phrase combinations.

1. The doctor — **advised me to stop** smoking.
2. This hospital — **does not allow patients to smoke** in their rooms.
3. The hospital director — **appointed Nurse Smith to report** any smoker.
4. Smoke — **causes my sister to cough.**
5. Anticigarette ads — **cannot compel anyone to stop** smoking.
6. The hospital — **commanded its staff to give up** cigarettes.
7. The people who smoke — **encouraged each other to protest** this command.
8. The director — **forbids anyone to ignore** this regulation.
9. My doctor finally — **got me to think about** the dangers of smoking.

Exercise 7: Complete the following sentences with a noun/pronoun object + infinitive. Choose object + infinitive combinations that will fit the meaning of the sentences. For some sentences, more than one answer may be correct.

1. On the airplane, the hijacker forced _____
                                          (object)

   _____ in their seats.
      (infinitive)

2. The man beside me helped _____ _____ calm.
                                      (object)   (infinitive)

---

* The verb **help** is followed by nouns or object pronouns and the simple form of the verb, without "to."

3. Our stewardesses instructed _____ _____ the hi-
   (object)   (infinitive)

   jacker's commands.

4. A little boy was crying, so I invited _____ _____ with
   (object)   (infinitive)

   me.

5. The hijacker commanded _____ _____ talking.
   (object)   (infinitive)

6. His accomplice ordered _____
   (object)

   _____ .

   (infinitive phrase)

7. They didn't permit _____
   (object)

   _____ .

   (infinitive phrase)

8. Our captain finally persuaded _____
   (object)

   _____ the women and children.
   (infinitive)

9. The captain warned _____ _____ all the
   (object)   (infinitive)

   passengers with care.

10. The airlines should hire _____ _____
    (object)   (infinitive)

    every flight.

Exercise 8:   Answer the following questions in complete sentences. Several different answers are possible in most sentences.

1. What did your parents **advise you to do** before you left home for the first time?
2. When you were a child, what are some of the things your father **did not allow you to do?**
3. What did your father **show you how to do** when you were a child?
4. What **have** your parents always **encouraged you to be?**
5. What are some of the adjustments a new culture **has forced you to make?**

6. Have you been able to **help another student adjust to** a new culture?
7. What did the director of your English program **get the teachers to do?**
8. If you were the director, what would you **require the teachers to do?**
9. On an airplane, what won't the stewardesses **permit the passengers to do?**
10. If a burglar broke into your apartment, what would you **persuade him to do?**
11. What do you have to **remind your roommate/husband/wife to do** before tomorrow?
12. Has a friend ever **challenged you to do** anything risky? What?
13. Have you ever **urged anyone to do** anything silly, just for fun? What?
14. What would a million dollars **tempt you to do?**

Infinitive/Infinitive Phrase as Direct Object

Group III: Verbs followed by object + infinitive construction *or* by an infinitive construction only.

Pattern: subject + verb + object + infinitive phrase
        I   want   you   to help him.
                   OR

Pattern: subject + verb   + infinitive phrase
        I   want   to help him.

The following verbs may be followed by a noun or pronoun object + infinitive phrase or by an infinitive phrase only. However, notice that the *meaning* of each pattern is different. Discuss the differences between each group of sentences in the example sentences.

ask	expect	promise
beg	like	want
choose	need	wish
* dare	prefer	

NOTE: Only the verb "promise" keeps the same meaning in both patterns.

He promised to be on time.   He promised us to be on time.

The verbs "expect," "hope," "need," "promise," "want," and "wish" may indicate future time although they are in the simple present tense.

* In interrogative and negative statements "dare" is used without "to" if no object follows the verb. "Do you dare **jump off** that building?" "No, I don't dare **do** that." "Do you dare **me to** jump off that building?"

Examples:

Verb + Infinitive	Verb + Object + Infinitive
1. I have **asked to see** the doctor.	I have **asked** *my husband* **to see** the doctor.
2. The little boy **begged to go** home.	The little boy **begged** *his friend* **to go** home.
3. The committee **chose to investigate** the hospital.	The committee **chose** *Jim* **to investigate** the hospital.
4. I **expected to be** in the hospital for a week.	I **expected** *my best friend* **to be** in the hospital for a week.
5. I **promised to take** better care of myself in the future.	I **promised** *my mother* **to take** better care of myself in the future.
6. Most people **don't like to be** in the hospital.	Most people **don't like** *the members of their family* **to be** in the hospital.
7. My brother **dared to leave** the hospital without our doctor's permission.	My brother **dared** *me* **to leave** the hospital without our doctor's permission.
8. I **prefer to have** an older doctor.	I **prefer** *you* **to have** an older doctor.
9. I **want to get** a check up next week.	I **want** *you* **to get** a check up next week.

Exercise 9: Complete the following sentences with either an infinitive/infinitive phrase or an object + infinitive/infinitive phrase as indicated. Be careful of meaning.

1. Yesterday, I spent three hours in the ladies department of the store. I was trying to find a birthday present for my mother. Finally, I asked

    _____the clerk_____
    (object)

    _____to give me some suggestions_____ .
    (infinitive phrase)

    Because I looked frustrated, the clerk asked _____ me.
    (infinitive)

2. Our grammar teacher puts a check by our incorrect answers, but she never gives

    the correction. She expects _____
    (object)

    _____ the corrections.
    (infinitive)

    I completed yesterday's grammar assignment very carefully, so I expect

    _____.
    (infinitive phrase)

3. When Sue took her two little brothers to the zoo, the older brother dared

   _____ _____
                    (object)   (infinitive)
   close to the lions' cage.

   The younger boy, however, didn't dare _____ it.
                                           (infinitive, without to)

4. When the dentist entered the room, my son begged _____
                                                          (infinitive)
   home.

   The dentist begged _____ not _____ while
                            (object)   (infinitive)
   he was trying to pull his teeth.

5. My father has always worked hard to save money so that I could study at a university. Because of his hard work, I promised _____.
                                                          (infinitive phrase)

   I promised _____ _____.
                   (object)   (infinitive)

6. After my sister married, she and her husband chose _____ a small
                                                              (infinitive)
   economy car.
   They couldn't decide on the color they wanted, so they chose

   _____ _____ them.
             (object)   (infinitive)

7. I missed the last week of classes because I was sick. Before the next test, I really

   need _____ _____ with me.
              (object)   (infinitive)

   I especially need _____ the chapters I missed.
                              (infinitive)

8. I'll help you review since I would like _____ _____ a
                                                 (object)   (infinitive)
   good grade.

   Thanks a lot. I like _____ with you.
                              (infinitive)

9. Yuko expects _____ well on the next test.
                     (infinitive)

The teacher expects _____ _____ all sec-
                              (object)   (infinitive)
tions of the test carefully.

10. José met with the director last week because he wanted _____
                                                                    (object)

_____ him permission to take his finals one week early.
    (infinitive)

His parents are coming to the States, and José wants _____
                                                              (infinitive)

around America with them.

11. They prefer _____ by car.
                    (infinitive)

His mother prefers _____ _____ by car so that they
                          (object)   (infinitive)
can stop whenever they wish.

12. Excuse me, I wish _____ with the manager.
                          (infinitive)

Infinitive/Infinitive Phrase as Adjective

Exercise 10:   Complete the following sentences with a simple infinitive (to + verb)
that will modify the underlined nouns and complete the meaning of each statement.

Example: The best **place** _____ to fish _____ is Wilson's Lake.

1. In 1979, the top **movie** _____ was *Star Wars*.

2. When we entered the theater, the only **places** _____
   were in the front row.

3. The first ten **people** _____ the theater received free *Star
   Wars* T-shirts.

4. If a person is being unnecessarily loud in a theater, the **person**

   _____ is the manager of the theater.

5. In case of a fire, the safest **place** _____ is near an exit
   sign.

6. Today, food at a theater is very expensive, so the **thing**

   _____ is take your own snacks in a bag.

7. The first time we went to see *Star Wars*, the **line** _____
   tickets was all the way around the theater.

8. Because of the long line, we made the **decision** _____ and see it on a week day.

9. The best **time** _____ to a movie is during the week when there aren't large crowds.

10. Our son's **desire** _____ every *Star Wars* record, book, poster and toy was unbelievable.

11. He tried to learn the words in every book, but he had a lot of **words**

_____

12. He was so interested in learning the words that he didn't have **time**

_____ with his friends.

13. My husband couldn't go to the movies with us because he had a **report**

_____ for the following day.

Infinitive/Infinitive Phrase as Adjective Complement

As complement of an adjective, the infinitive or infinitive phrase completes the meaning started by the adjective.

I am glad **to have you here.**

I will be sorry **to see you leave.**

As complement, the infinitive/infinitive phrase is usually used after adjectives expressing emotion, such as the following:

amazed	disappointed	horrified	sorry
angry	disgusted	pleased	surprised
anxious	disturbed	proud	upset
ashamed	eager	relieved	(and so on)
astonished	glad	sad	
delighted	happy	shocked	

Exercise 11:   A.   Complete the following statements with an infinitive phrase.

1. When my mother called last night, I was **sad** . . .
2. When I finished talking to her, I was extremely **anxious** . . .
3. At her high school graduation ceremonies, Gail was **proud** . . .
4. While watching the news on television, I was **disgusted** . . .
5. When I read the newspaper last night, I was **shocked** . . .
6. Although our last reading test was difficult, our reading teacher said that he was **pleased** . . .

7. When I looked at my reading test, however, I was **disappointed** . . .
8. Even though I was disappointed with my grade, I was **relieved** . . .

B.   Change the following statements as shown in the example.

Example: I was surprised **when I saw an A** on my last composition.
I was surprised **to see an A** on my last composition.

1. The students in the Section 1 grammar class were glad **when they learned** they would not have a grammar final.
2. The students had done so well all quarter that their instructor was happy **that he did not have to give** the class a final.
3. The director, however, was disturbed **when he heard about** this decision.
4. The students in Section 2 were angry **when they found out** about this.
5. In fact, they were shocked **when they discovered it.**
6. Don't be surprised **if you see them** protest this decision.
7. The grammar teacher for Section 1 said that he would be delighted **if he had** a class like Section 1 every quarter.
8. I really don't blame the students in Section 2 for getting angry. I'd be eager **if I could forget about** taking a final, too.

Infinitive/Infinitive Phrase as Adverb

As an adverb modifying a verb, the infinitive/infinitive phrase expresses purpose. It answers the question, "Why?"

When an infinitive construction is used as an adverbial to modify a verb, it is usually a substitution for a prepositional phrase beginning with "in order."

He is going to Spain **to study.** He is going to Spain (in order) to study.
Why is he going to Spain? He's going there **to study.**

Sue quit her job **to get a better one.**
Why did she quit her job? She quit it **to get a better one.**

Exercise 12:   Answer the following questions with an infinitive/infinitive phrase.

1. Why did Mr. Turner make an appointment with his banker?
2. Why is he planning to borrow five thousand dollars?
3. Why does he want to open his own business?
4. Why has he been talking to real estate brokers?
5. Why do many people keep their money in savings accounts?
6. Why do other people invest in the stock market?

7. Why have you decided to major in economics?

8. Why did you choose to study in another country?

9. Why are you returning home next quarter?

10. Why did you call your parents last night?

Infinitive Phrase to Replace Adverb Clauses

Infinitive phrases are commonly used to replace the following kinds of adverb clauses.

1. adverb clauses beginning with "so that"

2. adverb clauses beginning with "if"

3. adverb clauses beginning with "because"

Study the following examples. Notice that the subjects in both the dependent and independent clauses are the same.

    a. We arrived at the ticket office early **so that we could be sure to get tickets.**

       We arrived at the ticket office early **to be sure to get tickets.**

    b. Basketball fans must often stand in line for long hours **if they want to get good seats.**

       Basketball fans must often stand in line for long hours **to get good seats.**

    c. I took my camera to the last game **because I wanted to take pictures of** my favorite players.

       I took my camera to the last game **to take pictures of my favorite players.**

Exercise 13:   Replace the underlined adverb clauses in the following sentences with infinitive phrases.

1. In the United States, candidates for the presidency campaign so that they can present their views to the public.

2. Most candidates buy T.V. time because they can reach a large number of people at one time.

3. All candidates ask for money so that they can pay for campaign expenses.

4. Many private citizens must make financial contributions to their favorite candidate if they want to keep their candidate in the race.

5. A candidate has to study national and international issues if he wants to address the voters knowledgeably.

6. All presidential hopefuls hire campaign workers in each state because they want to have good publicity on the local level.

7. These workers have to hold many meetings <u>if they expect to establish a good local organization</u>.

8. Campaign volunteers often go from door to door in their cities <u>so that they can tell voters about their candidates</u>.

9. These people must work hard <u>if they want to get the people to vote for their candidate</u>.

10. Voters should listen to all the individuals running for office <u>if they want to be able to make intelligent decisions</u>.

11. One year, I read three different newspapers every day <u>so that I could learn the candidates' views on various issues</u>.

12. During an election, T.V. stations cancel their regular shows <u>because they present the election results to the public</u>.

13. At this time, many people listen to the radio <u>because they can get relief from the many hours of election reporting</u>.

14. Most people would be surprised <u>if they knew how much money many presidential hopefuls spent to get elected</u>.

Infinitive Phrase to Replace Noun Clauses

Infinitive phrases are often used to replace noun clauses beginning with the words *who, what, where, when, which, how, how often, how much, how long.*

Study the following examples.

a. Sue asked me **which store she should shop in for inexpensive but good clothes.**
   Sue asked me **which store to shop in for inexpensive but good clothes.**

b. She was thinking about **how much money she ought to spend on a new coat.**
   She was thinking about **how much money to spend on a new coat.**

c. I finally decided **where I would take her.**
   I finally decided **where to take her.**

d. In the store, a friendly clerk explained **when we should look for certain clothing items.**
   In the store, a friendly clerk explained **when to look for certain clothing items.**

Exercise 14:   Change the underlined noun clauses into infinitive phrases.

Group 1

1. While Sue and I were talking with the clerk, we discovered <u>how we could find good bargains</u>.

2. During our discussion, we also learned <u>when we should check the newspapers for sales.</u>

3. The clerk also told us <u>how anyone can tell good shoes from poorly made ones.</u>

4. Now, I know <u>what I have to do before I make a purchase.</u>

5. I am wondering <u>whom I can talk to about getting a part-time job in a department store.</u>

Group 2

1. I'm going to ask my doctor <u>what I can give my son for his cold.</u>

2. It's difficult to know <u>which cough syrup I should buy.</u>

3. I can never remember <u>when I have to take medicine.</u>

4. Everyone would love to discover <u>how he could avoid catching a cold.</u>

5. Most people don't really know <u>how long they should stay in bed.</u>

Exercise 15: Student 1: Read one of the following sentences and ask the question that follows.

Student 2: Answer the question using the words in parentheses followed by an infinitive phrase.

Example: Student 1: You look very worried. What are you thinking about? (how)

Student 2: I'm thinking about **how to earn some extra money.**

1. The next vacation begins in two weeks. What are many students considering?   (where)

2. Most students know all the tenses in English; however, what don't they often understand?   (when)

3. Ana will complete her English studies this quarter. Concerning next quarter, what must she decide?   (which)

4. Some professors in university classes speak very quickly. What must students learn?   (how)

5. While you were making spaghetti sauce last night, what were you wondering?   (how much)

6. After the counselor's lecture on immigration services, what do you know? (who)

7. When you bought your new car, you received an operating manual. What is one of the things it tells the driver?   (how often)

8. We will soon have final exams. What are most of us worrying about?   (how many)

9. You are going away for two weeks, and you don't want to leave your dog alone. What are you wondering?   (what)

10. Since Yuko has been taking a course in public speaking, what has she learned? (how)

11. Your roommate wants to have a party, and your apartment is small, but he (she) has a lot of friends. What must he (she) decide?   (whom)

12. You are responsible for the refreshments for the party. What have you been trying to figure out?   (how much)

Infinitive Phrase to Replace Adjective Clauses

An infinitive construction is often used in the place of an adjective clause.

Study the following examples.

   a. I have a lot of dirty clothes **that I must wash.**
      I have a lot of dirty clothes   **to wash.**

   b. Carlos is the person **whom you can trust.**
      Carlos is the person   **to trust.**

   c. Can you lend me a good book **which I can read on the plane?**
      Can you lend me a good book   **to read on the plane?**

The infinitive construction is also used after *the first, the second, the last*, and *the only* to replace an adjective clause.

   d. The first student **who finished the exam** was Carlos.
      The first student   **to finish the exam**   was Carlos.
      The first student   **to finish**   was Carlos.
      The first   **to finish**   was Carlos.

   e. The only person **who didn't finish** was Sue.
      The only person   **not to finish**   was Sue.

   f. Of course, the last person **who left the room** was the teacher.
      Of course, the last person **to leave the room** was the teacher.
      Of course, the last person   **to leave**   was the teacher.
      Of course, the last   **to leave**   was the teacher.

Exercise 16:   Replace the adjective clauses in the following dialogue with an infinitive construction as shown in the examples.

Student: Does this store have a manager **whom I can complain to about my problem?**

Clerk: On Saturdays there is usually no one here **that can help you with a complaint.**

Student: I have a defective typewriter **that I must replace.**

Clerk: Just a minute. Perhaps I can find someone from that department **who can talk to you.**

Student: I must talk to someone. I have a lot of work **that I must complete this weekend.**

Clerk: Have a seat over there. I shouldn't be too long. There are some magazines **that you can read while you're waiting.**

Student: Am I the first person **who has had trouble with this brand?**

Clerk: No. But you're the only one **who has an immediate need for repair.**

Exercise 17: Replace the underlined clauses with an infinitive or an infinitive phrase.

1. Before Maria returns to Venezuela, she has a lot of presents that she must buy.
2. Can anyone suggest a nice gift that she could get for her father?
3. She wants to get him something that he can put in his office.
4. Her father is a businessman whom you have to admire.
5. He was the first businessman in his country who established a successful exporting business.
6. He is a good person whom you can consult if you have any questions about trade.
7. Maria doesn't have a lot of money that she can spend on a present.
8. She is from Caracas, and there are many beautiful places that you can visit there.
9. She hasn't taken final exams yet, so she has a lot of work that she must do before she goes shopping.
10. Before she returns to Caracas, she is going to Mexico where she will spend two weeks with her aunt Carla, who is her mother's sister.
11. Her aunt has a beautiful ranch and plenty of horses that she can ride.
12. The ranch is a good place where she can relax after finals.
13. Because she will have two entire weeks, she will have plenty of time in which to enjoy herself.
14. Maria's aunt is the only member of her family who has a ranch.

Additional Uses of the Infinitive and Infinitive Phrase

Infinitive with "Enough"

1. adjective + "enough" + infinitive/infinitive phrase

   The map we had wasn't excellent, but it was **good enough to get us to our destination.**

   Bob's car isn't very big, but it is **big enough to hold five people** comfortably.

2. adverb + "enough" + infinitive/infinitive phrase

We were driving **slowly enough to enjoy the beautiful scenery.**

At times, Bob played the radio **loudly enough to burst our eardrums.**

3. "enough" + noun + infinitive.

We only went on a short trip because we didn't have **enough money to take** a long one.

Furthermore, we didn't have **enough time to stay away for more than** four days.

Exercise 18:   Student 1:   Complete the question with an infinitive or infinitive phrase as shown in the sentences given.

Student 2:   Answer the question in either an affirmative or negative response.

1. I know that you and your roommate are planning to take a trip, but do you think the weather will be **nice enough** . . . ?
2. Are the tires on your car **good enough** . . . ?
3. Will you stay in Mexico **long enough** . . . ?
4. Are you planning to leave **early enough** . . . ?
5. Does your roommate drive **well enough** . . . ?
6. Will the check from your parents arrive **soon enough** . . . ?
7. Will you and your roommate have **enough money** . . . ?
8. Do you think that the weather will be **warm enough** . . . ?
9. Will you return from Mexico **early enough** . . . ?
10. This exercise has been **easy enough** . . . ?

Exercise 19:   Combine each pair of sentences using adjective + "enough" + infinitive phrase, adverb + "enough" + infinitive phrase, or "enough" + noun + infinitive phrase.

Example: This bicycle isn't strong. It can't hold two people.

This bicycle isn't **strong enough to hold two people.**

Group 1

1. Our candidate for president of the foreign student association isn't popular. He can't win the election.
2. He doesn't have many friends. He can't get the majority of the votes.
3. He doesn't have much time. He won't make many speeches.
4. He hasn't been on campus a long time. He doesn't know many people.

5. Most of the students don't know him well. They won't give him their support.
6. He really isn't very interested in the position. He won't campaign very hard.
7. For him, winning isn't important. It won't make him lose time from this studies.

Group 2

1. Ahmed's embassy didn't give him very much time. He couldn't finish his English studies.
2. Six months was not long. He couldn't complete all the levels.
3. He didn't realize the problem early. He didn't get permission to study longer.
4. This problem is not serious. It won't make him forget about beginning academic work.
5. He is a very good student, and his vocabulary is good. He can at least start part-time academic work.
6. Besides, he learns quickly. He will do well during his first quarter of study.

Infinitive with "Too"

1. "too" + adjective + infinitive/infinitive phrase

   When we returned from our trip Sunday night, we were **too tired to attend classes on Monday morning.**

   When I got home, my apartment was **too cold to sleep in,** so I slept at my neighbor's.

2. "too" + adverb + infinitive/infinitive phrase

   I woke up **too late to eat breakfast with her the next morning.**

   She left **too early for me to say good-bye.**

Exercise 20: Combine each of the following pairs of sentences, using "too" + adjective/adverb + infinitive/infinitive phrase.

   Example: I'm tired. I can't go anywhere tonight.
   I'm **too tired to go anywhere tonight.**

REMEMBER:

"for" + noun/pronoun may be used before the infinitive construction.

   I'm very tired. You can't come over tonight.
   I'm **too tired** for you **to come over tonight.**

1. Many big cities have become dangerous. Citizens cannot walk alone at night.

2. When I lived in Paris a few years ago, I was afraid. I didn't go out alone after dark.

3. Some people in large urban areas have become very suspicious. They don't trust anyone except their close friends.

4. In a big city, the pace of life is very fast. I would not enjoy it.

5. Many people are busy. They don't speak to their neighbors.

6. In most large cities, the cost of living is very high. The average citizen cannot have a comfortable life.

7. I am very happy in my small town. I would not move to a big city.

8. My brother, on the other hand, is restless. He will not stay here forever.

9. He says that our town is small. It is not interesting.

10. He says he's young. He will not die of boredom.

11. At the moment, however, he is broke. He cannot leave until he has saved some money.

12. I am very satisfied here. I don't worry about money.

13. Life is very short. I do not want to spend it living in fear.

List of Verbs Followed by Infinitives

> ***Group 1:*** Verbs followed immediately by an infinitive or an infinitive phrase

1.	**afford**	We can't **afford to take** a vacation this year.
2.	**agree**	The family **agreed to wait** until next year.
3.	**appear**	The children **appear to be** happy about this decision.
4.	**arrange**	We'll **arrange to go** to Hawaii.
5.	**be** (am, is, are)	We **are to leave** some time in July.
6.	**care**	I really don't **care to eat** out tonight.
7.	**choose** (prefer)	I certainly didn't **choose to come** to this restaurant.
8.	**claim**	It **claims to serve** the best Italian food in town.
9.	**come**	We **came to see** if the food is really good.
10.	**consent**	Everyone **consented to try** it tonight.
11.	**decide**	I **have decided to order** a chicken dish.
12.	**demand**	Why **is** that customer **demanding to see** the manager?
13.	**deserve**	Every customer **deserves to receive** good service.
14.	**endeavor**	That student **has** always **endeavored to do** well.

15.	fail	He **has** never **failed to get** a good grade on a test.
16.	forget	He never **forgets to complete** his assignments.
17.	happen	I **happen to like** him very much.
18.	hesitate	I don't know why the other students **hesitate to talk** to him.
19.	hope	He **hopes to receive** a scholarship for next year.
20.	intend	His teachers **intend to help** him all they can.
21.	learn	My children **are learning to ski.**
22.	manage	I **have managed to remain** calm so far.
23.	mean	I'm sorry. I didn't **mean to interrupt** you.
24.	neglect	You **neglected to tell** me that you had to study tonight.
25.	offer	Don't worry. The teacher **has offered to give** a review.
26.	plan	Many students **are planning to take** the review.
27.	prepare	The teacher is **prepared to spend** three hours on the review.
28.	pretend	At my surprise birthday party, I **pretended to be** surprised.
29.	proceed	I **proceeded to act** and **look** as if I hadn't known about it.
30.	prove	Your decision **proved to be** the wrong one.
31.	refuse	Never **refuse to tell** the truth.
32.	regret	I **regret to tell** you that your luggage is missing.
33.	remember	Did you **remember to put** an address label on each suitcase?
34.	seem	You don't **seem to be** very worried about it.
35.	struggle	The students **struggle to stay** awake in that history class.
36.	swear	The defendant **swore to tell** the truth in court.
37.	tend	Your child **tends to be** a little noisy at times.
38.	threaten	She **threatened to call** the police.
39.	volunteer	Who **will volunteer to help** us?
40.	wait	Have a good trip. I'll **be waiting to hear** from you.

Group 2: Verbs requiring a (pro)noun + an infinitive or infinitive phrase

1.	advise	Who **advised you to join** this soccer team?
2.	allow	Does the coach **allow the players to smoke?**
3.	appoint	Who **appointed John to be** the captain?
4.	cause	Bill's injury **caused him to play** poorly yesterday.
5.	caution	The referee **cautioned the members of both teams to play** fairly.

6. challenge	The losing team **has challenged our team to meet** again.
7. command	The police officers **commanded the thief to stop.**
8. compel	They **compelled him to drop** his weapon.
9. convince	I can't **convince you to do** anything you don't want to do.
10. direct	The usher **directed us to sit** in the third row.
11. enable	His strong desires **have enabled him to succeed.**
12. encourage	Parents should **encourage their children to do** their best.
13. forbid	Her mother **forbids her to tell** a lie.
14. force	Her son's refusal to obey **forced her to spank** him.
15. get	I **got my neighbor to take** me to the hospital.
*16. help	The police officer **helped me find** the address.
17. hire	He **has hired me to work** in his store this summer.
18. implore	I **implore everyone to help** the tornado victims.
19. instruct	Our teacher **instructed us to read** the directions carefully.
20. invite	After the exam, she **invited the class to come** to her house.
21. motivate	I don't know what **motivates some people to hurt** others.
22. oblige	Human decency **obliges us to treat** all people equally.
23. order	The court **ordered him to pay** for his parking tickets.
24. permit	The coach **permitted the players to take** a short break.
25. persuade	She **persuaded me to go** with her.
26. remind	I **reminded her not to forget** her driver's license.
27. request	The invitation **requested all guests to be** on time.
28. require	Does this school **require new students to take** a placement test?
29. show . . . how	Who **showed you how to do** that?
30. teach	My father **taught my brothers and me to play** chess.
31. tell	He **told us to concentrate** on the game.
32. tempt	You know that was wrong. What **tempted you to do** it?
33. urge	I **urge you to think** before you act.
34. warn	She **warned me not to do** it again.

* See note on page 228.

Group 3: Verbs followed by an object + infinitive construction
or by an infinitive construction only

Remember that the sentences in each pair differ in meaning.

1. **ask**

   She **asked to talk** with the manager.
   She **asked me to talk** with the manager.

2. **beg**

   He **begged to come** with us.
   He **begged us to come** with him.

3. **choose**

   The director **chose to investigate** the problem.
   The director **chose a committee to investigate** the problem.

4. **dare**

   They **dared to ask** the teacher for an answer during the test.
   They **dared me to ask** the teacher for an answer during the test.

5. **expect**

   We **expected to be** on time.
   We **expected you to be** on time.

6. **like**

   I **like to meet** new people.
   I **like you to meet** new people.

7. **need**

   We **need to help** your roommate with his math class.
   We **need your roommate to help** us with our math class.

8. **prefer**

   The children **prefer to tell** stories.
   The children **prefer their teacher to tell** stories.

*9. **promise**

   My brother **promised not to tell**.
   My brother **promised me not to tell**.

10. **want**

    The nurse **wants to give** the injection.
    The nurse **wants the doctor to give** the injection.

11. **wish**

    I **wish to consult** with my lawyer.
    I **wish you to consult** with my lawyer.

* See note on page 239.

LESSON FOURTEEN: PRACTICE EXAM

Before completing Part I, review pages 228 and 229.

Part I: Identification. Identify each underlined infinitive phrase according to its function in the sentence. Be careful of the false subject, "it."

Subject = S   Adjective = A   Object = O
Subject   Adjective   Adverb = AV
complement = SC   complement = AC

_____ 1. Because of the complexity of the world's problems today, to find proper solutions is a difficult task.

_____ 2. Today's world leaders have an extremely difficult job to do.

_____ 3. Indeed, it is not easy for any leader to govern his or her country wisely.

_____ 4. Every head of state needs to have well-informed advisors.

_____ 5. The president of one country recently fired his defense minister to get someone more knowledgeable.

_____ 6. He was anxious to have someone who could look at the subject of defense rationally.

_____ 7. His chief concern was to have a strong yet rational policy of defense.

_____ 8. It is disturbing to think about the effects of war today.

_____ 9. Few individuals want to see their country engaged in war.

_____10. Every sane person's desire is to live in peace.

Part II: Use each of the following verbs in a short sentence. Remember that some verbs require an *object* before the infinitive.

    Example: afford: I cannot afford **to buy a new car.**

                 advise: My friend advised **me to get a used car.**

1. allow _____

2. command _____

3. decide_____

4. demand _____

5. direct _____

6. encourage_____

7. forget _____

8. hesitate_____

9. intend_____

10. neglect _____

11. offer_____

12. order _____

13. persuade_____

14. refuse _____

15. seem_____

Part III: Change the underlined adjective, noun, and adverb clauses into infinitive phrases.

1. Rosa registered for the TOEFL exam early <u>so that she would be sure to have a seat</u>.

   _____

2. One month before the test, she asked her grammar teacher <u>which points of grammar she should review</u>.

   _____

3. Her teacher gave her the lesson <u>that she should study</u>.

   _____

4. As she was reviewing, she realized there were many rules <u>that she had to remember</u>.

   _____

5. After she had talked with her teacher again, she discovered <u>how she could review quickly yet thoroughly</u>.

   _____

6. Most students have to review a little <u>if they want to get a high score</u>.

   _____

7. Next quarter, the director is giving a special class once a week <u>because he wants to help the students review before the test</u>.

   _____

8. In this class, he will explain <u>how the students should prepare for the test</u>.

   _____

9. Last quarter, Mirko was the only person <u>who received a score above 550</u>.

   _____

10. Mirko had spent a lot of time preparing for the test <u>so that he would get a high</u> <u>score</u>.

_____

11. Since he had taken the practice tests in the TOEFL book, he knew <u>what kind of</u> <u>questions he should expect on the test</u>.

_____

LESSON FIFTEEN

GERUNDS

The Simple Gerund

A gerund is a noun that has been formed from a verb. Any verb can be turned into a gerund by adding "-ing" to the simple form of the verb.

   walk, walk**ing**   play, play**ing**   be, be**ing**

When changing some verbs into gerunds, changes in spelling may be necessary.

   lie, ly**ing**

Gerunds function as nouns in a sentence.

   Jogging is good exercise.   (subject of the sentence)
   My favorite form of exercise is **jogging**.   (subjective complement)
   I have always enjoyed **jogging**.   (direct object)
   My roommate is against **jogging**.   (object of a preposition)
   His favorite form of exercise, **dancing**, is more enjoyable.   (appositive)

The Gerund Phrase

Although gerunds function as nouns, they are similar to verbs. Like verbs, a gerund may take an object, a complement, and other modifiers.

   Interviewing **small children** is amusing.
   Playing **tennis** is fun.

The nouns "children" and "tennis" receive the actions of the gerunds "interviewing" and "playing." "Children" and "tennis" are used as the direct objects.

In the sentences given, "Interviewing small children" and "Playing tennis" are gerund phrases.

The gerund with its object, adjectival modifiers, or adverbial modifiers is called a *gerund phrase*. In the following sentences, the gerund phrases are underlined.

I have always enjoyed **cooking Italian food.**

Listening to the radio in the evenings is a good way to relax.

Her beautiful singing pleased everyone in the audience.

Functions of Gerund/Gerund Phrases

As a noun, the gerund/gerund phrase can be used in the following ways:

1. **Subject**

   Traveling is enjoyable.
   Traveling with young children can be difficult.
   Finding a good hotel is not always easy.

2. **Subject complement** (as subject complement, the gerund/gerund phrase renames or identifies the subject)

   My mother's hobby is **cooking.**
   My father's favorite **pastime** is **collecting foreign stamps.**
   What he really enjoys is **getting rare stamps.**

3. **Direct object** (after certain verbs)

   My family has always enjoyed **traveling.**
   We have always dreaded **staying in one place.**
   At one time, my father considered **moving to Europe for three years.**

4. **Object of a preposition**

   I have always been interested *in* **learning about different cultures.**
   My brother is thinking *about* **spending a year in Italy.**
   The whole family has become accustomed *to* **eating different kinds of food.**

5. **Appositive** (an appositive merely repeats or adds information about a person or thing already identified)

   My mother's hobby, **cooking,** is enjoyable to her.
   My father really enjoys his favorite pastime, **collecting stamps.**

Making Gerunds Negative

To make a gerund negative, "not" is placed in front of the gerund.

   a. Bob regretted **not seeing** that movie.
   b. The students proposed **not having** final examinations.
   c. My doctor thought about **not letting** me go on a vacation.

It is important to put the word "not" immediately before the gerund. Look at the following sentences where the main verbs are negative.

    d. Bob **did not regret** seeing that movie.

    e. The students **did not propose** having final examinations.

    f. My doctor **did not think** about putting me into the hospital.

Notice that the meanings of sentences d, e, and f are different from the meanings of sentences a, b, and c. In sentence a, Bob did not see the movie, and he regretted having missed it. In sentence d, Bob saw the movie, and he was not sorry that he had gone to it.

Exercise 1: Complete the following sentences with either a gerund or gerund phrase.

    Example: I really miss **not** . . .

                     I really miss not **having my television set.**

1. Please, would you mind **not** . . .
2. Does the teacher remember **not** . . .
3. Are you going to propose **not** . . .
4. Have your parents ever regretted **not** . . .
5. Can you imagine **not** . . .
6. Has your roommate ever considered **not** . . .
7. On Saturday, would you prefer **not** . . .
8. Concerning the next test, would you advise **not** . . .
9. As a child, I hated **not** . . .
10. Because of the bad weather, I really prefer **not** . . .

Exercise 2:   Student 1:   Complete the following questions.
                      Student 2:   Answer the question in a complete sentence.

    Example: Student 1:   Do you sometimes miss not **being able to talk to your parents?**

                     Student 2:   Yes, sometimes I really miss not **being able to speak with them.**

1. When you were a child, do you **remember not** . . .
2. As a child, can you **deny not ever** . . .
3. When you were small, did you **regret not** . . .

4. As a mother, do you **prefer not** . . .

5. As a parent, have you **minded not** . . .

6. Can you **imagine** a six year old child **not** . . .

7. Whenever you get married, **are** you **considering not** . . .

8. As a married person, will you **miss not** . . .

9. As a single person, have you **enjoyed not** . . .

10. Does your married brother regret **not** . . .

11. After I get married, do you suggest **not** . . .

12. Before you got married, did you and your loved one **discuss not** . . .

13. As a married student, do you sometimes **resent not** . . .

14. With seven children at home, do you usually prefer **not** . . .

Gerund/Gerund Phrase as Subject of the Sentence

Exercise 3: Complete each of the following sentences with a simple gerund or gerund phrase as subject of the sentence.

> Example: **Listening to the news** really depresses me sometimes. (gerund phrase)
>
> **Sleeping** is my favorite pastime. (simple gerund)

1. _____ is an excellent form of exercise.

2. _____ has changed my life.

3. _____ is going to be very difficult for me.

4. _____ has always been important to me.

5. _____ is not easy in a foreign country.

6. _____ has been one of my country's most important goals.

7. _____ will be the most difficult thing for me to do when I return home.

8. _____ is foolish, considering the price of gasoline.

9. _____ seems to be a favorite American pastime.

10. _____ has never made me comfortable.

11. _____ will be a difficult job for the next U.S. president.

Exercise 4:   Complete the following sentences with a gerund or gerund phrases.

1. After school, _____ is the first thing many children do.

2. _____ really annoys most mothers.

3. If it is raining, and they can't go outside, _____ appeals to most children.

4. My parents didn't have a television when they were young, so

   _____ was their way of relaxing after school.

5. _____ takes a lot of time for both mothers and fathers.

6. _____ is a big responsibility for every parent.

7. _____ demands a lot of time from both parents.

8. In many families, _____ has always been the father's job.

9. In many countries, _____ has usually been the woman's responsibility.

10. Nevertheless, _____ is a source of pleasure for most parents.

11. _____ is not easy for children in any part of the world.

12. As a child grows up, _____ is very difficult.

13. My grandparents loved children, so _____ was an enjoyable experience.

14. I have six sisters and four brothers, but as a parent

   _____ does not appeal to me.

Gerund/Gerund Phrase as Subjective Complement

Remember that as the subjective complement, the gerund construction renames or identifies the subject.

Exercise 5:   Answer the following questions with a gerund or gerund phrase as subjective complement.

> **Example:**   What would be your ideal **summer job?**
>
> My ideal **summer job** would be **guiding tourists around my city.**

1. What has been one of your biggest **problems** this quarter?
2. What is your favorite **form of recreation?**
3. What has always been your **hobby?**
4. When you worked in your country, what was your **job?**
5. If you were the leader of your country, what would be your **main concern?**
6. Your wife wanted to go to the movies last weekend, but what was your **suggestion?**

Exercise 6:   Complete the following sentences with a gerund or gerund phrase as subjective complement.

> **Example:**   One **solution** to the large number of cars on the roads is **car pooling/ riding with a friend/taking the bus.**

1. After five hours of classes every day, my one **thought** is . . .
2. One of my **major goals** in life has always been . . .
3. An actor's **biggest dream** is probably . . .
4. When my roommate went to the car dealer, his **biggest mistake** was . . .
5. The police officer who stopped me said that my **violation** had been . . .
6. After Roberto completes his English studies, the next **step** will be . . .
7. Before my oldest brother left home, his one **fear** was . . .
8. When driving in the downtown area, a big **frustration** is always . . .
9. When I worked at the pool as a lifeguard, my **responsibilities** were . . .
10. Concerning Kenji's inability to sleep at night, his doctor's **suggestion** was . . .
11. If I had a million dollars, my one **desire** would be . . .
12. Generally speaking, John is usually a nice person; however, his biggest **fault** is . . .
13. Man's highest **aim** should be . . .

Gerund/Gerund Phrases as Direct Object

The gerund or gerund phrase may follow a verb and function as the direct object. However, not every verb in English can take a gerund construction as the direct object. The following verbs are commonly used in this pattern.

admit	enjoy	practice
appreciate	escape	prevent
avoid	*excuse	quit
can't help	finish	recall
consider	forgive	recommend
defer	imagine	resent
delay	keep (continue)	resist
deny	mention	risk
detest	mind (dislike)	suggest
discuss	miss	tolerate
	postpone	*understand

The teacher excused **my** coming late.

I appreciate **your** helping me with this problem.

The teacher understood **John**'s failing to do the assignment.

Examples:

1. Bob	admitted	**borrowing** Tom's car.
2. He	should appreciate	**having** such a nice room-mate.
3. I	can't help	**loving** him.
4. You really	should consider	**coming** to class on time.
5. After Christmas, we	defer	**paying** some bills.
6. Last year, we	delayed	**putting** anything on credit.
7. Tell the truth. Do not	deny	**copying** this composition.
8. I	detest	**cheating** in any form.
9. Tomorrow, I	will discuss	**giving** you another chance.
10. No teacher	enjoys	**failing** students.
11. However, it's difficult to	forgive	**cheating.**
12. No one	can escape	**being** punished.

* These verbs are always followed by the possessive before the gerund.

264

13. You	have not finished	**doing** the other assignment.
14. I	cannot imagine	**forgetting** about this.
15. You	must keep	**trying** to do your best.
16. I	have mentioned	**giving** you extra help many times.
17. I	do not mind	**helping** you.
18. Bob arrived late and	missed	**catching** his plane.
19. Due to snow, our captain	postponed	**leaving**.
20. While waiting to leave, I	practiced	**pronouncing** my French words.
21. After a while, the passengers	quit	**worrying** about the delay.
22. At the time, I	recall	**thinking** about the children.
23. An airline official	recommended	**buying** ice cream for the children.
24. Some passengers	resented	**being** in the airport so long.
25. I	could not resist	**worrying** about the weather.
26. The airlines	could not risk	**having** an accident.
27. One passenger	suggested	**playing** cards.

Exercise 7: Complete the following questions and statements with a gerund or gerund phrase as direct object.

1. In the courtroom, what did the defendant **admit?**
2. What couldn't the defendant's lawyer **avoid?**
3. The defendant had always been a quiet man, but on the night of the crime he **could not help** . . .
4. Because he had never been in trouble with the law, the judge **considered** . . .
5. The jury needed more time, so it **delayed** . . .
6. The defendant's wife **detested** . . .
7. That night he and his wife **discussed** . . .
8. The trial was interesting, but I don't really **enjoy** . . .
9. Actually, many times the defendant could not **finish** . . .
10. I have never been in jail, so I can't **imagine** . . .

11. While the defendant's lawyer was speaking, the lawyer for the prosecution **kept** . . .
12. Because the jury could not agree on the defendant's innocence or guilt, what did the judge **postpone?**
13. Finally, the judge gave his verdict, and the defendant's wife **quit** . . .
14. The defendant seemed to be such a quiet man that I can't **resist** . . .
15. Nevertheless, I really don't **understand** (his) . . .

The Possessive + Gerund/Gerund Phrase

In formal English the possessive is often used before the gerund construction.

> I couldn't understand **John's** coming late.
> I couldn't understand   **his**   coming late.

In informal usage, however, native speakers often use the object form of a personal pronoun or the noun without the possessive inflection.

> I couldn't understand **John** coming late.
> I couldn't understand **him** coming late.

When a possessive is used before a gerund construction, there is often a change in meaning.

> We enjoyed singing.   (We were singing.)
> We enjoyed the **choir's** singing.   (We were listening to the choir.)

Exercise 8:   Complete the following sentences with a possessive + gerund construction.

> **Example:**   The teacher did not appreciate **my interrupting his explanation.**

1. Because of the snow storm, the instructor excused . . .
2. The students really appreciated . . .
3. One very late student who lives near the university tried to defend . . .
4. During the exam, the instructor didn't permit . . .
5. I studied very hard for the last test, so I couldn't understand . . .
6. Because so many students did poorly on the test, the instructor suggested . . .
7. We have a good class; however, a few students constantly speak out of turn. I hate . . .

8. I saw one of my classmates at the movies last night, but he pretended not to see me. I can't imagine . . .
9. He invited me to his home last weekend, and I really enjoyed . . .

Verbs Followed by Gerunds or Infinitives as Direct Object

The following verbs may be followed by either a gerund or an infinitive construction with *no change in meaning*.

advise	dislike	love
allow	dread	need
attempt	forbid	neglect
begin	hate	permit
cannot bear	intend	prefer
continue	like	start

1. Bob	attempted **bringing** in attempted **to bring** in	fruit from Mexico.
2. The customs officials	began **searching** began **to search**	his suitcases.
3. They	continued **questioning** continued **to question**	him for several hours.
4. Many people	dislike **visiting** dislike **to visit**	warm countries.
5. I	love **traveling** love **to travel**	by plane.
6. Nonsmokers	hate **sitting** hate **to sit**	in the smoking section.
7. On a trip, many women	prefer **dressing** prefer **to dress**	in pants for comfort.

NOTES:

1. After *advise*, *allow*, *forbid* and *permit*, a noun or pronoun object is necessary before the infinitive. Compare the following sentences.

   a. Our travel agent advised *us* **to take** a European vacation.

      Our travel agent advised **taking** a European vacation.

   b. Professor Jones does not allow *anyone* **to leave** the room during an exam.

      Professor Jones does not allow **leaving** the room during an exam.

c. My father forbids *me* **to smoke** in his house.

My father forbids **smoking** in his house.

d. This apartment building does not permit any *resident* **to have** a pet.

This apartment building does not permit **having** pets.

2. The words *begin* and *start* take either the gerund or infinitive. However, if the verb following *begin* and *start* is a verb of "knowing" or "understanding," (for example, **reflect, contemplate, perceive**) it is more common to use the infinitive.

a. After a few minutes, we **started to understand** the teacher's explanation.

b. As I watched the report of the earthquake victims, **I began to perceive** the horror of such a disaster.

3. After *attempt* and *intend* gerunds are possible, but infinitives are more common.

a. She **attempted to do** the work by herself. (is more common than: She attempted doing the work by herself.)

b. **I intended to help** her, but I was too busy. (is more common than: I intended helping her, but I was too busy.)

4. With *need*, the passive infinitive is used.

a. My car **needs to be washed.**   (or)   My car **needs washing.**

Exercise 9:   Answer the following questions using a gerund if an infinitive is used or an infinitive if a gerund is used.

Example: If it **begins to rain,** are you going to cancel the picnic?
Of course, we'll cancel it if it **begins raining.**

Did the radio announcer **continue asking** for donations?

Yes, he **continued to ask** for donations.

1. I understand that Robert is looking for a new job. Doesn't he *like to work* here anymore?

2. Is it true that he *dislikes being* inside all day?

3. Wouldn't he *prefer to have* a job where he could travel once in a while?

4. Hasn't he *neglected doing* much of his work lately?

5. When will he *start looking* for another job?

6. Did you *advise going* to an employment agency or *checking* the want ads in the newspaper?

7. Haven't you noticed that he *dreads to attend* the morning staff meetings?

8. He has excellent sales experience. Couldn't he *begin working* as a salesman?

9. Does he *intend leaving* before he finds another job?

10. Doesn't our company policy *forbid quitting* without giving at least two weeks notice?

11. He really looks depressed. Don't you agree that he *needs cheering* up?

12. He is such a nice person. Don't you *hate to see* him so depressed?

Verbs Followed by Gerunds or Infinitive as Direct Object

The following verbs may be followed by either a gerund or an infinitive construction, but the *meaning changes*.

forget	regret	try
mean	remember	used to
propose	stop	be used to

1. The infinitive after the verbs *forget*, *remember*, and *stop* refers to an action that happens AFTER the action of the main verb.

2. The gerund after these verbs refers to an action that happens *before* the action of the main verb.

Study the following pairs of sentences:

a. Fadel forgot **to come** for the test. Action 1: forgetting
   He will never forget **missing** the
   test Action 1: missing

b. We stopped **to eat**. Action 1: stopping
   We stopped **eating**. Action 1: eating

c. I remembered **to write** down the
   assignment. Action 1: remembering
   I remembered **writing** down the
   assignment. Action 1: writing

d. I regret **to tell** you that you failed
   the test. Action 1: regretting
   I regret **telling** you this bad news. Action 1: telling

3. The verb *mean* meaning *intend* is followed by the infinitive. *Mean* meaning *result in* is followed by the gerund, and is used only with an impersonal subject.

e. The police detective **means to solve** this crime even if it **means forgetting** about his other work.

f. I'm tired of smoking. **I mean to stop** even if it **means gaining** weight.

4. The verb *propose* meaning *plan or intend* takes the infinitive. *Propose* meaning *suggest* takes the gerund.

g. We **propose to leave** early tomorrow morning. (plan to leave)

h. I **propose leaving** before 6:00 A.M.   (suggest leaving)

5. The verb *try* meaning *to make an effort* takes the infinitive. *Try* meaning *experiment* takes the gerund.

i. I **try to take** notes carefully, but I miss much of the information.

j. **Try taking** a tape recorder to class.

6. The verb *used to* referring to an *habitual past action* takes the infinitive. The verb *be used to* means *accustomed to* and takes the gerund.

k. We **used to drive** to New York from Nevada every other month to see our parents.

l. We **are used to driving** long distances, so the trips didn't bother us.

Exercise 10:   Answer the following questions. Several correct answers are possible for each question.

1. As a student, what do you sometimes *forget to do?*

2. What does being a full-time student usually *mean?*

3. What incident in your life will you never *forget?*

4. What do you *propose to do* about the test you missed last week?

5. What did you *remember to do* this morning?

6. Why did the teacher *stop* in the middle of her explanation?

7. What did Hassan *propose* concerning the end of the quarter party?

8. Why did Yuko *stop studying* with her roommate?

9. Since your friend has been working on his new job, what *is* he *used to?*

10. Last semester, what did you *use to do* every Saturday morning?

11. Because the teacher couldn't read Ali's writing, what did Ali *try to do?*

12. Everybody makes mistakes once in a while. What is something that you have always *regretted?*

13. Since your every effort to stop smoking has failed so far, what will you *try* next?

14. I really didn't like what you told my roommate about me. Did you really *mean to say* what you said?

Exercise 11: Oral review. Complete the following sentences with either an infinitive or a gerund.

1. When you get married, will you **begin** . . .
2. Will you **allow** your husband . . .
3. Have your parents ever **regretted** . . .
4. As a mother, will you **attempt** . . .
5. Are you planning to be a working mother, or do you **prefer** . . .
6. Does any member of your family **hope** . . .
7. As a husband, will you **refuse** . . .
8. Who in this class **dreads** . . .
9. Your cousin is forty-five years old. Hasn't he **decided** . . .
10. Does your aunt **intend** . . .
11. Have you ever **tried** . . .
12. If you were having trouble with your mate, would you ever **consider** . . .
13. Your cousin is a very nice person. Don't you think he **deserves** . . .
14. Before he gets married, my brother has to **quit** . . .
15. When you get married, I will **promise** . . .
16. A single person cannot **imagine** . . .
17. My parents have been married for ten years; however, my father **continues** . . .
18. My mother told me that after their ceremony, she **enjoyed** . . .
19. For their honeymoon, my father **proposed** . . .
20. After they had been married for several years, my mother **attempted** . . .
21. You didn't attend my wedding last week, but I will **forgive** . . .
22. Before my sister and her fiancé get married, they really **need** . . .
23. While my brother and his wife were driving to the mountains on their honeymoon, they **stopped** . . .
24. They had a nice drive, but when they arrived at their cabin, they discovered that they **had forgotten** . . .

Exercise 12: Think and respond. Read the following paragraphs and answer the questions that follow.

Campus Disorder

In the 1960s there were many demonstrations on university campuses around the world. In the spring of 1969, my sister was a graduate student at New York University, which is an excellent institution. At that time, however, there were many demonstrations and bomb threats. Both professors and students were forced to leave their classes in the middle of a lecture because of these disturbances. In many instances, university officials **considered closing** the university **instead of endangering** the lives of innocent people, but many students **resented missing** their classes. Due to the disturbances on campus, some teachers **tried holding** classes in their apartments, and several had to **postpone giving** final examinations. They **regretted doing** this, but they could not **finish presenting** the content of their courses because of the disorder and interruptions.

During the demonstrations, the police said that they could not **avoid hurting** some people since many of them **resisted following** their orders. The students **denied disobeying** the police, and a large number of them stated that in many instances, the police **continued hitting** them even after they had **stopped pushing** and **shoving**. After a demonstration against the war in Vietnam, students met and **began planning** for their next protest. At this meeting, some students **proposed having** other students keep order instead of the police. They complained that they **disliked seeing** police officers on the campus.

Hundreds of parents wrote to the university and stated that they did not **like having** their sons and daughters in danger; furthermore, they did not **appreciate** their children's education **being** interrupted.

In the fall of 1969, the demonstrations had subsided somewhat, and the university opened its doors to new and old students. Most of my sister's friends are now married with families of their own; however, they **remember participating** in the protests, and some **admit feeling** regretful about the parts they played.

Answer the following questions on the reading. In your answers, use a gerund that is different from the gerund in the question or reading, but keep the same meaning. You may use the words from the following list if you need to.

cancel	have	teach	be disorderly
give	postpone	injure	take part in
be absent from	be disorderly	refuse to obey	
choose	think about	beat	

> **Example:** Did university officials **consider closing** the university?
> Yes, they **considered canceling** classes.

1. Did many students resent missing their classes?
2. Where did some teachers try holding their classes?
3. Did several teachers have to postpone giving final exams?
4. Could the teachers finish presenting the content of their courses?
5. During the demonstrations, could the police have avoided hurting some people?
6. What did the students deny?
7. What did the students say about the police?

8. After the demonstration against the war in Vietnam, what did the students begin planning for?

9. Instead of having the police keep order, what did some students propose?

10. What do many of the former students remember today?

Gerunds after Prepositions

When a verb is placed immediately after a preposition the gerund form must be used. Study the following sentences.

a. The children insisted **on going** to the zoo.

b. Their mother had no objection **to taking** them there.

c. However, she was not interested **in staying** all day.

d. The father avoided going to the zoo **by saying** he had a lot of work to do.

There are many verb + preposition, adjective + preposition, and noun + preposition combinations in English. We will study a few of the most commonly used ones.

Verb + Preposition + Gerund/Gerund Phrase

The verb + preposition combinations listed below can be used in the following patterns.

Pattern A:	**subject +**	**verb**	**+ gerund phrase**	
	He	approved of	writing the story.	
Pattern B:	**subject +**	**verb**	**+ possessive +**	**gerund phrase**
	Bob	apologized for	his	being late.

apologize for	depend on (upon)
apologize to (someone) for	dream about
adjust to	forgive (someone) for
agree with	forget about
approve of	insist on
argue about	look forward to
believe in	object to
blame (someone) for	plan on
care about	refer to
comment on	see about
complain about	talk about
concentrate on	think about
consist of	warn (someone) about
care for	worry about
deal with	

The following verb + prepositions can only be used in pattern A.

subject   + verb + indirect object +   gerund phrase
The police officer   accused me of   speeding on the freeway.

accuse _____object_____ of   pay _____ for

congratulate _____ on   prevent _____ from

devote _____ to   thank _____ for

Oral Drill: Answer the following questions.

1. What did the sales clerk **accuse** your friend **of?**
2. This quarter, what are you **devoting** yourself **to?**
3. What did you have to **pay** the doctor **for?**
4. What did your roommate **prevent** you **from** doing?
5. What are you going to **thank** me **for?**
6. What did you **congratulate** your teacher **on?**

Exercise 13:   Student 1:   Ask the question.
            Student 2:   Answer the question in a complete sentence.

1. What did you **apologize to** the reading teacher **for?**
2. When you came to the United States, what did you have to **adjust to?**
3. What have you and your roommate been **arguing about?**
4. What doesn't your father **approve of?**
5. What did the police **blame** you **for** last night?
6. As a student, what do you really **care about?**
7. When you were in the director's office, what were you **complaining about?**
8. Since this quarter began, what have you been **concentrating on?**
9. What did you **dream about** last night?
10. When you were a little child, what did your mother always **forgive** you **for?**
11. What are you trying to **forget about?**
12. After this quarter, what are you **looking forward to?**
13. What has the grammar teacher always **insisted on?**
14. What do you **plan on** doing this weekend?
15. After class today, what do you have to **see about?**
16. Excuse me, what are you **talking about?**
17. What does keeping your scholarship **depend on?**

18. Before you left your country, what did your mother **warn** you **about?**
19. What does being a good student **consist of?**

Adjective + Preposition + Gerund/Gerund Phrase

The following adjective + preposition combinations can be used after the verbs *be seem appear remain look become.*

*accustomed to	*excited about	responsible for
afraid of	famous for	sorry about
angry at	generous about	suitable for
appropriate for	good at	sure of (about)
ashamed of	grateful to, for	*surprised at
*concerned about	incapable of	*tired of (from)
content with	*interested in	used to (accustomed to)
*delighted at	lazy about	*worried about
essential to	proud of	

Oral Drill: Answer the following questions.

1. Since you've been away from home, what have you become **accustomed to?**
2. When you were a small child, what were you **afraid of?**
3. Before you left your country, what was your mother **concerned about?**
4. For you, what is studying English **essential to?**
5. What do you usually feel **excited about?**
6. What would you like to become **famous for?**
7. What have you always been **interested in?**

Exercise 14: Complete the following sentences.

1. After each Olympic game, the winners look **proud of** . . .
2. When a country hosts the Olympic games, it is **responsible for** . . .
3. All athletes feel **sorry about** . . .
4. Until the last moment every athlete seems **sure of** . . .
5. Were you **surprised at** . . .
6. A hopeful athlete can never become **tired of** . . .
7. During the games, I am sure that some coaches are **worried about** . . .

*Note: These words are past participles used as adjectives.

8. For an Olympic athlete, eating properly and training hard is **essential to** . . .

9. Because they train so much before the games, a serious athlete appears **used to** . . .

Noun + Preposition + Gerund/Gerund Phrase

The following is a list of commonly used noun + preposition combinations. These combinations may be followed by a gerund or by a possessive form and a gerund except for the four combinations with asterisks.

*difficulty in	interest in
in addition to	in the course of
*in charge of	in the middle of
*in danger of	need for
in favor of	reason for
in return for	*technique for
instead of (in lieu of)	the point of

a. Professor Smith stopped speaking **in the middle of giving his lecture.**

b. He asked the two students in the back of the room to state their **reasons for having a private conversation.**

c. He warned them that they were **in danger of failing his course.**

d. They apologized and said they were having **difficulty in understanding** his lecture.

f. Professor Smith took time out to explain a few **techniques for taking good notes.**

Exercise 15:   Complete the following sentences.

1. As they were driving to the mountains, Sue told Bob to slow down because she did not see the **need for** . . .

2. She also warned him that they were **in danger of** . . .

3. Because the road was clear, Bob said he did not see **the point of** . . .

4. Sue reminded him that **in addition to** . . ., they could get a ticket.

5. When Bob saw a police car in his rear view mirror, he was suddenly **in favor of** . . .

6. It was too late. After the police officer had checked Bob's license, he asked him if he had **difficulty in** . . .

7. The officer sarcastically asked if he had an **interest in** . . .

8. The officer also reminded Bob that as an officer of the law, he was **in charge of** . . .
9. Surprisingly, **instead of** . . ., the police officer told Bob to report to the police station every Wednesday night for safe driving lessons.
10. Sue mentioned that because of his poor driving record, Bob really needed to review the **techniques for** . . .

Exercise 16: Fill in the following paragraphs with the correct preposition and a gerund which completes the meaning of the sentences. Try to use a *different gerund* for each blank.

You may want to use some of the verbs from the following list. Many have the same meaning.

mug	help	live	change	do
walk	wait	reside	improve	keep
rob	assist	spend	solve	enforce
see	have	use	correct	insure
be	bring up	contact	look for	combat
serve	rear up	ask	find	fight

The Changing Quality of Life in Many American Cities

Few would deny that the quality of life has changed in many big American cities. Many people can remember a time when it was very safe to walk to the

corner store after dark; however, today they are afraid _____ _____

alone. Store owners find that they are constantly in danger _____

_____ robbed. Some of them have been threatened in the course

_____ _____ their customers. Many people agree that a big city is no

longer suitable _____ _____ children.

People who live in the big cities are concerned _____

_____ these conditions. They say that the city governments do

not really seem interested _____ _____ solutions to
the problems. On the other hand, the city officials maintain that they are

incapable _____ _____ very much without money from
the state and national governments. The mayors of the big urban areas ad-

mit that they, too, are worried _____ _____ the
quality of life in their cities. The majority of citizens believe that their police

forces have not been good _____ _____ law and

order. Everyone feels that a good police force is essential _____

_____ a safe environment.

The citizens in these areas are also tired _____ _____
such high taxes. Again they complain that the city and state governments are

responsible _____ not correctly _____ the money
available to them.

Violence and high taxes are only two of the problems that city dwellers face.
Many Americans who move to the big cities from small towns have been used

_____ _____ in an atmosphere that is friendly and

quiet; therefore, they are not accustomed _____ _____

in an environment that is cold and impersonal. No American is proud _____

_____ about these conditions, and all agree that there is a need

_____ _____ the situation. Everyone feels that the problems are

very serious, but no one seems to know the best technique _____

_____ these problems. Some officials are in favor _____

_____ the law enforcement officials of certain European
cities for advice.

While it is true that many European cities, as well as others around the world,
have some of the same problems, it is also true that they seem to have found successful solutions to many of them.

Exercise 17:   Read the following paragraphs, paying particular attention to the verb/
adjective/noun + preposition combinations.

The Year Following Watergate

Even after the news of the Watergate break-in and cover-up was almost a year
old, the American people had not yet become accustomed to hearing new stories of
corruption and dishonesty in the Nixon administration. Each new incident was just
as surprising as the previous ones. Consequently, the president was becoming in-
creasingly unsuccessful in restoring confidence in his administration.

On Saturday, October 20, 1973, Nixon's dismissal of Special Prosecutor Archibald Cox created massive headlines. Nixon had ordered Elliot Richardson, who
was the attorney general, to fire Cox. However, Elliot Richardson was opposed to
getting rid of him; as a result, Richardson resigned from his position as attorney
general. The president then ordered former Deputy Attorney General William
Ruckelhaus to fire Cox, but like Richardson, Ruckelhaus could not see the need for

releasing Cox from his duties. Millions of Americans were surprised and shocked. They accused Nixon of acting irresponsibly and recklessly.

The country soon learned that Cox had been fired because of his intense efforts to secure the White House tapes. Nixon had previously said that he was not afraid of releasing the tapes because of possible evidence that might prove he was guilty. On the contrary, he stated, he was only concerned about preserving the confidentiality of presidential material. Moreover, he had claimed, on numerous occasions, that the tapes contained information essential to maintaining national security.

In spite of his past refusals to surrender the tapes, Nixon finally announced that he would do so. He made this announcement on Tuesday, October 23, 1973, just three days after Cox had been released. A large number of people felt that he had changed his mind because of the thousands of telegrams for impeachment that were sent to the White House by disapproving citizens.

These people had become tired of listening to the daily reports of crime and dishonesty in Nixon's administration. Even past supporters felt that Nixon could no longer be responsible for keeping law and order in the country since his administration had become infamous for breaking and ignoring the law. They were convinced that he was no longer suitable for running the country, and they believed that in the interest of preserving the dignity of the presidency, Nixon should resign.

Answer the following questions based on the reading in complete sentences. Some answers may require a possessive before the gerund construction.

1. Concerning Nixon's actions, what did the American public **disapprove of?**
2. What did the public **blame** Nixon **for?**
3. What had Nixon not **succeeded in doing?**
4. What did Vice President Gerald Ford find himself **looking forward to?**
5. What had Archibald Cox been **concentrating on** before Nixon fired him?
6. What did Nixon and Elliot Richardson probably **argue about?**
7. Could Ruckelhaus see the **need for firing** Cox?
8. Before Nixon fired Cox, what should his advisors have **warned** him **about?**
9. What did the protest of the American public **prevent** Nixon **from doing?**
10. What did many people believe concerning the presidency?
11. What will many people never **forgive** Nixon **for doing?**
12. Through all of this, what should Nixon have **insisted on?**

List of Verbs Followed by Gerunds

Verbs followed immediately by a gerund or gerund phrase

1.	admit	He **has admitted taking** the money.
2.	appreciate	We **appreciated his telling** the truth.
3.	avoid	Sue **avoids having** a conversation with Jim whenever she can.
4.	**can't help**	Sometimes, however, she **can't help asking** him a question.
5.	consider	We **are considering moving** to Hawaii.
6.	defer	We **have deferred making** a final decision until next month.
7.	delay	I can't **delay telling** you the truth any longer.
8.	deny	Why did you **deny being** at the party?
9.	detest	Most people **detest waiting** in long lines at the movie.
10.	discuss	We **discussed going** to the mountains for the weekend.
11.	enjoy	Everyone **enjoys being** in the fresh air.
12.	escape	How did you **escape taking** the makeup test?
*13.	excuse	The teacher **excused my being** late.
14.	finish	Has everyone **finished doing** the assignment?
15.	forgive	She **forgave my shouting** at her yesterday.
16.	imagine	Can you **imagine winning** a thousand dollars?
17.	keep (continue)	**Keep working** until you finish page thirty-four.
18.	mention	I didn't **mention seeing** you yesterday.
19.	mind (dislike)	Do you **mind not smoking** in class?
20.	miss	Do you sometimes **miss being** with your high school friends?
21.	postpone	Susan had to **postpone taking** her trip.
22.	practice	I'm going to **practice giving** this speech all night.
23.	prevent	Sometimes it's impossible to **prevent fighting** among children.
24.	quit	Please, children! **Quit shoving** and **pushing.**
25.	recall	I don't **recall promising** to have lunch with you.
26.	recommend	She **recommended getting** a tutor.
27.	resent	I really **resent being** the last one in line.
28.	resist	I'm on a diet, but who can **resist eating** your good cooking.
29.	risk	I will not **risk failing** tomorrow's test, so I won't go out tonight.

* See explanation page 264.

280

30. **suggest**	The football coach **suggested swimming** as a means of relaxation.
31. **tolerate**	Be quiet. Professor Smith does not **tolerate talking** during a test.
*32. **understand**	I can't **understand your getting** angry with me.

List of Verbs Followed by Gerunds or Infinitives

A.   The following verbs may be followed by either a gerund or an infinitive construction with *no change in meaning.*

1. **advise**	Jim's high school counselor **advised going** to a small college.
	Jim's high school counselor **advised him to go** to a small college.
2. **allow**	Most restaurants **allow smoking** only in certain sections.
	Most restaurants **allow diners to smoke** only in certain sections.
3. **attempt**	To forget our fear, we **attempted singing.**
	To forget our fear, we **attempted to sing.**
4. **begin**	It **has begun raining.** Roll up the car windows.
	It **has begun to rain.** Roll up the car windows.
5. **cannot bear**	I'm taking you to the hospital. I **can't bear seeing** you in pain.
	I'm taking you to the hospital. I **can't bear to see** you in pain.
6. **continue**	Although we were tired, we **continued working.**
	Although we were tired, we **continued to work.**
7. **dislike**	Most people **dislike hearing** about their faults.
	Most people **dislike to hear** about their faults.
8. **dread**	I really **dread being** alone in a big house at night.
	I really **dread to be** alone in a big house at night.
9. **forbid**	The law **forbids driving** over the speed limit.
	The law **forbids motorists to drive** over the speed limit.
10. **hate**	I **hate asking** such a big favor from you, but I need help.
	I **hate to ask** such a big favor from you, but I need help.

* See explanation page 264.

11. intend   Who **intends staying** here tonight?
                    Who **intends to stay** here tonight?

12. like   Nobody **likes being** embarrassed in front of others.
                    Nobody **likes to be** embarrassed in front of others.

13. love   I **love spending** time with young children.
                    I **love to spend** time with young children.

14. need   This shirt really **needs ironing.**
                    This shirt really **needs to be ironed.**

15. neglect   **Have** you **neglected doing** the review again?
                    Have you **neglected to do** the review again?

16. permit   I'm sorry. We do not **permit loud talking** in this
                    theater.
                    I'm sorry. We do not **permit anyone to talk** loudly
                    in this theater.

17. prefer   The students **prefer not having** a final exam.
                    The students **prefer not to have** a final exam.

18. start   She **started giving** a long explanation to the police
                    officer.
                    She **started to give** a long explanation to the police
                    officer.

B.   The following verbs may be followed by either an infinitive or a gerund construction, but there is *a change in meaning.*

* 1. **forget**   I **forgot to take** my camera to the mountains last
                        weekend.
                        I'll never **forget taking** those beautiful pictures on
                        our vacation last month.

  2. **mean (intend)** We **mean to find** a solution to this problem before
                        we go home.

     mean (result in) It may **mean staying** up all night until we arrive at
                        an answer.

  3. **propose (plan)** As the chairman, I **propose to start** the meeting on
                        time tomorrow.

     propose (suggest) May I **propose starting** at nine instead of ten
                        o'clock?

* 4. **regret**   I **regret to tell** you that History 203 has been
                        cancelled for this quarter.
                        I **regret not being** able to take that course.

* 5. **remember**   I **remembered to lock** the door before we left.
                        Don't worry. I **remember doing** it.

* 6. **stop**   Sue **stopped to talk** to Bob.
                        She **stopped talking** to him five weeks ago.

* Review explanation on page 269.

7. **try (make an effort)**   They **tried to warn** him of the danger of speeding.
    try (experiment)   They even **tried showing** him pictures of accident victims.

8. **used to (habitual past)**   I **used to walk** to classes at the university every day.
    be used to   I **am used to walking** everywhere, so I enjoy it.
    (accustomed to)

LESSON FIFTEEN: PRACTICE EXAM

Before completing Part I, review page 259.

Part I: Identification. Identify each of the underlined gerund phrases according to its function in the sentences.

Subject = S   Subject complement   Object = O
                      = SC

Appositive = A   Object of preposition
                      = OP

_____ 1. Having a summer job is the only way many students can pay for their college tuition.

_____ 2. When my father was in college, his favorite summer job was working in a restaurant.

_____ 3. He has often said that he didn't mind serving the customers, but he dis-

_____ 4. liked removing the dirty dishes from the tables.

_____ 5. After only two weeks at one restaurant, however, he was fired for eating too much on the job.

_____ 6. A waiter doesn't make a large salary, but being polite to customers can

_____ 7. result in getting big tips.

_____ 8. The best part of his job was waiting on attractive girls.

_____ 9. My father and mother often recall meeting each other for the first time.

_____10. My mother's job, working as a cashier, was in the same restaurant.

Part II: Infinitive versus gerund as direct object. Use each of the following verbs in a short statement or question.

    Example: admit: My father admitted **eating on the job.**
                agree: After the manager had spoken to him, he agreed **to stop.**

  1. appear _____

  2. avoid _____

3. can't help _____

4. consider _____

5. choose _____

6. consent _____

7. deny _____

8. discuss _____

9. finish _____

10. forget _____

11. miss _____

12. offer _____

13. postpone _____

14. practice _____

15. refuse _____

16. resent _____

17. seem _____

18. suggest _____

Part III: Verb, adjective, noun + preposition + gerund. Complete each sentence with the correct preposition followed by a gerund phrase.

1. Most employers do not **approve** _____

2. Last week, two secretaries were **arguing** _____

3. When interviewing for a job, I have never **believed** _____

4. In a noisy office, it is difficult to **concentrate** _____

5. I have often **dreamed** _____

6. Al worked in a dentist's office last summer, and he will never **forget** _____
_____

7. Last summer, I had two good job offers, and I had a lot of **difficulty** _____
_____

8. I finally made up my mind **in the course** _____

9. Next summer, I am **looking forward** _____

10. Since I have always been a good employee, I have never **worried** _____

_____

11. Some people are lazy, but most people **devote** _____

12. Understanding the rules in an office is **essential** _____

13. The manager of an office is **responsible** _____

14. Since a five-day workweek is very long, most employees would be **in favor** _____

_____

APPENDIX

IRREGULAR VERBS

NOTE: Some verbs have two past forms: -ed and -t, as in *burned, burnt*. The -ed form is generally used.

Present and Infinitive	Past	Past Participle
awake	awoke	awaked
be	was/were	been
bear (bring forth)	bore	born
bear (carry)	bore	borne
become	became	become
begin	began	begun
bend	bent	bent
bite	bit	bitten
bleed	bled	bled
blow	blew	blown
break	broke	broken
bring	brought	brought
build	built	built
burn	burned, burnt	burned, burnt
burst	burst	burst
buy	bought	bought
catch	caught	caught
choose	chose	chosen
cling	clung	clung
clothe	clothed, clad	clothed, clad
come	came	come
cost	cost	cost
creep	crept	crept

Present and Infinitive	Past	Past Participle
cut	cut	cut
deal	dealt	dealt
dig	dug	dug
dive	dived, dove	dived
do	did	done
draw	drew	drawn
dream	dreamed, dreamt	dreamed, dreamt
drink	drank	drunk
drive	drove	driven
eat	ate	eaten
fall	fell	fallen
feed	fed	fed
feel	felt	felt
fight	fought	fought
find	found	found
flee	fled	fled
fling	flung	flung
fly	flew	flown
forbid	forbade, forbad	forbidden
forget	forgot	forgotten
forsake	forsook	forsaken
freeze	froze	frozen
get	got	got, gotten
give	gave	given
go	went	gone
grind	ground	ground
grow	grew	grown
hang (suspend)	hanged, hung	hung
hang (kill)	hanged, hung	hanged
have	had	had
hear	heard	heard
hide	hid	hidden, hid
hit	hit	hit
hold	held	held
hurt	hurt	hurt
keep	kept	kept
kneel	knelt	knelt
know	knew	known
lay (put, place, prepare)	laid	laid
lead	led	led
leap	leaped	leaped, leapt
leave	left	left
lend	lent	lent

Present and Infinitive	*Past*	*Past Participle*
let	let	let
lie (tell a falsehood)	lied	lied
lie (recline, be situated)	lay	lain
light	lighted, lit	lighted, lit
lose	lost	lost
make	made	made
mean	meant	meant
meet	met	met
pay	paid	paid
prove	proved	proved, proven
put	put	put
read	read	read
rid	rid	rid
ride	rode	ridden
ring	rang	rung
rise	rose	risen
run	ran	run
say	said	said
see	saw	seen
seek	sought	sought
sell	sold	sold
send	sent	sent
set (place, put)	set	set
shake	shook	shaken
shine	shone	shone
shoot	shot	shot
show	showed	shown, showed
shrink	shrank	shrunk, shrunken
shut	shut	shut
sing	sang	sung
sink	sank	sunk, sunken
sit	sat	sat
sleep	slept	slept
slide	slid	slid
sling	slung	slung
speak	spoke	spoken
speed	sped	sped
spend	spent	spent
spin	spun	spun
spread	spread	spread
spring	sprang	sprung
stand	stood	stood
steal	stole	stolen

Present and Infinitive	*Past*	*Past Participle*
stick	stuck	stuck
sting	stung	stung
stink	stink, stank	stunk
strike	struck	struck
string	strung	strung
swear	swore	sworn
sweep	swept	swept
swell	swelled	swelled, swollen
swim	swam	swum
swing	swung	swung
take	took	taken
teach	taught	taught
tear	tore	torn
tell	told	told
think	thought	thought
throw	threw	thrown
understand	understood	understood
wake	woke	woken
wear	wore	worn
weep	wept	wept
wet	wet	wet
win	won	won
wind	wound	wound
wring	wrung	wrung
write	wrote	written

Index